Surviving Your First Five Years As A Faculty Member:
Living and Prospering in Academia, Book 2

J. Timothy Lightfoot

This edition first published in paperback in the United States in 2019 by
Presyncopal Press, a division of Academic Career Development Services.
904 University Oaks. #65
College Station, TX 77840
www.AcademicCareerDevelopment.com

For bulk and special sales, please contact Questions.ACDS@gmail.com, or write us
at the above address.

Copyright © 2019 J. Timothy Lightfoot

Cover Design by Kim Topp, KimTopp.com

All rights reserved. No part of this publication may be reproduced or transmitted in
any form or by any means, electronic or mechanical, including photocopy,
recording, or any information storage and retrieval system now known or to be
invented, without permission in writing from the publisher, except by a reviewer
who wishes to quote brief passages in connection with a review written for
inclusion in a magazine, newspaper, or broadcast.

Library of Congress Cataloging-in-Publication Data

Lightfoot, J. T. (John Timothy), author.
Surviving Your First Five Years As A Faculty Member: Living and Prospering in
Academia, Book 2 / J. Timothy Lightfoot
p. ; cm
ISBN: 0-578-57735-6
ISBN-13: 978-0-578-57735-7

Manufactured in the United States of America
ISBN-13: 978-0-578-57735-7

Testimonials for *Surviving Your First Five Years As A Faculty Member*:

"For all the things about the tenure and promotion process that you should know but didn't, or didn't know to ask, this book is an all-in-one guide to helping young new faculty navigate one of the most critical processes in their academic career." – Dr. H Vellers, Assistant Professor, Texas Tech University

"Dr. Lightfoot has helped me navigate the complex and ever-changing world of academia for over 10 years. Without Dr. Lightfoot's guidance and expertise, I would have been extremely lost in making some of the difficult decisions surrounding my career path. By reading this book, you too will feel better equipped to make some of the challenging decisions that come in the first 5 years with a job in academia." – Dr. E Schmitt, Assistant Professor, University of Wyoming

"Dr. Lightfoot has put together what may be the first, and certainly the most comprehensive, how-to guide for new university faculty. His ability to weave the critical details of success with his 30+ years of experience, creates an insightful and invaluable resource for all new or nearly new faculty. The topics in this book are the same topics I as a Dean address on a weekly basis, therefore, I will be purchasing this book for all new faculty hires, not only to help them succeed, but to reduce some of the ambiguity and uncertainty that comes with the tenure process." – Dean and Professor G Liguori, University of Rhode Island

"The process of tenure and promotion is difficult to navigate, but Dr. Lightfoot has provided elegant guidelines for young faculty so they can have a successful and enjoyable career. I will be providing a copy of this book to all my students and post-docs as I feel it is crucial information for their success." – Dr. D Ferguson, Assistant Professor, Michigan State University

"This is a concise yet comprehensive text detailing the framework for surviving your early career as a faculty member and for preparing your professional self for promotion and tenure material submission." – Dean and Professor J Potteiger, Grand Valley State University

"This book should be studied carefully by every aspiring professor who enters academia. Once published, I intend to equip each of our new hires with their own personal copies." – Dean and Professor M Reid, University of Florida

"By itself, *Surviving Your First Five Years as A Sciences Faculty Member* is remarkably insightful and useful. Combined with its predecessor – *Finding the Best Faculty Job for You* – it answers nearly all the tough questions about tackling and thriving in academia. From addressing the 'elephants-in-the-room' – such as how to deal with departmental dynamics, or the pitfalls of securing external funding – to highlighting the importance of *professional grace*, Lightfoot's insights, tips and strategies are vital! Lightfoot candidly shares some of his own experiences, and adds a much-needed touch of humor to difficult topics – making *Surviving Your First Five Years* a joy to read and an indispensable tool for success!" – Professor P Goodson, Presidential Professor for Teaching Excellence, Texas A&M University

Other books From This Author:

Physiology Phil's True Life Lab Experiments

Finding the Best Faculty Job For You: Living and Prospering in Academia
Book 1

To my wonderful, brilliant, and beautiful wife, Faith, who is my inspiration, muse, and partner in all.

CONTENTS

Welcome to the Academy! Or, Be Careful What You Wish For! i

1 Starting Your New Job: Some Assembly Required 1

2 Who is Going to Help You Succeed? Finding People who won't remember when you ate dirt 17

3 Can you hear me now? Communication is key 35

4 Funding your research and Scholarship: The skills that will set you apart 59

5 Scholarship as a Faculty Member: All You Need to Know, But Didn't Know You Needed to Know 85

6 Teaching: How to Give Your Students Their Money's Worth 121

7 Service: Necessary, yet learn to say 'no' 175

8 Building toward promotion and tenure: The time to start is now! 183

9 After promotion/tenure: What to do when the smoke clears and the fog lifts 215

Index 235

About the Author 239

PREFACE

WELCOME TO THE ACADEMY!
OR, BE CAREFUL WHAT YOU WISH FOR!

This is an exciting time for you! You've just graduated with your PhD[1] (or you've finished your post-doc) and you're starting a new career as a faculty member! It's an exciting time and finally after years of work, you are a member of academia; a part of that select group known as 'faculty'. As a faculty member you're going to be responsible for decisions that affect your career and impact students and maybe even the University and profession!

But the realization all this responsibility is yours can also be overwhelming. Even though I've been a faculty member for over 30 years, I still remember my first day as a faculty member, alone in my new office, struck by the realization that I now had to make all the decisions. I was the one that would be making all the decisions about my research – what I studied, who I hired in the lab, what equipment I bought – and I also had to make decisions that were previously made for me – like what textbooks I used in my classes, how I taught the classes, and what committees I would serve on, etc. etc. Wow! That was a sobering thought at the time. As I've worked with new faculty members over the years, I've found I wasn't the only one that ever had those thoughts; most new faculty members, about the time they start their position, get hit with similar sobering concerns, and as a result feel overwhelmed and sometimes, even an 'imposter'[2].

In fact, as a new faculty member, around August 15 if not earlier, you'll feel overwhelmed with all the things that are suddenly your responsibility. You'll be responsible for planning, organizing, and managing classes; responsible for setting up your lab, picking lab personnel, and writing grants and funding proposals; responsible for the myriad small things faculty members must do like attending faculty meetings, lab meetings, and committee meetings; and

---

[1] You may have finished some other terminal degree (MD, DVM, JD, DDS, etc.) and I am no less happy for you. However, to make the text flow easier, I'm going to refer to all terminal degrees as 'PhD' throughout the book.
[2] The 'imposter syndrome' is a real thing in faculty and is defined as a feeling of incompetence despite accomplishments or a feeling that you've succeeded due to luck and not because of your talents or qualifications. Here's a great article by J. Sakulku from the J. of Behavioral Science (2011) to get started on the topic: http://bit.ly/Imposter_SyndACDS.

responsibility for small things like finding your way around a new campus! If you have a family, you may also face upheaval with having to move to a new community, finding a new home, and figuring out how to navigate your new community and your children's schools. Looming over all these responsibilities is the evaluation called 'Promotion and Tenure' happening in five years[3] that will determine whether you keep your job or must move on to something different. And you thought your last year as a doctoral student/post-doctoral fellow was tough? How do you cope with all of this, continue to be successful, enjoy your life, and keep your sanity? Read on, there's hope ahead.

This book is about figuring out how to navigate the first five years of your life as a faculty member without losing your sanity, your relationship(s), and your self-respect, while getting through the promotion/tenure process in one piece. While there are also a few other sources of information you might want to consult[4], there will be many times you will wish you had a guidebook for transiting your first five years and the aim of this book is to be that guide. There will be times you can't ask your colleagues for advice, nor should you. And frankly, there will be times no one has the answer, not even this book. However, by having a resource like this book and your mentoring network, you will gain perspective so you can make the best decision for your situation and career.

While this book is generally aimed at those faculty members that are in the life sciences and 'hard sciences', as opposed to the humanities, I believe all the strategies and concepts in this book will apply equally well to all faculty disciplines with the biggest exception being in regards to the research and funding chapters. As a result of my training as an exercise physiologist, I present topics in this book using a linear approach Chapters 2 through 8 each emphasize a facet of your first five years and then dive deep into that topic to give you guidance, advice, and tips on how to deal with that facet. Tying it all together, Chapters 1 and 9 provide bookends to the other information presented and provide a critical integrative overview of all the topics. The

---

[3] If you are on a non-tenure track position, you may not have to worry about the tenure and promotion process, but more than likely, you'll be on a five-year contract. So, the five-year timeframe is just as critical to you because your concern may be whether your contract will be renewed. If it is not mentioned when I talk about promotion and tenure, you should just substitute the words 'contract review and renewal' when you see the phrase 'promotion and tenure'.

[4] One great source regarding setting up your lab is the free manual *Making the Right Moves* from the Howard Hughes Medical Institute and the Burroughs Wellcome Fund. While it focuses primarily on soft-money institutions, it is a wealth of knowledge. And it's free! http://bit.ly/HHMIRightMoves

integrative overview from Chapters 1 and 9 are important because as a faculty member, you won't just get to worry about scholarship one day of the week, teach on another day, have service obligations on a third day, and so on. Instead, you'll find each day is an 'exciting' mix of all these items, sometimes with several of them all happening at once!

In academia, you'll find to be truly 'successful' in almost every definition of that term, you'll need other supportive and caring people to help you not only in the first five years of your career, but throughout your life. You'll find the importance of supportive people in your life and career is a thread that runs throughout the book. To that point, I've been incredibly fortunate over my career to have both family and colleagues that have supported my sometimes wacky academic and personal efforts. Their support has certainly been critical to the writing and production of what you are holding right now. Besides my own experiences, a large influence on the content of this book have been the many professional colleagues I've had the pleasure of working with and mentoring through the early stages of their careers. However, mentioning names would just set me up to forget someone and so I will say 'you know who you are'.

No less important to the content of this book are those faculty who I worked with when they were undergoing very difficult times in their careers, whether it was promotion/tenure denials, post-tenure review problems, or just distressful student issues. Both good and bad, these are all situations where I have learned and observed so my goal is to relay those experiences throughout this book to help augment your experience as a new faculty member and minimize the tough times.

While the content of this book has been developed through interaction with literally hundreds of academics and professionals, there are some folks that certainly directly impacted this book. My colleagues (all Drs.) Pat Goodson, John Thornton, Adam Barry, and Melinda Sheffield-Moore have shared their insights and ideas over the years and I appreciate their input toward this project. My editor, Faith Lightfoot, who also is my wife, has once again endeavored to keep me from falling into the grammatical abyss and so to her I send a large "thanks" for her continued vigilance and for the saving anchor(s) she sent me when I started to slip into the abyss.

Lastly, a huge thanks goes out to my beta-readers who gave me wonderful insights, alternative ways of thinking about some concepts, and appropriate corrections where needed. These beta-readers provided additional material and quotes for the book, as well as sometimes providing alternative viewpoints that were important to augment the text. As such, I can't thank these beta-readers enough: Dr. Heather Vellers (Texas Tech University), Dr. Emily Schmitt (University of Wyoming), Dean and Professor Gary Liguori (University of Rhode Island), Dr. David Ferguson (Michigan State University), Dean and Professor Michael Reid (University of Florida), Dean and Professor Jeff Potteiger (Grand Valley State University), and Presidential Professor for Teaching Excellence Pat Goodson (Texas A&M University). I couldn't have done this without all your thoughts and support.

Lastly, I would not be where I am today without the two cornerstones of my life: my wonderful wife Faith and my faith. Both 'Faiths' guide me daily, give me support when I need it, and comfort me when I've had enough of the inanity that sometimes occurs in this business. They truly are the rocks upon which I've built my career and through which, preserved my sanity!

1

STARTING YOUR NEW JOB: SOME ASSEMBLY REQUIRED

Whew! You've arrived! You're a new faculty member and your accomplishments are the result of many years of education, research, and hard work. If you are like most junior[5] faculty you are eager, excited, and ready to get started, but how do you do that?

How do you make the transition from a doctoral or post-doc position and become a full-fledged and valuable faculty member? How do you make it through the first five years and achieve promotion and tenure? How do you balance research, teaching, service, and life, without working 24/7? I am going to assume if you are reading this book, you need answers to those types of questions, and that's what this book will give you.

When I first became a faculty member over 30 years ago, no one told me *how* 'being a faculty member' worked. In fact, some of my colleagues assumed I knew how to *be* a faculty member and, in many cases, expected me to step right in and start. However, I was overwhelmed and found that information and responsibilities came so fast, that I didn't know what to do first! Certainly, those first few months as a faculty member were often like trying to drink water out of a fire hose!

When I started as a faculty member, I felt like I was trying to build a piece of furniture with no instruction sheet and a handful of parts that didn't fit. It was like I

This Chapter:
First step, read the instructions 4
What is promotion/tenure or contract renewal? 4
Understanding the expectations 6
What your University really values 11
Putting your priorities in action 13
From the Flip Side 13
The Take Home Message 14

---

[5] I use the term 'junior faculty member' through-out the book to designate a faculty member in the first five years of their career vs. a senior faculty member that has moved past the promotion/tenure process. Remember, that junior faculty members are full faculty members and have all the same responsibilities as senior faculty members. As such, the term 'junior faculty member' is only meant to connotate a career stage!

had purchased a piece of 'build-it-yourself' furniture where the instructions are given only in pictures, with no words! I had seen faculty members, worked with them, and even spent time with faculty members but I never had anyone really tell me how to become a good faculty member. Just like the 'build-it-yourself' furniture, I had the picture, but I also needed the words!

All I knew at the beginning of my career was that this 'piece of furniture' I was assembling had four major parts – teaching, research, service, and developing funding – but how those parts fit together, I had no clue.

Even though I thought I knew what the furniture (i.e., faculty job) should look like, I realized I wouldn't know if I had enough parts, or even if I was putting things together correctly until the end of that first year.

Often my colleagues would offer to help when asked, but their piece of furniture or faculty position was different than mine. They had built their careers and it was now up to me to build mine! And now, it is up to you to build your own unique piece of furniture.

So, where do you start?

Info to Know – 1.1
Where Your Academic Furniture is Built Affects What It Looks Like

In the Preface, I noted that this book being aimed (primarily) at faculty members in the Life Sciences versus those in the Humanities. While much of the academic environment in Life Sciences and the Humanities are the same, there are some critical differences that will affect how your career – or your academic furniture – looks when you come up for P/T.

Most of this book will be equally effective whether you are in (Life) Sciences or Humanities. However, the major difference in approaching your career for Sciences and Humanities is how research and scholarship are approached. In general, research and scholarship in the Sciences is based on data-driven investigations, using what would be considered the traditional, 'scientific method'. However, scholarship in the Humanities is often more subjective and involves creative processes that are less easily described and evaluated. For example, I have colleagues in Dance Science and their scholarship is based on their choreography and development of dance pieces. The evaluation of their scholarly works is markedly different than the objective counting of papers and/or grants that often happens in the Sciences disciplines.

Thus, be aware that the 'discipline' where you are assembling your academic furniture may alter how your career looks, especially as to how your scholarship is evaluated.

This chapter is meant to answer the 'where do I start?' question. While your furniture (job) will look different than mine did, the process and timelines are the same. As such, this chapter will focus on giving you an integrated overview of what is coming and a sense of how to approach and attack this new position you have, especially for your first five years.

We are going to focus on the first five-year period[6] because that is the length of most pre-tenure and initial contract periods for academic jobs in the United States; this 5-year period is often called the promotion/tenure 'clock' and it begins as soon as you start your new position. How you fare as you go through these processes will dictate how stressful or successful your time will be as an academic. Your immediate daily focus as a faculty member will be on research and teaching. How well you perform in those areas will inform the University's decision on your promotion/tenure or contract renewal. This is why focusing on your first five years and promotion/tenure or contract renewal should be your overriding priority throughout the first five years of your career.

If you are in a non-tenure-track position, this five-year period also applies to you, maybe not for tenure-promotion reasons, but because in most cases, your first contract and most subsequent contracts will be three to five years in length. It seems like academia in general thinks five years is an adequate period to figure out whether you are capable of being a great faculty member. Just think of this first five-year period as being the 'test drive' phase for the department/college/university.

From your standpoint, you also must remember you have five years to 'test drive' the unit you are in to determine whether you want to stay *as well as* showing the search committee and Department Chair they were correct when they forecast your 'potential' and hired you.[7]

As you think about and focus on getting through promotion/tenure or contract renewal, it will be helpful to understand what the 'University Community' is thinking in regards to this and other topics. To help with this

---

[6] You may find that your pre-tenure period may be shorter or longer than a 5-year period. One of the newer trends is to adjust this pre-tenure period based on previous experience and accomplishment. Thus, while I'll use 'five-years' through-out the book, understand that you may need to alter the timelines to fit your situation.
[7] For more information about the hiring process, and why search committees focus on 'potential', check out book 1 in this series – *Finding the Best Faculty Job for You*. In short, I'll refer to that as 'Book 1' throughout this book.

perspective, I'll share with you the view from the 'flip side'. As you progress through academia, you may wind-up on the 'flip side' at some point, but currently, it'll help you to understand what those above you on the academic totem pole are thinking.

With all that said, let's get started!

First step, read the instructions
A great place to start understanding how to assemble your new faculty position is to thoroughly take the time to read and understand how your University is organized. For information on this topic, check out the first book in this series, *Finding the Best Faculty Job For You*.[8] However, in short, you need to make sure you understand the levels of organization in your department, College, and University. Certainly, you need to know who are the leaders of each of these units and who are the senior academic faculty members in your department. It is critical you understand these basic tenants of your organizational structure so you can begin to understand how you will be evaluated and judged when it is time for you to be reviewed for promotion/tenure or contract renewal.

What is promotion/tenure or contract renewal?
Before we dive deeper into assembling your job, it will help tremendously if I take a step back and talk about what is promotion/tenure or contract renewal. Looking back, I don't think I quite understood what 'promotion/tenure' really meant when I started, so this is a good place for a review.

As a new faculty member, you were hired either on a 'tenure-track' line or on a 'non-tenure-track' line. Tenure is a status given to faculty after a certain period, and is meant to provide protection for the faculty member so they can research, teach, and perform service in the way they see fit. In most cases, a tenure-track line will have research responsibilities (some non-tenure-track lines do as well). If you are on a non-tenure-track line, that just means your position is not eligible for tenure and you will not have to go through the promotion/tenure process. But you'll have your share of processes. In a non-tenure-track position you will likely be on a series of employment contracts with your first contract being for one to three years.

If you are on a 'tenure-track' line, this means you'll be eligible for review for tenure in five years. This timeline can vary a bit, but in most places, it is five years. As a new faculty member on a tenure-track line, you'll be an 'Assistant Professor' and at the same time you are reviewed for tenure in five years,

---
[8] Chapter 1 in Book 1 – *Finding the Best Faculty Job for You!*

you'll also be reviewed for promotion to 'Associate Professor'. That's why you'll often see tenure and promotion tagged together, even though they are two separate, but simultaneous processes.

In either case, whether you are on a non-tenure-line or on a tenure-track-line, there will be a step-by-step process your University has outlined that will be used to determine whether your contract will be renewed or whether you'll be awarded tenure and promotion. Because these evaluation processes differ at each university, there is no one process everyone uses. However, there are some generalities in these processes that apply in most cases (see Figures 1.1 and 1.2).

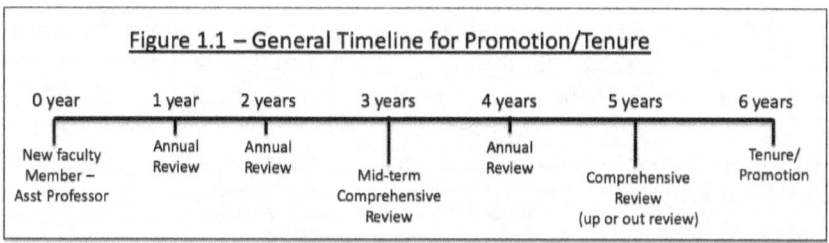

One of the things you'll note in the general process shown in both Figures 1.1 and 1.2 is the large number of evaluations that occur during your initial period. In my experience, Universities want you to succeed and have your contract renewed or have you awarded promotion and tenure. As such, most Universities really keep an eye on the progress of junior faculty to determine if they are moving appropriately toward either contract renewal or promotion/tenure. No university wants anyone to be surprised when it comes to how their faculty are progressing and so, there are a lot of reviews during the process. Think of it this way: Most Universities may metaphorically throw you into the deep end of the swimming pool as a new faculty member, but they will have a lifeguard standing by to make sure you are doing okay as you swim for the first few years!

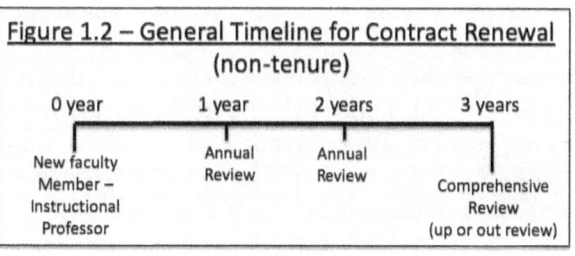

Annual evaluations: One of the ways the University keeps tabs on your progress is through regular and timely evaluations of your performance. In most cases, your Department Chair will formally evaluate you each year. Additionally, adding to this evaluation may be input from a committee of senior faculty set up to provide mentoring. These annual evaluations will normally lead to a comprehensive evaluation during your third year. After this comprehensive evaluation, your initial contract will be renewed (if you are on a non-tenure-track line) or you'll be allowed to continue toward promotion and tenure if you are on a tenure-track line. Universities do this 'third-year review' to correct any problems and to have a formalized record of whether you are progressing appropriately (or not) toward contract renewal or promotion/tenure.

If you continue toward promotion/tenure, you will go through another comprehensive evaluation during the fifth year of your faculty appointment. This is an 'up or out' evaluation meaning if you are not 'promoted up' you will be 'out' of a job (the same with the comprehensive evaluations for non-tenure-track faculty usually happening at the third year). However, if you are not awarded promotion/tenure, or a contract renewal, in most cases you'll be granted another year to work, often called a 'bridge year', which gives you time to find another job.

There are times when the University will 'pause your promotion/tenure clock', essentially allowing you extra time before you come up for promotion/tenure. One of the more common reasons the promotion/tenure clock is paused is for childbirth. Beyond personnel reasons (like childbirth), there are other reasons the promotion/tenure clock can be paused. These reasons can include university-induced delays in getting your lab facilities ready or other issues that are out of your control. In short, these types of uncontrollable issues can be a rationale for pausing your promotion/tenure clock. If you believe that there is a rationale for pausing your promotion/tenure clock, you need to discuss this with your Department Chair as soon as possible. The further you are into your five-year period, the less lenient the University will be with granting a pause in your promotion/tenure clock.

In short, personnel decisions such as promotion/tenure or contract renewal are usually made following strict adherence to procedures and processes that are in place in your Institution. These procedures and processes can be a pain at times, but you should understand they exist not only for your protection, but also to insure fair treatment of everyone.

Understanding the expectations

The best way to increase your chance of success in academia is to fully understand the expectations the University has for <u>the position you are currently filling</u>. As you move up in the University and your position and rank changes, the expectations for your position and your performance will change. As

STARTING YOUR NEW JOB

such, you need to have an understanding as to what expectations there are for your current position and how those expectations relate to your ultimate priority of achieving promotion/tenure or contract renewal.

Hopefully the expectations for your current position were explained during your interview and hiring process. It is likely you were given some all-encompassing, generalized version of these expectations; these expectations were probably were expressed as something like 'be a great teacher, publish and fund your research, and do great professional service'. Those are expectations, but they aren't very clear or detailed. The details of the expectations are critical, but can seem infinite. For example:

- Can you be an excellent teacher, but mediocre in research and still get tenure?
- How much funding will you need to find?
- How many publications will you need to have?
- What kind of journals should you publish in?
- How much professional service should you do?
- Does university service count more than service to professional organizations? etc.

The details of the expectations of your position, which may seem trivial and unimportant, are very critical and important. The details allow you to understand what you need to do as a faculty member and will help you prioritize your activities as you move forward in the first five years of your career.

To understand the expectations of your job, there are five primary sources I suggest you consult. The first source of expectations for your job to understand is your contract. In most cases, the contract you signed will delineate what your duties will be and the general expectations for your position. If you are asked to do duties that are outside of what has been described in your contract, you should quickly see your Department Chair and get clarification. If you are tasked with taking on duties like developing an additional class in a different disciplinary area, make sure that you help your administration understand that these extra duties may pull you off your promotion/tenure pathway.

> **Info to Know – 1.1**
> **Sources That Can Help You to Understand Expectations**
> 1) Your contract;
> 2) Written Department, College, and University expectation documents;
> 3) Your Department Chair;
> 4) Senior Faculty on P/T Committees;
> 5) Pivot Faculty in the Department/College.

The second source that will go hand-in-hand with your contract, is to read and *understand* whatever departmental/college/university documents cover the promotion/tenure process (or the contract renewal process). There will usually be specific documents pertaining to these topics at each of the organizational levels, with the Departmental documents being specific and the University documents being broad (with the College documents somewhere in between). These approved documents are official and must be used throughout the process; i.e., the Department Chair can't change a written process as s/he wants; it must be followed as written. Thus, one of your greatest strengths will be when you thoroughly understand the process. The sooner you understand the process you are going through, the more you'll feel confident about your place in the process and you can make sure the process is playing out as written. Additionally, understanding the process can be quite an advantage for you if the process, for whatever reason, doesn't work out in your favor.

The third through fifth sources that can help you understand the expectations are all human; these are the people you will be working with who may also be judging you in the promotion/tenure process. These human sources are critical in understanding the expectations of your job and consist of your Department Chair, senior faculty, and your mentors.

Department Chair: Unless the Chair changes during your first five years, your Department Chair will be one of the three primary 'Deciders' in the promotion/tenure/renewal decision tree (the other two Deciders usually being the Dean and the Provost). These Deciders are the ones that will officially decide if you should be awarded promotion/tenure or contract renewal. These Deciders get input from what are called promotion and tenure committees (aka: P/T Committee; see below).

However, you need to remember the P/T Committees are just <u>advisory</u> to these Deciders; I have seen the Deciders recommend the opposite action the P/T committees recommended, so it is really the opinion and experience of the Deciders that will be key in whether you will get promotion or tenure (or your contract renewed). Thus, very early on in your time as an Assistant Professor, you should schedule a meeting with your Department Chair to talk about the specific expectations of your job.

If you had this type of conversation before you got the job, which I hope you did, I would still recommend having this conversation with your Chair in the first month of your time as a faculty member, but only <u>after</u> you have thoroughly digested all the department/college/university guidelines regarding promotion and tenure. I've put some sample questions you can use for the conversation with your Department Chair in Table 1.1.

Because the Department Chair is often the first Decider in the chain and will carry a lot of weight in the process, it is critical for you to understand your Department Chair's expectations for your position as soon as possible, so you can move forward toward promotion/tenure confidently.

Table 1.1 – Questions to ask to understand the expectations of the job	
Suggested question	**What this question is really asking**
1. Are there quantitative expectations for research production?	How many articles and presentations do I have to have every year?
2. Is quality of outlet considered in determining my research productions? If so, how is that measured?	Does it matter the journal I publish in? If so, how do you rank the different journals; how do you determine good quality from poor quality?
3. Do book chapters, books, and reviews count the same as published original data articles?	Are some types of publication more valued than others?
4. How are funding attempts counted in my performance? If so, how does that work?	Do I get credit for trying to get funding, even if I don't get funding? What type of criteria are used in this determination?
5. When I come up for promotion/tenure, will I need to be considered 'excellent' in both teaching and research?	Is it expected that tenured faculty excel in all aspects of the academic life, or can I excel in research and be good in teaching? (or excel in teaching and just be good in research?)
6. How much service am I expected to do as a new faculty member? How should I balance department, college, university, and professional society service requests?	Should I get involved in a lot of service within the first five years of my career? If so, which is more important to the unit?
7. How would you advise me to keep my service load appropriately balanced with my research/teaching expectations?	Will you help me keep from getting overwhelmed with service?
8. Who are the influential faculty in the department I can talk to for historical perspective?	Who can I talk with to get insight into the expectations for my position?
9. Who will the University seek as 'outside-reviewers' for my P/T packet?	Where will be the pool of experts that the University consults on my P/T packet.

Senior Faculty: The fourth source of information to further understand your job expectations are the senior faculty in your department, both those on or not on the P/T Committee. Find out which of the senior faculty are on the P/T Committee and talk to each individually. Ask each of them the same questions you ask the Chair (see Table 1.1). This repetition will help you understand what the faculty value versus what the administration values. In most cases, for a junior faculty member, both the Department Chair and the senior faculty will have the same values.

If the senior faculty responses don't match with the Department Chair's responses, you should talk to the Department Chair again and share the inconsistencies you've learned about (without necessarily identifying your sources). You'll want to get some resolution to these inconsistencies before you go too far into P/T so you can work to develop your academic activities appropriately. You may even want to get clarification in writing so that you will be able to point back to that document as the guidance you used. In short, if you hear inconsistencies between the Department Chair's expectations and the Senior Faculty's expectations, you'll need to resolve that issue.

In addition to talking to the senior faculty on the P/T Committee, it is important to identify and get to know all senior faculty that exert leadership in your department. Every Department (and College for that matter) I've ever worked in has had a few senior faculty who exerted quite a bit of influence; sometimes these faculty were also former departmental/college leaders (i.e., they had had official leadership roles) and sometimes these faculty did not have formal leadership roles. I've often thought of these influencers as 'pivot faculty' for the department or college; usually, these senior leaders' thinking plays a large role in guiding the department and as such, their thoughts and opinions (and experience) can pivot the department in many different directions. Getting to know these pivot faculty can also help you understand how to function effectively in the department and they can also be a great historical resource for how the department functions.

Mentors: Most Universities will assign one or more senior faculty to each junior faculty member to serve as a mentor(s) which will be a fifth source of job expectation information. These mentors may or may not be within your department – and there are some good reasons to have mentors outside of your department – but regardless of where they are located, they can also give you an experienced perspective on the required processes and expectations of your life as an academic.

One note of caution: many junior faculty, while wanting to appear as if they belong as a faculty member, get the notion they shouldn't ask for help or ask questions. Whether this hesitation to ask questions is a result of the fear of being perceived as weak, incompetent, or not deserving (or some combination of these), you should immediately release these concerns. The other faculty in your department understand where you are in your professional development and they will welcome your questions especially if those inquiries will help make you a better faculty member. Besides, do you really want to make a mistake that could cost you promotion and tenure, if that mistake could have easily been prevented by asking a few simple questions?

Once you understand the process and the expectations, you now have a better sense of what your job should look like as you construct it. Using our earlier metaphor, it is so much easier to assemble a piece of furniture if you know what the end-product should look like. Having a sense of what the job should look like is critical to how you build your career and how you conduct yourself as a professional. To that end, I would encourage you to keep a '30,000-foot overview' perspective about what your job is supposed to be. At the end of the day, your job and how you do it should result in you getting either tenure/promoted or having your contract renewed.

What your University really values

So, how do you work toward achieving that '30,000-foot overview' of your position? Simply put, understand what your University values most. As part of this understanding, you need to understand what your Department and College values most and work to fulfill those values. Remember, as you are reviewed during your first five years, you will be compared to an expectation set by those three units (department/college/university) and members of those three units will judge you on how well you've met those expectations.

The starting point to understanding what your University values is to figure out what the Carnegie Classification of your University is. The Carnegie Classification is a categorization of the different types of Universities in the United States[9] which assigns a category to a university based on its research and teaching output. Universities classified as Research 1 or 2, (or R1 or R2 in 'academic-speak') focus primarily on research, with teaching a secondary priority. In short, if you are in an 'R' institution, your University's primary value is creating and disseminating new research. Teaching is still important at R-Universities, but research takes priority. Similarly, Institutions that are

---

[9] You can find copious details about the Carnegie Classifications and what they mean at http://carnegieclassifications.iu.edu/. As of this writing, Carnegie just changed some of the classifications that had been used previously, including dropping the R3 category and adding the D/PU – Doctoral, Professional University – category.

ranked as 'Masters 1, 2, or 3' (or M1, M2, or M3) focus more on teaching with some emphasis on research. As you move down the classifications below the M-Universities (Baccalaureate, Associates, etc.) the Universities become more education focused and less research focused. None of this discussion is value-driven; being at an R1 is no better or worse than being at an Associate classified Institution. However, understanding the classification of your University is a key to understanding what the University, and likely your College and Department, wants their faculty to do. After understanding your job expectations, this is the starting point for how you should mold your job actions to fulfill your overall priority.

As an example, let's assume you are at an R1 University on a tenure-track line. Certainly, R1 Universities value great teachers. In fact, it will be difficult to get promotion/tenure at an R1 if you are not a good teacher, however, teaching will not be the cornerstone of your evaluation at an R1. The cornerstone will be your research production (both funding and/or publications). Conversely, if you are at a Baccalaureate university, they will be thrilled if you conduct research, especially if you get students involved in your research. However, if you do not excel in the classroom, it is unlikely you'll receive promotion/tenure because the key mission of a Baccalaureate university is teaching.

If you are on a non-tenure-track line, the examples aren't as clear-cut since there are several different types of non-tenure-track positions that are hired. Most often, faculty members on non-tenure-track lines classified as either 'Instructional' or 'Clinical' are hired based on their teaching ability (either in the classroom or in the clinic). These types of positions, regardless of the Carnegie Classification, are very specific in their expectations. Additionally, you may be on a 'Research' non-tenure-track line; as you might guess, the focus of this non-tenure-track position is on research. However, Research non-tenure-track lines are unusual at Universities other than R1 Institutes where research is already the priority.

Whatever type of faculty position you are in, you need to constantly remember the overall priorities of your University. If the overall priority is research (e.g., R1-R2 Universities), put up a sign in your office you see daily that says something like "I'm here to produce funding and new knowledge" to remind yourself everyday what you are *supposed* to be doing. If your Institution's primary goal is education, make that sign read "I'm here to educate the next generation" as a reminder of the Institute's goals. If you understand what the key priorities of your University are and remind yourself of the expectations they have of you as a faculty member, you will have a clear focus on how to assemble your job.

Putting your priorities in action

The rest of the chapters in this book are going to detail key skills you need to develop to help you fulfill your primary priority of gaining promotion/tenure/contract renewal AND fulfilling the expectations of your University. The skills and the tips in the upcoming chapters will help you build an action plan that will serve to get you from where you are now to a successful completion of promotion/tenure/contract renewal. You should strive to use all your skills in communication, teaching, research, and service to make yourself invaluable within your unit and to make sure you have a smooth and easy first five years of your career.

From the Flip Side

As I noted above, as you begin to think about assembling your career, it is helpful to get a general sense of what your Institution is looking for in new faculty members. You'll get great insight from talking to your Department Chair and the senior faculty in your department. Having been a faculty member for over 30 years, a department chair for 11 of those 30 years, and having played some role in administration for another 14 of those 30 years, I can tell you in general, your colleagues (and your Institution) are expecting you to be a member of the scholarly community by doing your job, caring for students, and working hard and diligently.

You should understand most faculty members, especially those that have been around awhile, will not expect you to come in and have all the answers. In fact, the expectation will be that while you may be a whiz in research and bring knowledge no one else in the department has, you'll be naïve when it comes to being a faculty member. To a large extent, faculty appreciate that only experience can teach you what it takes to be a great faculty member. As such, what faculty respect is a new faculty member that doesn't act like they know it all, but rather a faculty member that knows their strengths, but also is aware of and willing to work on their weaknesses. The faculty you work with will, in most of the cases, help you become a better faculty member; that's one of the reasons you'll see in the upcoming chapters a focus on showing people how you are getting better in your job. In fact, your greatest advantage as a junior faculty member may be that you have access to 'more experienced' faculty members you can tap for their knowledge and expertise.

However, a warning is in order here: don't expect respect if you are continually leaning on others to pull your load, do your work, or provide answers that are easily found elsewhere. There are many indirect ways experienced faculty learn and understand whether new faculty are going to prove to be a valuable addition to the community or will be a drag on its time and resources. Scattered throughout the rest of the chapters are some of these 'indirect ways' other faculty learn about you and your role in the community. Pay attention to these factors and make sure you don't trip up your own career.

The Take Home Message

As you start your position, you need to remember your end goal – at least for the first five years of your position – is to either get promotion/tenure or get your contract renewed. It is too easy – and way too common – for junior faculty to get bogged down and anxious about their day-to-day responsibilities and to lose sight of their end priority. Being a faculty member can certainly be a classic case of 'not seeing the forest because of the trees.'

Many people go into academia for altruistic reasons; they want to help students learn, they want to add new knowledge, or they want to advance the profession. All these reasons focus on others – the students, the profession, known knowledge – and none focus on the individual. That's why it is often difficult for junior faculty to focus on their primary priority, promotion/tenure or contract renewal. Don't mistake my emphasis on your primary priority to indicate you shouldn't care about others or care about the general welfare of the learning community you are in. I'm not saying that at all. But what I am saying is that over the first five years of your career as a faculty member, you need to be selfish and remember first and foremost, your actions need to contribute to your primary priority. Again, too many times I've seen junior faculty get to promotion/tenure reviews and almost seem surprised when they had difficulty because they had not focused on the important pieces of their job. So, while I'm not advocating for you to be selfish and become an insufferable narcissist who thinks it is all about you, you *must* remember the primary outcome you are striving for at the end of your first five years is promotion/tenure or contract renewal.

In closing, as you start your position, the other faculty in your unit will be thrilled to have you onboard. New faculty bring an increased sense of enthusiasm, energy, passion, and new skills to an academic unit. The increased enthusiasm, energy, and passion can be contagious and help bring excitement to a program and to its students. In the second year of my Master's degree, we had a new faculty member in the department (Dr. Kelly Stuart) who happened to be in Exercise Physiology – in fact, he was our first 'modern' exercise physiologist in the department and the first new faculty member hired in the department in several years. As a student, there was a great sense of excitement as Dr. Stuart started and brought new ideas like building a stand-alone exercise physiology lab and metabolic carts and such. His hire brought such a sense of excitement amongst the students and the faculty that it really transformed our small department. Keep that in mind as you start your career as a faculty member – you too are bringing new skills, excitement, enthusiasm, and passion to add to what is already in the department. And sometimes, the factors you bring can be synergistic and affect students and other faculty for the rest of their lives – but don't forget your priorities!

2

WHO IS GOING TO HELP YOU SUCCEED? FINDING PEOPLE WHO WON'T REMEMBER WHEN YOU ATE DIRT

As you assemble your career, it is always helpful to have people you can call on for advice. Just like putting together that piece of furniture that has no written directions, it always helps to have other people around. As alluded to in the last chapter, no matter what your subject matter or content expertise, you will have to work with people when you are a faculty member. Whether it is working through a thorny discussion with your colleagues, working to teach difficult topics to students, working to move the Institution forward with administrators, or working to propel your discipline forward within your professional organization, every day of your life as a faculty member will include working with other people. Simply put, how you work with people will determine your success in assembling your faculty career.

While we can think of success as a faculty member on a day-to-day basis, my focus in this book is on the first five years leading up to that all-important contract renewal or promotion/tenure (P/T[10]) decision. Thus, as you interact and work with people, you need to think of those interactions in terms of your eventual success in P/T. So, how can you work with people to increase your chances of success at the end of that five-year period? In total, I believe working successfully with others in the academic environment is a combination of interpersonal skills, developing a supportive network of advisors/mentors, and developing appropriate relationships with mentors, collaborators, and colleagues. As such, this chapter is broken up into various sections that when considered together, should give you a holistic approach to working with people that will maximize your success during that five-year period.

> **This Chapter:**
>
> Interpersonal skills 18
>
> Developing your network 23
>
> Finding Mentors 25
>
> Your colleagues 29
>
> Finding collaborators 30
>
> The Take Home Message 32

---

[10] By now, you understand that P/T stands for Promotion and Tenure, as well as a stand-in for contract renewal, so I'm going to use 'P/T' through-out the rest of the book.

But first, what is the difference between mentors, colleagues, and collaborators? While all these people play a part in your career, they serve very different roles. Sometimes individuals will change categories (e.g., from a collaborator to a mentor) and that is why it is important for you to understand the difference(s) among the three categories. While I'll say a lot more about each of these categories as we go through the chapter, a good basic understanding of the different roles for each of these categories is in order. *Mentors* are usually individuals that act as a personal advisor to you; usually a mentor is someone a little older that has been through what you are about to go through. Conversely, *colleagues* are those individuals you work with in your academic unit. Usually you and your colleagues are associated by unit – i.e., you are in the same department, college, or university – but do not necessarily have any stronger tie than that. Importantly, because they are in your same unit, colleagues usually will have some say in your P/T efforts because they may serve on various P/T committees in your department or College. Lastly, a *collaborator* is someone you work with on a joint basis to produce work; this could be a scientific collaborator, a course collaborator, or a collaborator in your discipline you are working with to advance your profession. Collaborators can be in your department, at your University, or even at another institution.

Are there times when an individual may fill all three roles for you? Yes, but that may not be wise for a variety of reasons I set out below. For our purposes, I am going to consider these three types of individuals as separate individuals and (spoiler-alert) I'm going to encourage you to do the same.

Before we jump off into how to develop your network of colleagues, collaborators, and mentors, it is critical you are aware of and think about your own interpersonal skills. If you don't understand your own interpersonal strengths and weaknesses and how to work on those, understanding others you work with will not be possible because of your own interpersonal skill blind spots. So, we'll take a bit of a journey through 'interpersonal skill-land' before we talk about the other people that are going to help you in your career.

Interpersonal skills

There was a moment of clarity for me that occurred during a faculty meeting when I was not yet an administrator. At the time, we had a small core of senior faculty, six or seven junior faculty, and another 10 or so instructional faculty. Thus, when an intense 'discussion' broke out at a faculty meeting regarding whether a certain subgroup of students needed to take a laboratory class, I was amazed to observe the rancor exhibited between the departmental faculty members, even though I had known these academics for almost 10 years! While I was wise enough to stay out of that fray - and I'm fortunate to still have great relationships with all the parties involved - it is sad to me that many years later, some of the rancor from that meeting still exists between my former colleagues. What started as a simple disagreement, got heated, branched off into other areas and has hurt the working relationships of some of those faculty since that time. Now I don't bring this example up to discuss whether a laboratory was needed (I'm not sure that point was ever decided), I bring it up to point out how important your interpersonal skills are in maintaining a productive and facilitative place as a faculty member in an academic community. When you lose control of yourself – even verbally - you are putting yourself in a position where you can be considered as less than mature. And you should be aware the times you lose control will always be remembered by your colleagues. And if you think the above example is silly, minor, or trivial and you wonder how faculty members could get upset by such a thing, believe me, it happens frequently. There is a famous quote attributed to Henry Kissinger: "Battles in academia are so vicious because the stakes are so small."[11]

When children grow up, it's often hard for parents to think of their children as adults because parents remember when their child 'ate dirt' because the child didn't know better. As a junior faculty member, one of your goals in interacting with other faculty members should be to not do anything others would remember and hold against you during review of your P/T documents. While many senior faculty members will be able to forget your growing pains as a junior faculty member, there may be some that won't be able to forget. In other words, you don't want to let others see you 'eat dirt'[12] as a junior faculty member, because they may remember it!

Unfortunately, most of us, at least implicitly, understand people judge other people quickly; for those of you that need hard numbers, it has been reported you are judged by others in about 100 milliseconds[13]. Whether you consider this 'speedy judgment' to be right or wrong, just understand research clearly

---

[11] While that quote is most often attributed to former US Secretary of State Henry Kissinger, when he was a faculty member at Harvard, it has also been attributed to many others as well.

[12] This phrase 'eat dirt' is meant to convey the stupid things we all do as a kid as we are figuring out how the world works. Unfortunately, one of the things that most of us do when we are very young is trying to eat dirt. Most of us find out quickly, that dirt is not edible, just as junior faculty, we all find out things we shouldn't do, but usually we don't figure that out until we've done these things.

[13] And if you want to read the research that came up with that number, here's a great place to start: Willis, J. and A. Todorov. First Impressions. Psychological Science. 17(7): 592-598, 2006.

shows people will judge you very quickly and it is difficult to alter that initial judgment. In fact, when the time people had to make their judgments was lengthened from 100 milliseconds to 500 milliseconds, the judgments tended to become more negative! As an example, during the first seminar I gave as a post-doctoral fellow at Johns Hopkins, a professor stood up about 15 minutes into my talk and loudly stated "You don't know s*^&. I don't know how you got here, but I'll never come to another of your talks" and then stormed out of the seminar room. This professor's initial judgement – even though he did take 15 mins to come to his conclusion – meant that he and I rarely talked over the next three years even though our offices were less than 20 feet apart. While my experience was shocking and a relatively rare example of faculty judgment, it is an example of how you will have people that unfairly judge you during your career. Your challenge as a junior faculty member is to have the best interpersonal skills possible so you reduce your chances of being judged negatively.

There are literally hundreds of books and articles on how to develop interpersonal skills and you can't go wrong reading most of them. However, I've found interpersonal skills start with your overall attitude toward people. As such, you need to think about your general attitude toward people. Are you demanding with high expectations or are you a 'live-and-let-live' sort of person? Do you forgive people their mistakes or do you hold mistakes against people? Are you generally willing to work for the good of your unit or are you primarily concerned about your advancement and thus, always ask "what's in it for me"? None of these attitudes are necessarily better or worse and I've worked with academics over my career that have exhibited all these attitudes. But those academics that succeeded, in my observation, generally had an overall attitude toward people I call being *'professionally graceful'*.

I define being *professionally graceful* as being kind, considerate, thoughtful, and having a sense of propriety in the work environment with everyone you encounter. Being professionally graceful many times can be very difficult, whether we're talking about academia or in the 'real world'. It's too easy to want to verbally 'hit back', especially with today's easy accessibility to social media. It is hard to be professionally graceful when you get criticism on your research or on your teaching or on any other

---

Info to Know – 2.1
Being Professionally Graceful

As noted in the text, you often succeed with a healthy attitude toward other people. I've defined this type of attitude as being *professionally graceful*. While the definition is in the text, having a professionally graceful attitude will allow you to live and prosper in an academic setting, while helping you keep a healthy life balance. Those academics I've seen succeed in their careers were always professionally graceful.

aspect of your professional life. Having said that – and probably most of us recognize how difficult assuming an attitude of professional grace is – your best shot at navigating through your first five years is if you assume an attitude of professional grace.

One of my earliest interpersonal skill problems as a faculty member was expecting that everyone had the same drive, passion, and determination I did. My biggest issues were with my colleagues and students who weren't working as hard as I was or who weren't putting in the same amount of time. I couldn't understand why they weren't striving as hard as I was. My problem wasn't with my colleagues and students – they had their own journey to walk. My problem was I had expectations for them that were not appropriate. Projecting my expectations on others around me did nothing but hurt me by causing me frustration, anxiety, and worry. Now don't get me wrong; just because I don't generally have expectations of those individuals around me doesn't mean I just roll-over and take whatever they throw at me, on the contrary. Having few expectations of those around me makes it easier for me to pick and choose who I work closely with, because I gravitate towards those individuals that have a similar work ethic as do I. In short, they become collaborators. Those that don't have the same work ethic? I don't let it frustrate me; those folks become colleagues. Not having expectations is part of an overall attitude of professional grace; when you let people fulfill their expectations versus judging them because they don't fulfill your expectations, it is easier to be kind and considerate of those individuals and that leads to you acting in an appropriately mature manner.

Another key to taking on an attitude of professional grace is to always remember to listen first and then speak. There's an old saying that since God gave us two ears and only one mouth, we should listen twice as much as we talk. In general, that's a great rule of thumb. Probably the only critical point I distinctly remember from any of my counseling classes that I took during my Master's program was the continued emphasis on listening versus talking. It is amazing how much people will tell you if you just show a willingness to listen. Great counselors don't tell their clients what to think, they simply listen and guide the client through their feelings and emotions. As a faculty member, listening and helping to guide others through their feelings and emotions will be a critical skill you'll use with students, parents, colleagues, collaborators, and administrators. The best academics I've worked with are those that listened first. In fact, high up on my list of pet peeves for academic administrators are those that don't listen (usually to anyone). People that don't listen may be following their own knowledge, but without listening to others, they often end up being ineffective and close-minded.

Another interpersonal skill that will serve to foster an attitude of professional grace is developing calmness as opposed to anger in the face of setbacks. Anger rarely solves any problem; it may help get you attention, but often your anger will be remembered as a sign of immaturity (remember that phrase about not letting people see 'you eat dirt'?). Children have temper tantrums, faculty shouldn't. Many years ago, we were working to move the department into a new building and I had been put in charge of the organization of the necessary laboratory renovations. One of our junior faculty members rarely replied to my requests for input; however, one week before we were supposed to move into the new space, I found him outside some of the new laboratories cursing and berating some of our construction workers because the laboratory wasn't being painted the right color! Not only was his behavior incredibly inappropriate, it made me question his maturity and fitness to be a faculty member. So, when you are faced with a situation where you can be angry - and you will be faced with those situations – choose to step back, take a deep breath, and figure out how to solve the problem calmly. Your calmness can defuse the situation and prevent a small problem from becoming a larger problem that haunts you for the rest of your career.

One last factor that is important in developing a professionally graceful attitude is resilience. The concept of 'resilience' in professional situations has received quite a bit of attention in recent years and has been defined as 'an ability to recover from or adjust easily to misfortune or change'[14]. The most successful faculty members are those that are resilient, especially to change. Higher education is under pressure to change from many quarters and as such, the higher education situation you will be in will likely change drastically over your career. Since I began my academic career, I've seen at least three boom and bust economic cycles that have altered higher education funding (and research funding), the development and use of email, the internet, and online education, as well as working under numerous Department Chairs, Deans, and Provosts, all of whom brought change (like the Provost that abolished all departments one week and then reinstated them two weeks later). You too will see marked change over the course of your career and maybe during the first five years of your tenure. Thus, your resilience in the face of these changes will greatly determine your emotional and academic success.

Much like general interpersonal skills, developing professional resilience is the topic of many books and articles[15]. As you look through the books and articles on resilience, you'll start to see some consistent trends. One trend is

---

[14] This definition of resilience comes from Merriam-Webster.
[15] Here are a couple of good ones for you: http://bit.ly/B2Resilient1 and http://bit.ly/B2Resilient2.

that most of the tips on developing resilience include developing both a sense of optimism and compassion (or kindness). You'll remember that professional grace includes both kindness and optimism. Another factor in developing resilience is 'kaizen' which is a Japanese word meaning improvement. Generally, 'kaizen' is used to denote your commitment to daily improvement and an openness to getting better in all things you do. The concept of kaizen is one we'll come back to in almost every chapter going forward because one of the most important things you are judged on in Academia is your ability to grow and develop as an academic.

In summary, developing an interpersonal skill toolset is incredibly important for all academics. This toolset starts with an attitude of professional grace and includes developing appropriate expectations of others, having great listening skills, practicing calmness, and developing resilience. While there are multiple other characteristics you'll discover that will add to (or subtract from) your interpersonal skillset, work on those four core skills as you develop professional grace and you'll have a better chance in your P/T review.

> **Info to Know – 2.2**
> **Keys in Developing Professional Grace**
> 1) Be careful of having expectations of others.
> 2) Listen first
> 3) Develop calmness instead of anger
> 4) Develop resilience

Developing your network

Most of us have a sense of what a network is – a network is generally thought to be a system of linkages between different objects that serve to enable function. We are all parts of many networks; you have a family network, a friend network, maybe a faith-based network. These networks - you could also call them communities – support you in a variety of ways. While we are born into our family network (or at least a part of it), the other networks that are part of our lives must be developed. Since our focus in this book is on your development as a faculty member, your 'academic' network will be a collection of individuals you are linked to that will serve to enhance your career. So, when should you develop your academic network? That's easy: as soon as possible!

You probably began developing your professional network when you were an undergraduate, even if you didn't know it or didn't mean to. But since you are beginning your professional career now, you need to take every opportunity to develop your network of professionals. The development of this network will give you access to the knowledge, skills, and experiences of other professionals and so it is critical to begin building right away.

How do you develop your network? Again, the answer is easy: you just remain open to meeting and getting to know other people that are in your profession, in your department, in your College, and in your University. As noted earlier, you probably started doing this when you were an undergraduate; the professors in your specialty area as well as your co-students in your degree program were the beginnings of your professional network. From that point on, whether you knew it or not, as you progressed through your education, you continued to add members to your network.

While the start of your professional network may have happened without your knowledge, as a working professional academic, it is critical you actively work to build your network. You can't wait for people to come to you, you must be open and actively seek out people that can help you. This suggestion may be very difficult for you because it has been suggested in some forums that academics can be shy and introverted.[16] I am by nature a shy individual who would rather observe and listen. I had to be strongly encouraged by one of my doctoral committee members (thanks Dr. Franks!) to have a conversation with another scientist at a scientific committee that ultimately led to my doctoral dissertation work and my post-doctoral fellowship. So, even though you may be shy and introverted, you still must build your professional network.

I noted above this process is as simple as being open to meeting people in your academic circles; make sure you introduce yourself and get to know as many people as you can in your University and in your professional societies. However, because your job as a faculty member is more than just research, you also must diversify your professional network to include professionals in all aspects of your position (e.g., teaching and service). For example, one of the best 'network expansion' opportunities I had as a junior faculty member was to serve on the human subjects institutional review board and on the animal care and use committee at my University. While those were service commitments, those activities also put me in contact with individuals across the University who could provide research, teaching, administrative, and service expertise and advice. And that's what you want in a network; you want to develop your network so when you have a question, a concern, or a problem in your career, you have someone you can contact that has experience and/or advice for how to deal with that issue.

To a large extent, the challenges any academic faces over her/his career often require advice and guidance and not having a network to help you with these

---

[16] And if you're interested in whether academics are shy and introverted, here's a good link from the *Chronicle* to get you started: http://bit.ly/shy_introvert.

issues can be viewed as a deficiency. For example, a few years back, I was on a search committee for an upper-level university administration position. One of the committee members asked the following question of all the candidates we interviewed: "Do you have a network of professionals you rely upon when you have a tough decision to make? If so, how do you interact with that network when making the decision?" You can understand the committee was stunned when our leading candidate stated that s/he didn't depend or ask for anyone's advice when making tough decisions! That answer alone – at least in my mind – cost that candidate the job because it showed s/he didn't think input was necessary for tough decisions and thus, relied solely on her/his own experiences to make decisions (and this candidate's experiences were limited compared to the University they were applying to). Unfortunately, this candidate's lack of a network, removed the 'multiplier' factor a good network can bring to exponentially increase the experiences and expertise this candidate could have brought to bear on any problem.

Understand that during your career your professional network will change; your network will grow and evolve based on the challenges you face. As part of this growth and evolution, it is likely you will lose touch with some colleagues in your network. For example, it is likely that the early faculty members and colleagues you had as an undergraduate will not continue to be an active part of your professional network. I recently 're-met' another professional who had been a master's student when I was a doctoral student. We had only overlapped by a year, but for that period (and a small time afterward), we had been part of each other's professional network, but really had not been a part of either's networks since. However, upon getting reacquainted 33 years later, we'll now be a part of each other's network for the foreseeable future. Networks are like that; they change and evolve; people enter them, leave them, and then sometimes reenter them. The key is to be open to meeting (or re-meeting) people so your network continues to be a source of experience you can tap into when you need to.

> **Info to Know – 2.3**
> **The Key to Developing Your Network**
> The key to developing your network is to remain open to meeting and interacting with new people, both in your University and in your profession. The more people you meet and know, the greater the chance that you will add people to your network that will support you and facilitate your career.

Finding Mentors

As noted earlier, a mentor is someone who will provide their support, expertise, and experiences to help guide you in your career when you face specific issues. As such, mentors can be considered part of your professional network. Mentors can come from many different areas; however, in general, you'll find mentors usually fall into one of four categories:

- Professional mentors – people in your research or scholarly discipline that can advise you;
- Local university mentors – people that are in your University, but are not necessarily in your research or scholarly discipline;
- Departmental mentors – people that are your departmental colleagues you may work with; and
- Peer mentors – people that are at the same rank as you are that can provide advice.

Each of these different types of mentors can provide differing types of advice and experiences, and all are important to have in your professional life. For example, a professional mentor may be able to help you navigate publishing or grant study sections because of their knowledge and expertise in this area. It may be true you'll have a departmental mentor that can also help you with your research or scholarship activities, but it is likely you'll also have some professional mentors that will be outside of your University that will be with you throughout your career. In the same manner, an individual who is a local university mentor will be able to help you with university issues, but may not be able to give you advice in your research area. Further, you may find that the mentor that is the most help for your research program, may not be the best to mentor you through the P/T process (and vice versa). Because the challenges you will face as an academic will be broad, you need mentors that can help you across a wide-range of potential experiences.

How do you find and ask professionals to be your mentor? Much like building your professional network, be open-minded and take every opportunity to meet and talk to other people. Go to seminars, go to college get-togethers, even look around and meet people at your University orientation sessions when you start your job. As you meet and talk to people, be aware of the experiences they've had and how you interact with them. Are they easy to talk to? Do you get the sense they'd be willing to be supportive? If you can interact with a potential mentor easily, that will make your relationship easier. Additionally, as you think about meeting mentors, your new University may appoint mentors to you, or specifically ask you to identify people who can be your mentors. In either case, these are additional opportunities for you to add to your mentoring network.

Once you've identified a potential mentor, asking them if they would be your mentor is as simple as inquiring if they would have time to be your mentor. Be prepared to give the potential mentor an idea of how many times you'd like to meet and what areas you think you'll need advice in. You may find after a few meetings, you and your mentor decide to change the frequency of your meetings to an 'as needed' basis. However, I would recommend that you meet at least once every 6 – 12 months with your mentor(s); this type of meeting should be documented so you can prove that you were meeting with your mentor(s) on a regular basis as you develop your P/T portfolio. In the end, as you think about asking someone to be your mentor, one thing above all that you must remember is your potential mentors are also very busy and they are doing you a service to help your career.

When you meet with your mentor, be respectful of their time. As such, make sure you have an agenda for your meeting – a listing of the concise topics you want to tackle. These topics should focus on building toward P/T; every item on your agenda that you discuss with your mentor, you should be able to tie directly into P/T. With your agenda, also bring potential solutions with you; don't expect your mentor to solve your problems. You are working to become a fully independent and functional professional; believe me, figuring out the solutions to your problems on your own is a big key to being successful in academia, so be prepared with some possible solutions. The mentor's role is to help you figure out the advantages and disadvantages of the various possible solutions you've come up with. In this way, you'll learn appropriate solutions for what you're dealing with and can use this information in the future without having to tap your mentors' expertise.

Along with knowing what issues to cover when you meet with your mentor, there are some clear subjects with which you should not spend your mentor's time. Specifically, your time with your mentor should not be:
    1) A crying session;
    2) A therapy session; and/or,
    3) A complaint session.

Remember, you should discuss issues with your mentor in a professional manner with your goal of bringing potential solutions for the professional issues you have and discussing those solutions with your mentor.[17]

Where should your mentors come from? There is one last item to consider as you think about whom to ask to be your mentors: where should they come from?

---

[17] If you need therapy or someone just to listen to you, seek out professional counseling at your University. Most Universities have counseling centers for just such things and will handle your participation in a discrete and confidential manner! There is nothing wrong with seeking counseling if you need it. Just don't expect your mentor to be a counselor – in most cases, they don't have the training for it!

Should you have mentors from your department or from outside of your department? Should they come from inside your University or outside of your university? There are pros and cons to both questions, so, let's touch on a few.

- From inside or outside your department? In most cases, you can think of your department as a small community; it is filled with people you will interact with daily. These people are the staff and faculty that know the processes and history of the department. Because they have the knowledge and expertise, having an 'in-department' mentor is not necessarily a bad thing; the 'in-department' mentor can help you figure out how to get things done within the department (and many times, within the University). However – and it's a big 'however' – an in-department mentor is someone that will likely participate in your future reviews. As such, that potential mentor will also be making judgements about your future in the academic community. Also, an in-department mentor may be involved in departmental politics, which may (or may not) be detrimental to your career. I have known of departments where there were clear divisions between faculty members and if you aligned yourself with a particular faculty member, you then were automatically pegged as being on the 'other side'. As a result, getting full consideration for P/T would become more difficult. Thus, you need to pay attention to these potential disadvantages in having an in-department mentor. I'm not saying it is a bad idea to have an in-department mentor, just be aware of the potential disadvantages and be careful.

- From inside or outside your College/University? The same rationale goes for whether you should have a mentor(s) just from within your College/University. I will often advise junior faculty to look for mentors in a related department within the University (and often in a different college). Having mentors from within your College brings you back to the same potential disadvantages with politics and history (and remember there will be college faculty that vote on your P/T). However, an in-college mentor can also bring expertise regarding the processes within the College. One potential way to get around the disadvantages of both in-department and in-college mentors is to find mentors that work in a similar research or scholarly area but are in a different department or college in your University. With a mentor in a related research area, you get someone who is knowledgeable about what it takes to succeed in your research area, as well as getting someone who is familiar with how your University works and who can give you advice on that aspect. Additionally, with this type of mentor, you then have a mentor who is removed from having to serve or give opinion about your P/T, as well as being removed from the local department and college political issues.

If you are now confused about how to pick a mentor, you're not alone. Most new faculty need time to process and think about who their mentor should be. Picking mentors is an incredibly important task for your future success; I have seen poor mentoring make it incredibly difficult – if not impossible – for a junior faculty member to get P/T. So, you should think long and hard about whom you put on your mentoring team!

> **Info to Know – 2.4**
> **Characteristics of a Great Mentor**
> As you look for potential mentors, keep these characteristics in mind:
> 1) Do you feel comfortable talking to them?
> 2) Do they have experiences and expertise that will add to your career development?
> 3) Are they willing to help and support you?

Your colleagues

Your colleagues are often like your family or your neighbors in that you don't have much choice in who are your colleagues; they generally come with your department. As such, you have to remember your colleagues – usually those people who are also faculty in your department – will watch what you do, will judge you for what you do (remember, they may be involved in your P/T decisions), and will remember 'when you ate dirt' (or throw a fit, act out, etc.). It may seem unfair that how you interact with your colleagues may be used against you in the future, but unfortunately, your colleagues are human and humans let their perceptions affect their judgement. As such, I have continued to find that your best option is to take a professionally graceful attitude with your colleagues. You must work and interact with these people daily; why not make those daily interactions as pleasant as possible?

As referred to above, I have known departments where colleagues didn't get along; it's not a pleasant work environment to be in! Furthermore, it's not pleasant for the staff and especially for the students. As a senior colleague of mine has said, "These types of departments can foster exploitive senior faculty who use junior faculty to advance the senior faculty member's research and minimize the senior individual's teaching load." In other words, these types of work environments can exploit junior faculty. In one example (and no, I won't name the University), students of some faculty members were afraid to talk to certain other faculty members because their primary faculty member would then be angry with them for talking to those other faculty members! Yes, it can be like junior high school, and unfortunately, these types of situations do occur in academia. But the last thing you want is to find yourself in one of those dysfunctional departmental relationships. So, be professionally graceful!

You may be thinking – "geez, that's a cop-out; I have to take a 'get along to move along' attitude". To some extent, you are right. As a junior faculty member, you probably have thoughts and opinions about how the education of your students, curriculum issues, and other departmental issues should be resolved. But as mentioned earlier, academic politics can get extremely petty and nasty. And remember your priority as a junior faculty member is to get P/T. It will do you no good to get involved with all the departmental issues/politics and to take sides in the arguments no matter how well justified, if you torpedo your chances of P/T in the process. Don't get me wrong, honest and forthright communication amongst faculty members is valuable because it helps outline the different parameters of an argument, but honest communication can be fragile because words spoken in anger can take on a life of their own that can have ramifications for many years down the line. As academics, we are all good with words, so academic arguments, no matter how well intentioned, are fraught with the opportunity for misunderstanding and misapplication. You may find you are in a departmental situation that is just not tenable and it may be better for you to look for other positions[18]. Regardless, you must remember, the more neutral and professionally graceful you are, especially as a junior faculty member, the better chance you have of moving up in academia.

Finding collaborators

As you work to establish your academic career to give yourself solid footing for P/T evaluations, you will hear the word 'collaboration' used quite a bit. In fact, one of the constant conversations in most universities today, especially in research-focused universities, is on developing 'collaborations'. One of the reasons this is such a hot-topic is your chances for external funding increase if you are part of a collaborative team, especially one that stretches across multiple-disciplines. As an example of this trend, at the time of this writing, I am currently on four external grants – none of which originated in my home department; in fact, I do more collaborating with investigators in other departments than in my own department. My example is not because I dislike or can't work with any colleagues in my department, it's primarily because most of the funding I go after requires multi-disciplinary collaborations. You will find research development officers at most Universities know this and as a result, talk about collaboration a lot[19].

Because of the importance of collaboration, your University will encourage and work to develop collaborations amongst faculty. There are a variety of

---

[18] See Chapter 9 about this very tough, and touchy issue!
[19] There's also good economics data to support scientific collaboration as being more productive and efficient. This data is provided in an interesting book by Paula Stephan, *How Economics Shapes Science*, 2012.

approaches I've seen used, including scientific 'speed-dating' programs where people stand-up and have one slide and one minute to describe what they do, interest group lunches, and multi-disciplinary seminars focused on a specific research topic. You should take advantage of every opportunity you get – even the scientific speed-dating ones. Not only will you learn who is doing what at your University, but you may be able to develop collaborators and mentors from these sessions. For example, about seven years ago, I was asked to attend a large meeting concerning a potential on-campus NIH-funded Center focused on Environmental Health. There were about 40 investigators around the table and we each took 30 seconds to describe what we did. Environmental Health is not normally the purview of Exercise Physiologists, and indeed, I was the only person at the table from my discipline. Interestingly enough, by the end of the day, I had met many potential collaborators, two of whom turned out to become my close friends, co-grantees, and co-authors on many projects since. It's amazing how an exercise physiologist can add to environmental health! In short, take the time to go to all the research networking opportunities you can find.

One item that can be overwhelming when it comes to collaborations is determining how much of your time should be taken with collaborations. As a new faculty member with an exciting research area, you will probably be approached by others to participate in their research. Let's be honest: it's flattering to have someone be interested enough in your research area to ask you to be a part of their research. However, you have to remember that while collaborations are valued in academia and can lead to an expansion of your research impact, they can also take a lot of your time. Your focus must be on establishing your research agenda and not just helping others fulfill their research agendas. Further, you must establish your research independence away from your doctoral/post-doctoral supervisors and not allow continued collaborations with those scientists to be construed as a lack of research independence on your part. It is too easy to fall back on established collaborations from your past, especially in the first few years of your career, but these 'easy' collaborations can hurt you because they can be seen as a lack of research independence on your part.

While I'm never one to think of research collaborations in selfish terms, during your first five years, a question you should ask yourself is "how is this collaboration going to strengthen my *independent* research agenda?" Too often I've seen junior faculty get so caught up in collaborating with others that they neglect their own research agenda. So, collaborate, but don't let those collaborations push your personal research agenda to the background.

Collaborations can be very exciting and can lead to fun discoveries.

However, if the collaboration is not defined well, it can also lead to hurt feelings, frustrations, and lack of product from your efforts. So, as you discuss a collaboration with a colleague, make sure that you have a clear and honest discussion about the collaboration. In particular, I would suggest that you discuss items such as your exact role, start/end dates, authorship roles on manuscripts, project timelines, and plans for manuscript and grant submissions. You may want to add other pragmatic factors to this list, however, it is critical that before a collaboration starts, you are clear on what the collaboration will entail. Some issues caused by the lack of understanding in collaborations was recently related to me by a junior faculty member I know:

> "Coming from a PhD program, or from a postdoc position, we are, in general, following the lead of another PI and simply performing the role(s)/task(s) we are given. In a faculty position, we then have a leadership role in leading/contributing to projects, and I did not realize the importance of setting clear goals, expectations, and particularly individual roles, until I started my current position. I found not doing so was a recipe for chaos and misunderstandings that, if not addressed, results in tension and anger/frustration/irritation between involved individuals."

As we wrap up collaborations, think about your research and scholarship 'story'. Your 'story' isn't just a recitation regarding the work you do and how you do it. It's also the 'why' you research what you do and the *potential applications* for your research. I would bet your 'research story' is what makes your work interesting for others. Because we are all often our own worst critics – and because we all know the flaws with our research - we often think others won't consider what we do is interesting (yes, that even happens to senior investigators). You need to immediately correct that thinking; polish up your research story and don't be afraid to tell people what and why you do what you do. The academics I *don't choose* to work with usually fall into two types: those people that are a pain-in-the-behind to work with and those that have no passion and can't articulate why they are doing what they're doing. Be open to meeting people, be fun to work with, have a great research story, and you'll find you'll have more collaborations than you know what to do with!

The Take Home Message
As you might gather from this chapter, it is incredibly important – and maybe more important than anything else you can do – to learn how to work with people and determining whom to work with. Whether they be mentors, colleagues, or collaborators, you will find you cannot assemble a great career – that unknown piece of furniture you are assembling - without the help of others. How you treat people and how you work with them will be the

deciding factor in how successful your career is. So, while you are striving for P/T (which is *your priority*), you must remember you won't get there on your own. How you interact and treat people in your career will often determine whether you meet your goals and how much you enjoy your academic life. However, you must remember that you are building your academic career and not others' careers. So, while you should collaborate and work with others, make sure that your actions go toward creating your own research independence.

3

CAN YOU HEAR ME NOW? COMMUNICATION IS KEY

As you put together your 'career furniture', how you and others communicate about your progress can affect other's perceptions of your success. Political strategist Lee Atwater once said "Perception is reality". This maxim has now been ingrained in many leadership and management philosophies and books. While we might discuss whether this maxim is true or not, in fact, this is one of the realities of your life as a faculty member. How people perceive you may or may not reflect who you really are, but in many cases, all they have to judge you by is how they perceive you[20]. How many of us have perceived celebrities to be nice people when the only basis for our judgement is what we have seen about those celebrities in the media?

As a faculty member, you will interact with many people and often the only basis upon which they'll judge you is their perceptions of you. You must remember that academics are especially prone to judging by perceptions because they have imaginations and they often try to fill in what they don't know with extrapolations based on their experience and perceptions of you. In many cases, academics work in isolation while writing, preparing class work, or working on research and scholarship, and thus, if people don't see you or witness what you do, it is easy for them to make false assumptions about you and your value to the department. For example, many years ago I worked at an institution where there was (supposedly) an Associate Professor who was never in their

This Chapter:
General Guidelines for Communication 36
Communicating with staff 39
Communicating with students 42
Communicating with your colleagues 45
Communicating 50
Communicating with the external world 54
The Take Home Message 58

---

[20] If you want to dive off into the philosophical debate about this, as well as whether the prevalence of social media has changed the perception/reality issue, a great place to start is this article by Shahar Silbershatz. http://bit.ly/reality2perception

office, specifically asked for online courses so they didn't have to come into the office, and always seemed to be traveling. This Associate Professor never participated on departmental committees and didn't even post a picture on their university directory page. The rumor was that this Associate Professor was mythical; however, their supervisor swore that the faculty member existed. Regardless of whether this Associate Professor was productive or a good department citizen, their behavior and lack of communication with any other faculty established the perception that they were not a part of the department and was largely trying to get by without working.

Right or wrong, the point is that this person's behavior and lack of communication with the rest of the department led to the perception that a mistake had been made in hiring. Instead of having a fellow academic that was part of our community, we hired someone who purposely went out of their way to dodge their responsibilities. While the last chapter dealt with personal interactions and how that can lead to a favorable perception of you as a faculty member, this chapter will deal with other forms of communication – primarily written and verbal – and how those forms of communication can form the perceptions that people have of you.

General Guidelines for Communication

Communicating as a faculty member takes many different forms and uses many different media with many different populations. As a junior faculty member, my communication with others largely consisted of face-to-face verbal interactions or written/typed memos. With the advent of word processing, computers on everyone's desks, email, texting, and ubiquitous and widespread multiple flavors of social media, we still communicate verbally, but more often through the written word. No matter the form, in general, the same tips and techniques apply to all communications when you're a faculty member, with the overriding concern being to engender the most favorable perception of you and your work as possible.

In academia, there are five general groups of people you'll be communicating with including staff, students, colleagues, supervisors, and the public. These groups will overlap to some extent, but there are specific things to keep in mind

> **Info to Know - 3.1**
> **The Groups of People You Will Communicate With**
> As a faculty member, you have a large constituency to communicate with! This constituency can be broken into five primary groups:
> - Staff
> - Students
> - Colleagues
> - Supervisors
> - The Public
>
> How you communicate with each of these groups can greatly influence the perception they have of you as a faculty member.

about each group that make your communication with them unique. However, as unique as these groups are, there are four commonalities that apply to communication with all these groups.

1) Never write or say anything that you don't want people to remember or publicize. As a faculty member, you are a public figure. Your words and writings can be taken as a representation of your University. Thus, a good rule of thumb is to always remember to not say or write anything that you wouldn't want on the front page of the newspaper (or to be tweeted to millions of people). More and more, especially in legal proceedings and academic disagreements, faculty member's emails and text messages are being subjected to open records requests (or Freedom of Information Acts – 'FOIA' for short). So, you must remember that everything you say (especially if it is recorded) and/or write – even in emails – have the potential of being seen publicly. I was once on a grievance committee where the primary evidence against the faculty member came from text messages that had been saved by a student! Just accept that nothing you write, say, or put on social media is private. Make sure you would feel comfortable if the whole world read whatever you said or wrote. Remember you are focused on P/T[21] and because of your position, you are basically 'on stage' most of the time; make sure that your communications are such that you will not be perceived incorrectly by their contents.

2) Face-to-face communication is always better than written communication, <u>unless</u> you need exact documentation of the conversation. In today's world, it is much too easy and sometimes more convenient to communicate with people via email, text, or other means of 'instant communication'. I once asked one of my staff members to go ask our business office a fairly simple question. Later, when I asked what the outcome had been, my staff member said that they were waiting for the business office to respond to their email. What made this ludicrous was that the business office was only two doors down from us; a total of about 50 feet. Here we were waiting on a response to a very simple question because it was perceived that it was easier to send an email rather than walk 50 feet to get an immediate answer (which I told the staff member to go do and they had an answer in about three minutes when done verbally). To add to this, you must also understand that most academics get many, many emails every day. Why add to someone's burden if you can just go speak face to face?

Additionally, verbal communication is often easier because humans have developed ways to determine intent, emotion, and other context through verbal

---

[21] As in past chapters, P/T stands for Promotion and Tenure and includes those up for contract renewals as well.

communication; these are factors that don't become apparent in emails or texts (and no, emojis don't capture all the context). Thus, often a verbal communication can provide more detail and information than just a written request. Also, individuals tend to give you more information if you ask verbally. I've gotten to where I will not answer multiple questions through an email, but rather, tell people if they want the answers, they need to come see me. It is easier to answer multiple and complex questions verbally rather than typing/texting lengthy answers to multiple and complex questions. Lastly, I've observed that people have a harder time saying "no" to you if you ask them verbally. Having to look someone in the eye and tell them "no" is difficult and so, verbal, face-to-face communication is the best for asking and making difficult and challenging requests.

While I recommend verbal communication most of the time, there are times when written communication is preferred. For example, you may have a situation where you need a quote on a piece of equipment so your business office will purchase it. While you could get a verbal quote, in this instance, you need a written quote. Thus, if you have a situation where you must have documentation of exactly what was said, a text, an email, or a paper memo are all good ways to go, especially if you can show that the individual you sent it to received it.

In the end, always ask yourself if your communication should be verbal or written. Because most academics are inundated with written communication, it is often easier, more efficient, and more effective if you communicate verbally.

3) Tone of your voice – whether verbally or in writing – can be incredibly important in an individual's acceptance of your conversation. Humans are very good at picking up on a 'tone' or attitude of the speaker when either reading or listening to communication. Part of our facility with picking up tone comes from the non-verbal aspects of communication and so whether you appreciate it or not, the tone of voice you use in verbal communication as well as in written communication, can have an impact on how successful you are. Most readers of this book will be fairly masterful with language – both written and verbal – so it doesn't surprise you that 'tone' can come both verbally and in your writing. Academic administration taught me very quickly that having an inappropriate tone in my communications didn't help anyone be more efficient or respond more quickly. I found out quickly that I had to phrase all my communications with the spirit of being professionally graceful. As such, making sure that your tone is not egotistic, sarcastic, patronizing, arrogant, or condescending (just to name a few) in any of your communications will help set the correct tone for your communications.

4) Let communications, especially sensitive or difficult communications, 'breathe' for 12-24 hours. In some cases, a quick response to a communication you receive is appropriate or necessary. However, if you are in a difficult situation, or are faced with a controversial issue that you must respond to, in most cases, it does not hurt to compose your response (either verbally or written) and let it sit for 12-24 hours (or overnight) before you deliver that communication. You may find that after the heat of the moment has passed, you'll be calmer and better able to respond in a more effective, and more professionally graceful, manner. There have been few academic circumstances that I've seen over my 30 years that demanded an immediate reply. Letting my response sit for 12-24 hours always helps me craft a more professionally graceful response. So, if you are communicating about a difficult, touchy, or controversial topic, compose your response, step back and let that response breathe for a period, and then review and revise, your response. You'll find that just by letting your communication breathe, you'll be a lot more effective.

Info to Know – 3.2
General Rules of Thumb with Academic Communication

1. Don't write/say anything that you don't want spread all over the world.
2. Face-to-face verbal communication is always more effective than written communication (with some notable exceptions)
3. Make sure the 'tone' of your communication is professionally graceful.
4. If sensitive or controversial, let your communications 'breathe' for 12-24 hours and then re-edit.

The four general communication guidelines above will work with whatever group that you are communicating with. However, as noted above, there are five specific groups that as a faculty member, you will have some communication and/or interaction with which will demand different approaches.

Communicating with staff

One of the hardest working and most overlooked groups that you will be working with are university staff. Ranging from the administrative assistants that keep the University running, to the custodians that keep the buildings clean, to the repair people that keep everything functioning, to the Information Technology staff that keep our technology working, to the research compliance staff that make sure we don't violate federal laws in our research, a modern university cannot function without these valuable staff members. As such, as a faculty member, you would not be able to do your job if you didn't have staff supporting you in ways that you may not fully realize. As such, staff are incredibly important and can be a big help to you, or a big hindrance if you do not communicate with them properly.

For example, I was running a faculty search one time and as I did with all our searches, after all three candidates had their on-campus interviews, I sat with the staff that had interacted with the faculty candidates to get their impression. In one instance, we had a candidate that all the academics involved with the search were enthralled with – his CV was amazing, he had great skills in the classroom, and he seemed personally engaging. However, every one of my staff indicated that he was also rude, pompous, condescending, arrogant, and had been very difficult to deal with during his visit. Wow - talk about a wake-up call! In speaking to this candidate's references after his visit, they indicated that our staff's observations were primarily correct. This junior academic, though very promising, didn't communicate or interact properly with the staff and lost his chance for the position. Remember that staff, while often quiet, play a huge role in the University and as such, should be communicated and interacted with appropriately.

To that end, I think there are seven factors to make use of when communicating with staff:

1) *Always, always respect the staff.* If you recognize and accept the importance and critical nature of the staff in the daily operation of the University, respect will naturally flow out of that recognition. Therefore, in your communication and interaction with the staff, you should always work to transmit respect for who they are and what they do.

2) *Know their job profiles.* Staff members are different from faculty members in that their jobs are often tightly defined. Staff normally do not have the same autonomy as do faculty members and you must remember that as you communicate or interact with them. For example, I can't go into our business office and expect the business staff to help me with an IT issue – even if some of those staff are IT experts. It's not within their job profile to solve IT issues and thus, it is inappropriate of me to ask them to do so. As faculty, we often forget that everyone doesn't have the same flexibilities in their job as do faculty members, so remember that staff usually must work within specific parameters.

3) *You are not their supervisor.* In most cases, you are not the supervisor of the staff that you'll interact with. Those staff may be tasked with supporting you, but ultimately, as a new faculty member, they don't work for you. You are not their boss and you can't give them orders. Therefore, communication and interaction with staff, even if part of their job profile is to work to support your efforts, must be respectful and recognize that the staff's

instructions come from their supervisor and not you.

4) Respect the staff's privacy. As a faculty member, we are public figures to a large extent, especially if you work in a public university. However, staff are not considered public figures and thus, they aren't necessarily required to be public people. As a result, you should refrain from putting their names, information, or other types of information in the public arena. For example, in the states where I have been a faculty member, all faculty members were required to put their CV online (and sometimes their pictures), so parents, students, legislators, and the public can see the faculty members' background and training. Those types of stipulations do not usually apply to staff, so you should be respectful of their privacy and make sure you don't do anything in your communications that would breach their privacy.

5) Respect the staff's work habits. Much like faculty members, staff have specific work patterns. For example, in most cases, they are required to keep specific hours during the day, unlike faculty members whose work hours can vary greatly. Understand what the work habits are of the staff that you communicate with and do not expect them to change their work habits for you. For example, don't expect staff to work on the weekend because that is usually not in their job profile and they don't answer to you. Don't expect the staff to respond to emails after business hours. Even if you want to alter your work habits, do not expect the staff to alter theirs. And respect their right to their own work habits.

6) Don't use staff members as surrogates. As noted in the previous chapter, academic politics can be challenging at times. Refrain from getting the staff involved in these politics and don't use them as surrogates for your point of view. In most cases, staff must work with all faculty in the department and thus, they need to be neutral in all disputes, arguments, or departmental battles. Consider this from another perspective: do you want staff to take the 'other side' and be against you? If not, then help them stay neutral and keep them out of the conflict.

7) Be grateful in word and deed for all they do. Lastly, you should always remind yourself that staff are critical to what you and the Department do. All the work that staff do, they often do cheerfully despite usually lower salaries than yours and lack of

---

Info to Know – 3.3
Quick Guidelines to Communicating with Staff

1. Always respect the staff.
2. Know their job profiles.
3. Remember you are not their supervisor.
4. Respect the staff's privacy.
5. Respect the staff's work habits.
6. Don't use staff members as surrogates.
7. Be grateful in word and deed for all they do.

work flexibility. You may have found yourself reading the above paragraphs and thinking "wow, I'm glad I don't have that job!" Yet, remember that without these individuals doing what they do, much of the day to day work within the department would go undone. So, you need to be grateful and express your gratitude to the staff you work with in every possible way, with the easiest way being to be polite and kind in all your communications and interactions with them!

Communicating with students

While Chapter 6 extensively covers different approaches to communicating with students, there are some basic guidelines that are worth introducing here. Students are arguably the base reason why we have a job. I've often heard faculty talk about how peaceful the campus is during the summer semester when the students are gone, but this sentiment is quickly tempered by the realization that if there were no students, there would be no jobs! So, communicating and interacting with students is incredibly important. Also, given the proliferation of social media, your communications and interactions with your students can markedly sway public perception of your effectiveness as a teacher. So, it is critical that you carefully consider how you interact and communicate with your students. To that end, there are at least eight different factors that you need to consider when communicating with students:

1) Your students are not your friends. Especially as a junior faculty member, there may not be that much age difference between you and your students. However, there is tremendous life-experience difference between you and your students. Additionally, you have professional responsibility in the situation; you are paid to be their teacher, their Professor. You are not paid to be their friend. So, resist the temptation to friend all your students on social media, to hang out with them after class, or even to go out drinking with them. There are many stories about Professors who did those types of things not realizing that there were likely many conflicts of interests in such relationships and in the end, they wound up losing their integrity, reputation, and/or jobs. You can engage and interact with your students; you don't have to remain aloof and distance. However, you are the Professor. That is a special responsibility with specific judgement duties (like assigning grades). As such, treat your communications and interactions with your students as professional contacts.

2) There is a professional divide between you and your students. Related and intertwined with the last point is the realization that there is a professional divide between you and your students. The responsibilities that you have make your role in the student/teacher relationship one of privilege, responsibility, and trust. You are a respected figure and as such, you must make sure that your communications and interactions with your students support that relationship. Your communications and interactions should be respectful and professionally graceful. This type of approach is very hard sometimes, but if you remember that you have a responsibility to be professional, it should make deciding how to communicate and interact easier.

3) Remember your role and your responsibilities: The majority of your communications and interactions with your students, especially your undergraduate students, should be made within the spirit of you guiding and interpreting the content and information in your area with your students. It is critical that you remember that each communication and/or interaction you have with your students serves to support the students' learning and development. Thus, all communication should be with a supportive and positive tone; judgmental and negative communication will not move your students forward. There will be times that you will be frustrated with your students, but remember that words spoken (or written) in haste with an inappropriate tone will be remembered and many times be hurtful to your students.

4) Be engaged with your students: There is an old educational saying "They don't care how much you know, until they know how much you care" which I have repeatedly found to be true. You can try to communicate in every possible way, but only when your students know that you are engaged and you care about them and their learning will they truly listen. Simple approaches like knowing all your students' names (no matter how big the class) or speaking to them respectfully and setting appropriate expectations for your class will help your students realize you care and are engaged.

5) Remain calm in the face of everything: Panicking or getting overly excited does not help the learning environment remain focused. Also, if you get too 'ramped up' it is easier to slip and say or write inappropriate things. I've found that students will get excited enough for both of you – someone must be calm to handle what is going on. An unfortunate, but illuminating example of this guideline are the stories of teachers that have remained calm in the face of the school shootings. While distressing, it was heartening and rewarding to read the blog post from Dr. Adam Johnson[22] at UNC-Charlotte whose classroom was the scene of a shooting in May 2019. His account as well as the students that have talked about the event, illustrate the value of a faculty member remaining calm in the face of extraordinary events. While most of us won't face such extreme circumstances, remaining calm in the face of circumstances in your classroom (e.g., excitement over an exam return) will not

---

[22] http://bit.ly/mass_shoot

only help you as an instructor, but will also benefit your students.

6) Set appropriate boundaries: As you establish communication and interaction with your students, set boundaries for yourself and your students. When you set boundaries, you help students understand how it is appropriate to communicate and interact. Often, if you follow the notes from above, especially the note about you not being the students' friends, this will help them understand that you are a professional and should be communicated with as such. Simple items such as telling students you won't respond to emails after a certain time or that if they have questions about an exam they need to come see you, will help set boundaries so that you and your students can communicate and interact in an appropriate manner. One last boundary point, be careful what contact information you give students on your syllabus or in other avenues. Giving students social media contact information (as well as cell phone information) may lead to issues because these avenues of communication are often more informal and can infringe on your privacy. While it is up to you as to what information you are comfortable sharing, I would encourage you to consider setting up boundaries so that you can indeed have a private life and so that your students will interact with you on a professional basis.

7) Keep your office door open when talking to students: We live in an environment where every communication and interaction you have with a student can be questioned, judged, and/or misinterpreted. Thus, you should be extremely careful about having closed-door meetings with students, especially if you must give the student bad news (e.g., poor grade on an exam, poor behavior in class, etc.). This difficulty is further amplified because there is a power differential between you and your student. Thus, keep your door open to your office so that you have the potential for witnesses for your conversations. Further, if you anticipate a difficult conversation, you may want to arrange to have another individual sit in on your meeting. While most of your meetings with students will not be difficult or fraught with potential liability, it still is a good practice to keep your office door open where all interactions in the office can be easily observed from outside your door.

8) Listen to them: I've found that often, all students need is someone to listen to them. While many of us are not professional counselors, most of us understand that one of the biggest jobs faculty have is listening to students and helping them move to the next step. That next step may be a progression in their career, it may be what they are going to take next term, it may even be a great idea they have. However, faculty are like anyone else in that they are busy and have things that must be done and so sometimes, they pay only cursory attention to the people talking. As a junior faculty member, I once had a student come into my office with a class question. I told her to sit down and go ahead and ask; unfortunately, I was trying to finish up a memo (or something that I thought was important) and I famously said "go ahead and ask – I can listen while I finish this". Most of you cringed at my actions; I do as well. But being caught up in what I thought was important at the time – some meaningless document – caused me to ignore the important interaction that the student needed. That student – to her credit – replied, "No, if you can't take the time to look at me when we talk, then I can't take the time to ask" and went to get up to leave. That got my attention and taught me an important lesson – there is nothing more important than the person in front of you trying to talk to you. This lesson is more critical today with the proliferation of 'screens' all around us calling for our attention. Don't forget that there is nothing more important than that student in front of you. Listen and you'll be amazed at what you hear.

There is one last caveat to this whole section on communicating with students. When you become a faculty member, you are now going to be responsible for reporting certain conversations. Your University may be different than mine, but for example, if a student confides in me regarding sexual abuse or regarding several other protected areas, I am mandated to report these conversations to my superiors, whether the student wants me to or not. Thus, you should learn what areas where you are a mandated reporter and make sure that students know that in certain conversational areas, you have to report the conversation.

> **Info to Know 3.4 –**
> **Guidelines on Communicating with Students**
> 1. Your students are not your friends
> 2. There should be a professional divide
> 3. Remember your role and responsibilities
> 4. Be engaged
> 5. Remain calm
> 6. Set up appropriate boundaries
> 7. Keep your office door open
> 8. Listen when they speak to you

Communicating with your colleagues

You will often be interacting with your colleagues, collaborators, and mentors daily. You'll find that communicating and interacting with both colleagues and mentors are similar, even though your mentors will be more familiar with you. Your communication and interaction with colleagues is at a different level than your interaction with staff and students because the power dynamic has shifted. When you communicate and interact with staff and students, you have more power in those relationships. As you communicate with colleagues, the power differential is either equal or tilted against you (i.e., you have less power in the relationship). As such, you need to be mindful that your communication and interaction, while still following the same general rules as noted earlier, are of a manner where you are on the negative side of the power dynamic. There are eight general principles that should guide your communication and interactions with your colleagues.

1) You have few 'true' peer faculty: Many junior faculty mistakenly believe that their colleagues are their peers. While that thought is often promulgated by faculty and administrators, it is fundamentally flawed to think that your colleagues are your peers. You may have colleagues that have the same title as you do, but there are few that will be at the same time in rank or in the same discipline which makes your environment for communication unique. The most critical thing to remember is that those that are 'above' you in rank or in time in rank (e.g., an Associate Professor), have a high probability of being a mentor, or even a Decider in the evaluation and P/T deliberations in your future. Even though you would hope that you will be judged on your accomplishments solely, you should remember that how you communicate with your colleagues may affect your P/T deliberations. As such, you should treat your communication and interactions with your colleagues with the understanding that what you say and write could alter their perceptions of your fitness to be a faculty colleague in the department. Don't be paranoid about the situation, but do recognize that there is a probability that your colleagues will serve in a judgement role when you are evaluated.

2) Be honest and straight-forward: This principle you should generally practice, but at some levels, it is difficult to put into play. However, because many of us are in the business of determining facts (through science mostly), most of your colleagues will appreciate it if you are honest and straight-forward with them. Appearing to conceal the truth, or even to lie, will cause people to mistrust you, which will severely affect your credibility as a colleague. An important caveat to this guideline though is to use tact when being honest and straight-forward. Sometimes honesty can be perceived as a blunt instrument; often there are a variety of ways to be tactfully honest with people and you will never lose if you work to find the most tactful, empathetic, and caring way to be honest. Again, being professionally graceful encompasses the idea of tactful honesty because when you care about people you'll not only be honest with them, you'll also be sensitive to how you express that honesty.

3) Have appropriate expectations: Because faculty come in all types with their own measures of success, communication and interaction is easier if you have no prior expectation of what your colleagues should say or do. Your drive, your passion, and the measures of success that you use will likely be different than many of your colleagues. When you have expectations that your colleagues will act, think, or work like you do, that will only lead you to be disappointed in how they actually interact and communicate. It is likely your colleagues will have different opinions, work styles, and ideas from yours and as such, your expectations may prevent you from seeing the merit of their approach. So, let go of expecting people to be like you, have appropriate expectations, and you'll find that your interactions and communications are much better.

4) Be calm: Being calm was a guideline for communicating with students and for many of the same reasons, having a calm demeanor can only help the perception of you as a mature, thoughtful professional. Faculty often allow themselves to get excited, angry, and disturbed, so having a calm demeanor will be a positive characteristic that your colleagues will recall when you are being evaluated. This same calm attitude applies equally to your written communication; certainly, writing in a neutral, non-excitable tone will lend itself well to the perception of you being a mature academic. Besides, there will be enough excitable faculty in your unit without you becoming one of 'those faculty members'.

5) Document when needed: In most cases, verbal communication is much more effective than written communication. Unfortunately, you will have situations where you will need to have documentation of a conversation or topic and in these situations, you'll need to communicate through writing. In these situations, it is important to convey the facts of the situation in calm, non-emotional terms. Further, few people read lengthy emails; if you must use an email as documentation, make it as succinct as possible with other offline backup if the topic requires it. In essence, if you think you'll need proof of a conversation or documentation later, write it down. Sometimes, you just may be 'uncomfortable' with a situation and not sure that there is a real problem; this is a situation where you need to document whatever is going on.[23]

However, you can go too far with documentation. When I worked at a large governmental agency in the mid-80's, I was dismayed to find that the agency had a policy in place that required every employee, if they were asking another employee to do something, to write down and document the request. This agency even printed up sticky note pads that had the abbreviation 'AVO' on them which stood for 'Avoid Verbal Orders'. In the unit I worked, I quickly found that the edict on AVOs was absolute and included even the smallest things like 'please stop the treadmill, our subject is having difficulty keeping up with the treadmill pace.' Certainly, written documentation can go too far so you need to be sensitive to the difference of when you document and

---

[23] A great example of this is when James Comey had to testify in Congress. He repeatedly had taken notes throughout his conversations with all the major players in the issues that he was testifying about.

when it's not necessary.

6) Set boundaries: Much as you did with students, you need to set boundaries with your colleagues, but usually in a different manner. For example, most often as a faculty member, I've needed to set boundaries for when people come talk to me. Given that I keep my door open most of the time, there are always students or colleagues dropping by to chat. If you are professionally graceful, some colleagues will take that attitude as a sign that you have a lot of time for these spontaneous conversations. However, being professionally graceful also includes setting boundaries so you are treated well. For example, how would you handle a senior faculty member who comes into your office daily to complain about the University, your Department Chair, or other faculty members? It is easy just to sit there, listen, nod your head in agreement, or even join into the discussion! It is more difficult to recognize that by allowing this faculty member to vent every day, you are not only wasting your time, but because you allow this faculty member to share their negativity with you, it will probably increase your negativity. So, how do you solve this behavior issue?

The easiest way to handle this type of behavior issue is to be professionally graceful. However, once you realize that all the faculty member is doing is complaining, get them out of your office so you can go back to work. There are a variety of ways to get them out of your office; one of the easiest is to get up out of your chair and walk to the office door. Most of the time, when you do this, people interacting with you will get up and follow you. You can look at them and note that you must continue with the work you were doing when they walked in your office. This is usually enough to get them moving out of your office.

Another strategy is before you start talking to someone, give them a heads-up that you have another meeting in a certain amount of time (if that is true). It always seems that if I have a meeting in 10 minutes, people will come by to chat. In that case, I always note that I must leave in 5 minutes. If people ask you if you have time for a conversation, give them a bounded time (e.g., "Yes, would love to talk. But I've only got X minutes before my next appointment/experiment/meeting."). This plants in their mind that your conversation will only be of a certain length of time, and so when you get up and move toward the door, they'll understand and will be less likely to think you are rude.

While not allowing others to monopolize your time is one way of setting boundaries, it is also critical to set boundaries if you hear or observe unprofessional behavior such as a colleague saying inappropriate things to you or to students. You should not hesitate to deal with any unprofessional behavior immediately and appropriately. Often, dealing with inappropriate behavior is as simple as noting to the other individual "that is inappropriate, we shouldn't act or do such things". You may have times where you witness or are involved in inappropriate behavior that is more severe. These more severe cases of inappropriate behavior may be things like sexual harassment, or racial, ethnic, or gender hate speech. If you witness or are present for these types of situations you should leave immediately and seek out your Department Chair. Do not allow unprofessional behavior of your colleagues to continue without saying anything. Far too often, junior faculty think that they must put up with or accept unprofessional behavior of their colleagues. That is not true and you should deal with these items as soon as possible. These types of situations are not easy to deal with, but they will not go away if you ignore them and in today's university climate, there may be legal ramifications if you don't act.

In the end, when you set boundaries and stay consistent with your colleagues, they'll know how to interact and communicate with you which will serve to make your work life easier.

7) Resolve conflicts quickly: Just know that conflict will happen with your colleagues. It's inevitable. Sometimes these conflicts will be small ("hey, why did you throw hole-punch debris on the floor?") and some will be major ("These students don't need lab classes!"). As most of us can relate, even having two people in a relationship leads to conflict at times; imagine multiplying that possibility by the number of people in your new department! You and all your colleagues are different individuals, and as such, will have different approaches, opinions, and disciplinary standards. Thus, it is common that there are many conflicts that happen in an academic department. While you should not seek out conflict, you also shouldn't ignore conflict. Your goal should be to resolve the conflict as quickly as possible without damaging your working relationship with your peers. Most conflicts you have with colleagues will be relatively minor that can be resolved through further open and honest discussion. Work to not make the conflict personal – remember, you may just have different contexts for the issue. My experience is that in most cases, the other individual wants the same thing as I do, whether that is a better education for their students or better research. Rarely you will have a major conflict with another faculty member; however, if you do, the same advice goes for these types of conflict – try to resolve them quickly. If you need to get the Department Chair involved, do so, but continue to work on resolving the conflict. Your first step on all these processes is to talk to the Department Chair (unless your conflict is with the Chair), so if you find that you have a major conflict with a colleague, do not hesitate to bring the Chair into the loop.

Lastly, do not hesitate to use university reporting procedures if the conflict demands it. Many Universities have conflict resolution services, usually administered through the campus omsbudperson, who are people on campus specially trained in conflict resolution. For severe conflict – e.g., sexual harassment – do not hesitate to contact your University's Title IX office immediately.

Conflict is inevitable and how you interact and communicate when you have conflict with your colleagues is important in establishing others' perception of you as being a mature professional. Resolve conflicts as soon as you can so your conflicts don't poison your work environment. Unfortunately, too often conflicts aren't resolved quickly and can fester and grow into much larger issues that can affect you for years.

8) *Be professionally graceful:* By now, you've read this phrase many times. Remember that the perception that others in your Department, College, and University have of you will come from how you conduct yourself. If you are professionally graceful, regardless of the circumstance, this attitude will be reflected in your interactions and communications and as such, you will be perceived as a calm and mature professional, which will always be favorable for you during evaluations!

> **Info to Know – Box 3.5**
> **Guidelines for Communicating with Your Colleagues**
> 1. You have no true 'peers'
> 2. Be honest and straight-forward.
> 3. Have no expectations.
> 4. Be calm.
> 5. Document when needed.
> 6. Set boundaries.
> 7. Resolve conflicts quickly.
> 8. Be professionally graceful.

Communicating with your supervisors

As a junior faculty member, you will have no shortage of supervisors. They may have titles like 'Department Chair' or 'Dean' or 'Provost' or other titles that are unique to your Institution, but you will always have supervisors above you on the organizational structure chart. As such, how you communicate with your supervisors can often play a large role in how they perceive you as a faculty member. As a junior faculty member, I got a call from my Dean requesting an immediate meeting. I was smart enough to go see him as soon as possible, recognizing correctly that if he had skipped having my Department Chair talk to me, this was a serious meeting. I clearly remember my Dean looking at me across his desk and saying quite clearly "I'm tired of getting these radioactive memos from you. You need to learn how to communicate so I don't need nuclear-handling tongs to deal with these issues." I had been trained at a rough-and-tumble big science institution where these types of memos flew around and so I just assumed this was how all Universities worked. I didn't appreciate that my skills with writing pointed memos, and I admit, sometimes caustic and sarcastic memos, put me in bad stead when I became a faculty member at a different University. At that point, it was clear that I needed to figure out quickly the most appropriate way to communicate with my supervisors (as well as my other colleagues). Since that time, I've developed some guidelines I use in communicating with my supervisors.

1) Remember, these are your Bosses! Yes, academia may be set up differently from other large structures like businesses and corporations, but never, ever forget that the person you are communicating with is your supervisor. These individuals control many aspects of your work life from class schedules (do you really want to teach nothing but 8 am or evening classes?), to conducting your yearly and P/T evaluations, and generally are the ones that recommend and approve your pay raises. These items alone should help you remember that your communications with your bosses should always be calm, respectful, succinct, and to the point. Your boss has already got a full plate of issues, do you really want to be the one that adds more to their plate, especially if you are doing it in a disrespectful manner? You can quickly be perceived as a diva or divo[24], and you must remember that divas/divos always die in the end![25]

2) Never surprise your supervisor: Certainly, you will deal with issues as a faculty member where your supervisor will have to be involved. However, you will also have to develop a sense as to what issues have a possibility of landing on your supervisor's desk in the future. As a faculty member, there will be many small situations you will be empowered to handle, but you must realize that some of these issues might be eventually elevated up to the Chair. For example, if you have a disruptive student, you may be able to handle the situation within your classroom, but you should also make sure that your Chair is aware of the situation (and this is a time when you need to document). There is always a possibility that an issue with a student will be elevated 'up the line', so it will be helpful if your supervisor has a heads-up about what happened and how you handled it. So, whether a situation involves issues with a student(s), issues with research, or any other issue, always give your supervisor

---

[24] A 'divo' is the male equivalent of a diva, even though some have suggested that 'divot' may be a better term!
[25] Of course, that is metaphorically and operatically speaking. I don't expect you'll die if you don't communicate with your bosses in a respectful manner. If so, I would have been dead many times over!

a heads-up even if you have already 'solved' the problem. This type of heads-up can be as simple as a short email or a short conversation saying "Hey, this happened and this is how I took care of it. Just wanted to let you know." It is better to err on the side of caution, and as you have more experience as a faculty member, you will develop a sense of what is important to communicate and what isn't.

3) *Learn the management/work style of your supervisor:* The type of management and work style that your immediate supervisor uses should be a key to how to best communicate and interact with them. Here are a few work styles to consider and observe.

>a. Does your supervisor walk around and engage with you or sit in their office and wait for you to engage with them? If your supervisor comes to you, certainly it is easier to communicate with them, because often it will be spontaneous and verbal. If your supervisor stays in their office, it will be up to you to keep them appraised of your progress, maybe through drop-ins or a quick email when something goes well (i.e., you have a publication, etc.). This management style is a 'comes to you / you go to them' decision which depends on how much you want your supervisor to know about your progress. In general, it helps if your supervisor knows what you are doing and what your progress is, but don't wear out your welcome by dropping in every day. I used to have one colleague that seemed to wander the halls with frequent drop-ins when he was not teaching. After a while, this faculty member's incursions in my office became a bother; don't become that faculty member!

>b. Does your supervisor leave you alone to do your job or feel that they need to tell you what to do? This situation is where you have a supervisor that is comfortable with giving you responsibility versus one that feels the need to micromanage. Most of us don't like micromanagers, but, the type of management style in this situation boils down to trust. Some supervisors will trust you to do your job and others don't. You need to recognize which of these your supervisor is and communicate and interact appropriately. If your supervisor is the type to give you responsibility and let you run, you should update them on a regular (e.g., monthly) basis on your progress. During your first five years as a faculty member, it is critical that you keep your supervisors apprised of your progress. However, if you have a micromanager, you must work on helping the individual trust you enough so they do not micromanage you as much. Sitting with a supervisor and having a conversation about why they feel they need to micromanage is a conversation that may make you cringe, but, if done in a respectful manner,

you may find that they have reasons for keeping a close eye on you.

I've seen some faculty react to a micromanaging supervisor by avoiding their supervisor, but this tactic is ineffective because it just leads to a greater distrust on the part of the supervisor about whether you are really doing the job. In some situations, once your supervisor sees your progress – e.g., articles published, grants funded, and/or good teaching evaluations – they'll trust you more and micromanage less. However, this is the management scenario – trusting or micromanaging – that I've seen most often drive faculty to take a new position. If you can determine as early as possible what type of management style your supervisor has you will know how to interact and/or communicate appropriately so you can remain as productive as possible.

c. Is your supervisor open to conversation or do they lecture to you? Face it, as a junior faculty member, you are once again on the bottom of the totem-pole when it comes to experience and time serving. As such, there will be those colleagues and supervisors that don't think you know much yet, and will feel compelled to share with you their opinions. As you think about communication with your supervisor, determine how they communicate with you – are your conversations true conversations where your supervisor listens or do they become lectures with your supervisor telling you what to do? Whichever direction those communications go, use this information to determine how to best communicate. Certainly, it is easier to communicate with a supervisor who has open conversations. It is more difficult if your supervisor lectures. One approach I've seen a junior faculty member take with a supervisor that lectures, is that she prepares an agenda for their conversations and will send that agenda to the Department Chair the evening before their meeting. Thus, the junior faculty member has given the Chair a list of the topics they have to cover with points about her progress on these topics. This junior faculty member figured out that the best way to communicate with her Chair was to provide the narrative in advance, which helps control the conversation and decreases the lecturing.

d. Is your supervisor calm or emotional/excitable, professional/businesslike, casual/familiar, or disengaged/removed? While supervisors may show a variety of styles of communication, in most situations, it will not hurt you if you are professional/businesslike in all your communications and interactions with your supervisor. While I've talked earlier about setting boundaries with your students and colleagues, you should keep in mind that boundaries also need to be in place with your supervisor. Because there is a power differential favoring the supervisor in your relationship, your communications and interactions must be professional and businesslike. Over time, your communication style with your supervisor may become more casual and familiar just because you know each other better, but at the root, your communication still needs to remain professional.

e. Do they listen or rush you out of the office? In the last section, we talked about setting boundaries with your colleagues and 'helping' them out of your office if their visits go too long or are too many. You should be aware of a similar dynamic when you talk to your supervisor. Your supervisor may not have time for extensive face-to-face meetings and you need to recognize that and if appropriate, communicate through written means. At the same time, you need to be sensitive to the workload and schedule of your supervisor and recognize that your ability to have office visits with them will depend on their schedules.

In short, communicating with your supervisor is critical to do. You want to make sure that your supervisor is aware of your activities and aware of any issues that you've had to deal with in case they must get involved. Additionally, if your supervisor is aware of what you are doing, it will be easier for them to make positive decisions for you throughout your time as a faculty member.

> **Info to Know – Box 3.6**
> **Guidelines for Communicating with Your Supervisors**
> 1. Don't forget they are your boss.
> 2. Don't surprise your supervisors
> 3. Understand your supervisor's work style and communicate appropriately.

Communicating with the external world

As a faculty member, you occupy a privileged position in our society; you are trusted with young minds and often with a great deal of latitude in your schedule and the topics you investigate. As such, it is important that you are open with society about what you are doing. Lack of transparency is often why the public mistrusts Universities and that point is borne out in survey after survey about the public's perception regarding higher education. Thus, I continue to be an advocate for faculty members communicating with the public outside of the university. However, it is often easier to only communicate with those in our discipline because we all speak the same language, understand the underlying contexts, and have basically the same assumptions. It is much harder to speak to the public because they don't understand the verbiage of your discipline, you often have to start the conversation with first concepts, and the public doesn't have the same built-in assumptions and biases as we do. Because of these reasons, scientists and scholars are often hesitant to speak to the public (or talk to the media) for the fear of misinforming or being taken out of context.[26]

While it is difficult to communicate with the public, the danger of scholars not speaking to the public is that the public will then get their 'facts' from less reliable sources. Take an example from my discipline: all you have to do is look at the plethora of nutrition advice on the web and then carefully consider the sources of that advice – which mostly come from lay individuals, including movie stars and former athletes. Because experts in nutrition often abandon the public spaces, large numbers of uneducated, misinformed sources have arisen to provide commentary that is often incorrect, and many times potentially dangerous.

On the other hand, when scientists engage the public, understanding and more critical thought can arise. For example, Dr. Katherine Hayhoe at Texas Tech University is a Climate Scientist who has chosen to engage the public in a variety of formats[27]. She continues to present a remarkably calm, balanced, and scientifically-valid overview of climate change questions to the public in a wide-variety of settings. I would encourage all scientists to engage in similar types of interactions; not only do these types of engagements help the public understand the current scientific facts, but these engagements help the public see that scientists are human as well, just trying to do the best job they can.

You'll also find that many public outlets also want to talk to you; often it is as simple as reaching out to your local newspaper and volunteering your expertise. When I took over my current position, I immediately reached out to the editor of the local newspaper and met with her. She was glad to meet and noted that in her 10 years as editor, I was only the second faculty member to reach out to her. Given that our University has around 3,000 faculty members with many public-facing programs, it was astounding to me that others had not thought to just have a meeting. From that initial meeting with the editor, we've supplied a weekly science-topic blog to the paper's website, which as of this writing has garnered over 100,000 hits. As an educator and a scientist, I will never complain about potentially impacting thousands of

---

[26] It's also hard for the public to understand scientists when we use so much jargon. A great website that will tell you how much jargon you are using in your public writing is at www.scienceandpublic.com.

[27] An amazing example of Dr. Hayhoe's outreach is this TEDx talk she gave (http://bit.ly/KH_climate_TED). Watch it and note how she approaches the topic which makes the science and the conversation approachable and less divisive. Also, check out her website to see how she engages the public – what a great role model, http://katharinehayhoe.com/wp2016/.

people directly. This is the type of opportunity you have as a faculty member – reach out and interact with the public. You'll have to change your presentation style a bit, but it is worth the time and effort that you put into it!

As a public figure and a public speaker, there are some guidelines you need to keep in mind when you communicate with the public. Here are the three that I think are most important.

1) Familiarize yourself with your College's/University's policies for dealing with the external world. You may find that your College or University has a public relations office that requires you to go through them when you talk to the media. If so, go meet the staff in the public relations office and let them know you are willing to talk to the external world. They'll work to understand your areas of expertise and will help you understand the guidelines about what you can or can't say to the media. In many states, if you are in a public university, you are a public employee, and as such, there are often laws that prohibit you from talking about topics in which you are a non-expert or prohibit you from talking to policy makers without previous clearance. If you identify yourself as an employee of the University in public communications, you are acting as a representative of the University, and thus, the University will want to make sure you are not misrepresenting the University or your position. Conversely, as a private citizen (not claiming affiliation with the University), you are free to speak about any situation/topic. For example, if I wanted to lobby my congressman about climate change issues, I could do it as Dr. J. Timothy Lightfoot, private citizen, but because it is not my recognized area of expertise, I couldn't do the same lobbying representing myself as Dr. J. Timothy Lightfoot, Texas A&M Professor. This is just one example of a policy that your University may have regarding you interacting with the public; make sure you understand all the policies that are in place before you go out and give public talks or write public blogs.

2) Be cognizant of what you say/write in public: This guideline loops back to our general discussion of being careful about you say and write, but is certainly germane here because you are certainly speaking/writing in a public context, and methods such as social media can amplify your message quickly. Therefore, don't say or write anything you don't want potentially millions of people to see and comment on. In that same vein, I would be extremely careful of even saying anything 'off the record'. While most journalists I know will respect an 'off the record' request, some journalists may not and you do not want to deal with the fall-out from these types of comments. There are many, many examples of public individuals who have made inappropriate comments when they believed that they were 'off the record' or the 'mic wasn't turned on'. Be careful and don't let your inner-most thoughts out!

3) You are always on stage: You should always keep in mind that in all public venues, which includes your classroom, you are on stage. As such, you are representing yourself, your department, your College, your colleagues, your University, your discipline, and academia in general. With social media channels, there have been many examples where students record what happens in class and then broadcast that to the world[28]. While being on stage all the time may seem like a lot of pressure, that representation is at the heart of what academics need to keep in mind with their communication and interactions. As a public figure you should always convey a calm, professional demeanor. This type of demeanor – which is encompassed in your professionally graceful attitude – will always serve you well in the public eye and will help everyone have a positive perception of you.

4) Don't allow your efforts at communicating with the public to take priority over your research communication efforts. It can be invigorating to find that you have information that the public is interested in hearing. However, you want to make sure that your public outreach efforts do not interfere with your research communication efforts. After all, as a junior faculty member, you are being paid to primarily do research, develop funding, and teach; your University has a whole staff of communication experts whose job it is to talk to the public. While, none of us should ever hesitate to communicate with the public, you must be careful that you don't spend more time doing that than you do pursuing the dissemination of your research.

One of the recent conversations I've been having with my doctoral students is whether the use of some social media outlets (e.g., Twitter, Instagram) to promote science fulfills our mission to disseminate science. In the sciences, none of the social media outlets is currently considered an appropriate venue for science dissemination; thus, as a junior faculty member, time spent on pursuing these outlets is time taken away from disseminating your science in accepted and recognized scientific outlets.

In summary, speaking to the

> **Info to Know – Box 3.7**
> **Guidelines on Communicating with the External World**
> 1. Understand your University's rules for speaking to the external world.
> 2. Be cognizant of what you write/say in public.
> 3. You are always on stage.
> 4. Don't allow your efforts at communicating with the public to take priority over your research dissemination.

---

[28] If you are interested in this trend, a great article from the *Chronicle*, "What happens in the classroom, no longer stays in the classroom" (July 19, 2018) is a great place to start your reading. http://bit.ly/classroom_recording

world is fun and can be validating and gratifying, but don't let it get in the way of your scientific production!

The Take Home Message

Communication and interacting with other humans can be immensely rewarding but also extremely frustrating at times. However, appropriate communication is critical to assembling a successful academic career. As a public figure and one that has a societal responsibility, your methods of interacting and communicating will give others a perception of who you are. The tendency of humans to use perception as reality is a fact that we must accept and learn to deal with. If you work to keep a professionally graceful attitude, coupled with appropriate communication and interaction skills, others will see you as a calm and mature professional. And frankly, a foundational perception of you as a calm and mature professional will help others view your academic record in a positive light as they consider your research/scholarship, teaching, and service when they evaluate you for P/T.

4

FUNDING YOUR RESEARCH AND SCHOLARSHIP: THE SKILLS THAT WILL SET YOU APART

Sometimes, as you put together that piece of academic furniture, you'll have parts that you don't see how they fit, but in the end, they are critical to the successful assembly of the furniture. It is likely you have already heard one or more of the following phrases: 'writing grants', 'finding money for your research', or 'developing external funding' and you may not know how they apply to your career. These phrases all refer to the modern demand on faculty to support their research, preferably using money from outside of the university.

'External fund development', in addition to the traditional pieces of teaching, research, and service, started making its presence known in most Universities in the United States approximately 30 - 40 years ago. External fund development has always been a necessity in 'soft-money' institutions, this 'grant-getting' necessity has slowly crept into all areas of higher education as the leaders of higher education institutions have looked for ways to offset the cost of research. In short, in most aspects of higher education, external fund development has become a critical piece of most faculty members' careers to not only establish your scientific independence, but also to offset the cost of research. And while finding funding is difficult, if you work to develop funding, you'll find there are many advantages to your efforts, including helping your P/T application go much smoother.

As a junior faculty member, the 'encouragement' to develop funding always bothered me. My irritation was because I was trained as a scientist, not as a salesperson/marketer for my research ideas. In fact, I had and still have many conversations with faculty and administrators about whether external fund development should be a part of a faculty member's job. However – and this is the take home message – whether you like it or not,

This Chapter:
The Flip Side 60
Do you have to have funding? 67
The advantages and disadvantages of getting funding 70
Types of funding 75
How your department sees your grant efforts 82
The Take Home Message 84

external fund development has become a necessary and critical portion of many tenure-track faculty jobs. In fact, in many cases, if you – as a junior faculty member – do not work on procuring research funding, especially in R1-R2 Universities, it is likely you will not be given tenure or promotion. So, in short, developing research and scholarship funding is a critical piece of your job and is almost as critical as doing your scholarship and disseminating your results. However, writing for external funding is different than writing scholarly papers since it requires a different set of skills that you'll need to develop; that is why I've separated this topic from the research and scholarship chapter.

Before we jump into details of external fund development, you should understand that the amount of funding you need to procure will depend greatly on the demands and needs of your research and scholarship. Life sciences research programs cover a great range of research topics, methodologies, and philosophies, all requiring varying amounts of funding. For example, in my current department, I have colleagues in the divisions of Community Health and Sports Management that have relatively few needs for funding; in most cases, they don't need equipment and supplies, but rather need funding to support their salaries and graduate students. Conversely, in my lab – where we do a lot of molecular techniques in animal models – not only do I need to support researchers, graduate students, and animal costs, I must also purchase and maintain a wide variety of equipment and supplies. So, the amount, type, and sources for funding will vary greatly by discipline and research approach.

The Flip Side
The longer I've been in academia and the more administrative roles I've had to fill, I've developed a greater appreciation for why universities want their faculty to write for external funding. In my experience, universities want their faculty to be research-prolific; they want them to have an impact in their scientific area. After all, if your faculty are research-prolific, that is good for the University's image. However, to do research, it costs money. There are no research and scholarship areas where the cost to do research is zero. As such, there must be money available to do research and scholarship and therefore, most universities want their faculty to build external research funding because of the overall university budget.

Over the past 30 years, university budgets – especially public university budgets – have not kept up with inflationary increases. At the same time, state budgets have become tighter and politicians have decreased the amount they are willing to spend on higher education. Since 1975, when state spending on higher education peaked, the amount states spend on higher education has decreased by approximately 50%.[29] In fact, if trends continue, states will spend zero on higher education in the year 2059 (on average). What does this mean to you as a junior faculty member? You need to appreciate that your administrators are trying to find money to run your University. Since the continuing trend has been for states to decrease their support, to make up the shortfall, Universities raise tuition (it is now estimated student tuition pays ≈44% of the budget vs. 20% 30 years ago[29]) and search for other funding avenues. Your administrators need faculty to search for funding to help offset the cost of running the University, of which one of the largest parts is faculty salaries and the cost of research activities.

You may be thinking "Wait, if I find funding, that just pays for my research and scholarship. How does that help the University's bottom-line?". Part of your hypothesis is correct; external funding does pay for your research, which in many cases will include parts of your salary, which saves the University money. But there is also another aspect of external funding that can tremendously help the University's bottom-line and that aspect is known as 'Indirect Costs' (or IDC[30]). IDCs are technically cost recovery mechanisms and are the way universities can recover at least part of the costs associated with your research and scholarship. For example, one indirect cost of research is the cost to supply lights (and water, etc.) for your office and laboratory.

With potentially hundreds of labs at a university, these indirect costs add up. When the University tacks IDC onto your grant, those IDCs – theoretically – go to offset the costs of your research. And it is not just utility expenses making up indirect costs; there are all types of indirect costs to support your research including the actual costs of your laboratory space (i.e., rental costs for your space) and

> **Info to Know – 4.1**
> **Why is external funding important to your University?**
> 1) External research funds offset the cost of research and can help keep tuition lower for students;
> 2) Associated indirect funds (IDCs) help support research and general functioning of the University;
> 3) External research funds are often used as a marker for the amount and level of research done at the University (i.e., they are a 'research scorecard').
> 4) External funding can enhance faculty productivity, impact, and scientific reputation.

---

[29] There are several great reports that show this clearly. Here are a couple: one from the American Council on Education (http://bit.ly/2StateFunding) and one from the Center on Budget and Policy Priorities (http://bit.ly/2StateFunding2). Warning: these reports are depressing!

[30] These IDC are also known in some Universities as Facilities and Administrative Costs or 'F&A' costs

the cost of research administrative personnel (i.e., compliance, accounting, contracts, etc.) to name just a couple of common indirect costs. It takes a lot of money to run a research enterprise! As one example, our University estimated back in 2010 that to submit each grant, it cost the University almost $800. That $800 cost did not count the faculty member's time, but was just the indirect cost required for the *submission* of the grant. You can readily see why Universities want and need to charge IDCs; they must recoup the hidden and support costs of research. A handy way of thinking about how this all works is in Figure 4.1.

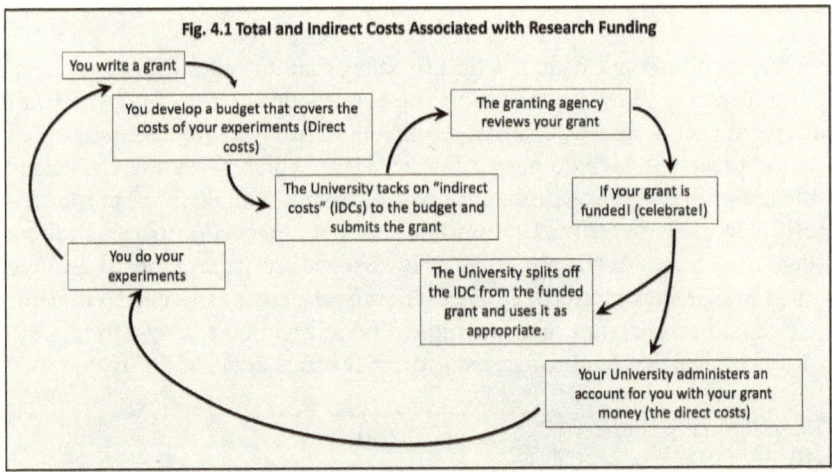

The IDC rate a university charges is normally set through an agreement between the University and the federal government. The Federal government gets involved because grants from the Federal government through the National Institutes of Health, National Science Foundation, Department of Education, NASA, and other federal granting agencies, are all federal monies. Thus, each Institution has an IDC that is negotiated with the federal government. The IDC that is negotiated is based on many factors, including the cost of utilities in the University's area and other local factors. So, your University will have a specific IDC rate they must use for federal initiatives.

This IDC rate is often expressed as a percentage of the total grant cost and varies across the country; IDCs can range from 100% to less than 30%. You will need to ask your Department Chair what the IDC rate is for your University. As an example, if your University's IDC is 50%, that will mean the total indirect charge tacked onto your grant will be 50% of the total amount it will cost you to do your research (aka: Direct Research Cost). Thus, the IDC amount will be added to the direct research cost for a total grant cost. Confused yet? An example may help.

Let's suppose you are going to ask for $1 million to fund your research project and your University charges 50% IDC. That $1 million is the direct cost of your grant, while the IDC amount that will be added to the $1 million will be $500,000. But don't panic, the IDCs are not normally taken out of your direct costs; instead they are added to it, so your University's IDC will not affect how much you ask for and potentially receive.[31] Given our example, the total grant request to the funding agency will be for $1.5 million; $1 million will be set aside for your research, while the University will take the $500,000 in IDC (see Figure 4.1 for the flow of this process).

Even though IDCs come as a result of research grant proposals, Universities do not necessarily have to spend IDCs on research costs; in most cases, Universities can spend IDC on whatever they want. While there is justification for the charging of IDCs, the University (usually the President/Chancellor/Provost) decides how those IDCs can be spent. And IDCs can be a big source of revenue for the University. As an example, it is not unusual for a large R1 university to have more than $100 million of annual research expenditures. If the IDC rate is 50%, you can quickly understand that anyone would welcome an additional $50 million to the University's revenue. The costs of research and the need to recover those costs, make research a business enterprise for the University - and that's before we even think about the revenues of patents and licensing of the discoveries from the research!

Here's one more example to help you understand why the University would be interested in research from a business perspective and the role of IDCs in offsetting the costs associated with research. Let's assume you are a Full Professor and a productive researcher who is successful at bringing in research money. Let's hypothesize you are bringing in $1 million/year in research grants (and for successful Full Professors in Life Sciences, that is not an unusual amount of grant funding). With an IDC of 50%, this amount of grant activity means you are bringing in an additional $500,000 per year to your University in the form of IDC.

Another university may try to recruit you away with a lucrative package - say they offer to spend $5 million to bring you and your team into their University. While that's great for you (and very likely your current University will work hard to keep you), the University that is courting you is doing it from a business perspective. They know if you have a record of successful grant

---

[31] In some European funding situations, the IDC is funded out of the direct research costs. In other words, the funding agency will only fund a specific total and this specific total includes both IDC and direct costs.

funding and bringing (on average) $500,000 of IDC every year, their $5 million investment will be paid off in just 10 years and then anything else you bring in will be bonus. In other words, to make money through IDCs, the University courting you spent money with the *assumption* you'll continue to bring in that amount of money on a yearly basis.

Often, the amount of start-up money a university offers a new faculty member is based on the same math. If you get a start-up package of $250,000, the University believes that by the time you receive tenure, you will have brought in enough IDCs to repay that initial start-up investment. In my field, it is hoped a starting faculty will land an independent federal grant (e.g., an NIH R01-level grant). This level grant is usually for five years at approximately $250,000/year direct cost. That means over five years, the direct costs will be about $1.25 million and the IDCs (if the IDC=50%) would be $612,500. You will have paid back your start-up costs and more, and the University will be happy. So, if you are uneasy with the financial side of the research enterprise, you should be aware the University has to treat it like a business to offset the costs of research. Research and scholarship are never free and the University has to offset those costs in some way. If you want to think of it in a more positive light, faculty bringing in IDCs may also help keep tuition from rising as fast and that's great for the University and students!

There can also be a financial impact on *you* when you bring in IDCs. A university will be quite clear about how they spend IDCs and will have an official document that describes how the IDC funds are used. For example, one University I was at took 92% of the IDCs and put them into a building fund. The other 8% was used by the President for special projects. However, most Universities are very good about including the College, Department, and the Investigator in the IDC benefits.

In many cases, your College will get a percentage of the IDC that comes from your grants (usually 10-15%), while your Department will get a percentage (again 10-15%), while you will also get a percentage. Thus, if you are awarded an R01 grant, you could wind-up with a fair amount of additional funds you can use for your research program. However, let me stress how a university uses IDCs are up to the University and can change at any time. Ask your Department Chair how the IDCs are distributed, or look on your University's Sponsored Research website, to get an idea of how your University handles IDCs.

As you move forward with your research, be aware that not all granting agencies are willing to pay 'full IDCs' and some will only pay a portion (or none) of the IDC. Large charitable organizations, like the American Heart

Association, often will only pay a partial IDC, so if you get a grant from one of these organizations, your University will be getting less IDC revenue. For example, in the past, the American Heart Association has capped their IDC payments at 8%.

From the University's perspective, if they don't get full IDCs when you have a grant funded, they view that as losing money because they are going to have to pay for your research costs from other sources. So, your University may strongly encourage you to apply for grants that pay full IDCs; in fact, they may not let you apply for grants that don't pay full IDCs. If you want to apply for a grant from an organization that does not pay full IDCs, you may have to get permission to get a portion of the IDC waived so you can apply for these grants or the University will want you to find funds to make up for the portion of the IDC that is not paid. This is one example where the University may look at you and say you must pay the rest of the IDCs from the direct costs of your grant! However, Universities want junior faculty members to get their research started and will often accept partial IDCs just so you can apply for those funds. After you get tenure, Universities are less willing to accept partial IDCs, so appreciate that your University wants to get your research going and will often take less IDCs in the early part of your career. Again, make sure you talk to your Department Chair about this if you are applying to a grant agency that pays less than the full IDCs. By the way, this applies to any external funding you get – whether it is a grant or a contract – the University will still want full IDCs.

> **Info to Know – 4.2**
> **IDCs are important**
> You need to understand that IDCs are incredibly important to your University and the administrators above you, and as such, are important to you. Understanding IDCs, how they work, and how they are distributed not only helps the University, but can help increase the amount of funding you have to spend.

Be aware that more cynical faculty might propose universities just want the IDC money and that's why they are pushing you to find funding for your research. However, it is a much more complicated story than just a drive for money and is wrapped up in declining state support for higher education and the need to keep tuition costs as low as possible. Certainly, your University also wants you to become a successful researcher, and the University understands – as you will eventually – in most cases, to have high impact in your field, you must get external funding.

Info to Know – 4.3
The Necessity of Funding - A Dean's Perspective

A good friend and long-time colleague and administrator from a large, R1 University offers the following thoughts regarding why developing external funding is a necessity for faculty members:

"Extramural funding allows investigators to expand their own research program, support their students, travel more freely, and free up more time for research. Used wisely, extramural funding increases an investigator's research productivity, scholarly impact, and intellectual reach. Extramural funding enables the investigator to pursue questions that would never be possible with the limited time and modest funding provided by university budgets. Extramural funding is the hallmark of a truly independent investigator.

Beyond money, the mere process of competing for extramural funding is hugely beneficial. Personally, I have never thought with greater rigor or creativity than when writing a grant. The process teaches intellectual discipline. It forces an investigator to understand the literature thoroughly. More importantly, the investigator must see and explain the unique contribution of his/her work to the broader field. The investigator must also learn to communicate ideas. To be successful, a grant application requires compelling reasoning and clear writing: skills that are honed by repeated efforts.

Once submitted, the application introduces a junior investigator and his/her ideas to senior scientists on the review panel who, by definition, are experts in the field. This is an early step to professional recognition. Reviewer comments usually contain frank appraisals of the junior scientist's ideas and informed suggestions for improvement. This evaluation-and-feedback process can help improve one's scholarship. So, applying for extramural funding has important benefits even when the application is unsuccessful.

This logic underpins the university expectation of extramural funding for P&T. Extramural funding objectively demonstrates that a faculty member's scholarship is respected in the field. The research has earned approval by outside experts and is worthy of significant investment by the funding agency. Implicitly, extramural funding also proves that the faculty member has the professional skills to create a compelling application and the persistence to succeed in a highly-demanding task. These are qualities that justify a long-term commitment by the institution."

Dean and Professor Michael B Reid, College of Health and Human Performance, University of Florida

Do you have to have funding?

Whether you have to find external funding for your research depends on many factors: 1) How much does your research cost to carry out; 2) What type of university you are in; 3) Do you need extra salary support; and 4) What is the cultural expectation at your University regarding funding?

The Costs of Your Research: We touched earlier on the cost of your research; some research just costs more to complete than other forms of research. But I would encourage you to consider that the direct costs of your research don't just include the cost of the actual data collection – and I'm not talking about indirect costs (covered above). Certainly, data collection costs can be a large portion of the cost of your research, but you also need to consider costs that are part of research, but aren't as apparent. One of these research costs you must consider and plan for is the cost of publication. What funds will you use when you get a paper accepted for publication? And yes, in many cases, it costs money to publish articles[32]. Because publishing a journal costs money, in many cases professional societies and publishers charge what are called 'page charges' to publish your article in a printed journal. These page charges can range from $50/page up to $600/page, so even a short 3-4-page article can be expensive! Additionally, with the acceptance of publication in an open-access journal, these open access fees can range from $2000 - $4500 for an article. As you can see, items like page charges can bring costs to your research endeavor, even if your research data doesn't cost anything to collect.

The Type of University You Are At: Another factor that will play a role in pursuing funding is the type of university you are at. For convenience I'm going to refer to universities by their Carnegie Classifications, which is a categorization of universities by the types of students produced and amount of research expenditures.[33] The more research the University does and the more doctoral students it graduates, moves it toward what are called 'Research' (or 'R') institutions. R-institutions are categorized as either R1, R2, or D/PU[34] institutions, with the R1 universities doing the most research and producing the greatest number of research-focused doctoral students.

---

[32] And I'm not even talking about the high costs associated with predatory publishers – a topic I'll get into in Chapter 5.
[33] If you want a detailed explanation and how the Carnegie Classification might affect your decision about where to apply for a job, check out Chapter 1 in Book 1 (Table 1.1 there should explain all you need/want to know.)
[34] Always adding to the complexity are new Carnegie Classifications. The new 'D/PU' classification designates a "Doctoral, Professional University" such as Law Schools and the like.

Many R1 Universities, especially those that are not state-supported, are often called 'soft money' institutions. These are universities where a large portion of their operating budgets, including your salary, come from grants and contracts which expire, thus the term 'soft' to describe the fact the funding is not necessarily always there. Soft-money institutes make up some of the largest research universities in the United States, with Johns Hopkins, Harvard, Yale, Princeton, and Baylor College of Medicine all being soft-money research universities (just to name a few). Given operating budgets at soft-money institutes depend on grants and contracts, if you are at a soft-money institute and you are a faculty member, you must find funding. Your ability to bring in funding will be a large factor in whether you get P/T.

R1 Universities that are state-supported are many times a blend of soft-money and 'hard money' programs. As you might guess, 'hard' money programs are those where the University has committed to paying for the salaries of the researchers regardless of grant or contract funding. However, as state-funding has fallen, so have the number of 'hard' money programs, so it is becoming more and more frequent where state-supported Universities act and operate more like soft money institutions, often with hybrid programs where faculty are supported by a combination of hard- and soft-funding sources.

If you are at a university that is not an R-institution, the chances are not as great you'll be required to find external funding. It's not that these Institutions don't want external funding; they do and frankly, if you get external funding at an institution that is not an R-level university, you will be prized greatly there. However, since those non-R-Institutions' primary mission is usually education first, in most cases, if you are a faculty member at one of these Universities, your funding expertise will not make or break your P/T aspirations.

Salary Support: Another factor determining whether you need to go after funding is whether you need extra salary support. You're probably thinking one of two things:
    1) "What? I'll need extra salary support?"; or
    2) "What? I can increase my salary this way?".
To answer both responses, we'll need to take a short detour and talk about how your salary is determined and funded (this may seem boring, but it is critical for you to know because after all, we are talking about how much salary you'll be making).

In most academic settings, as a junior faculty member, you will be on a 9-

month contract. In other words, your contract will pay you a certain amount for 9-months (but many Universities let you stretch this 9-month salary over 12-months so you'll have income in the summer). This is not the case in most medical, nursing, and health profession schools, where you'll usually be on a 12-month contract[35], but in most non-medical academic units, you'll be on a 9-month salary.

Your salary may be all soft-money (comes from grants), all hard-money (comes from the University), or some blend of the two. Many soft-money Institutions will provide 5-20% of a faculty member's salary while the faculty member must bring in the other 80-95% in grant support for their salary. So, if you are in a situation where part of your salary comes from your grants, you better write grants!

But even if you are on a hard-money salary, there's a way grants or contracts can augment your salary. In most cases Universities will not allow you to give yourself a pay raise from a grant. However, because you are on a 9-month salary, most Universities will allow you to use your grant money to pay your summer salary. That can be like getting a 33% pay raise, just by finding money to pay yourself during the summer. To illustrate how this works, let's assume you are getting paid $75,000 and you are on a 9-month contract. If you get a grant that has salary support on it, you can use that salary support to pay you up to $25,000 during the summer (since the three-month summer is equivalent to 1/3 of your 9-month salary). Voila! Your yearly salary is now up to $100,000. If you have more salary support on your grant than what you can pay yourself in the summer, you can then buy yourself out of classroom teaching, reducing your teaching requirements and giving yourself more time for research. Universities have different policies about how to buy yourself out of teaching time, so make sure you discuss this with your Department Chair as you are planning your grant. But there is no doubt that one of the best things about writing for external funding is the opportunity to augment your salary by paying for your summer salary.

Cultural Expectations: Lastly, an important factor determining whether you should develop external support for your research is the 'cultural' expectations at your University. This factor is a bit different than taking into the account the type of university you work at. Yes, if you are at an R1 university, in general, you'll be expected to pursue external funding. However, it is possible you'll be in a department or college that doesn't traditionally go after

---

[35] And even some medical, nursing, and health-professional schools are moving to 9- or 10-month contracts for their faculty. This is an area that is changing daily so check your Institution carefully if you are in one of these settings.

research funding, despite your University's R1 status. For example, colleagues of mine in Sport Management point out there are few external funding opportunities for them; instead, most of the time, they go after contracts with various business entities.

While contracts are still external funding, it is a different 'cultural' expectation than most external funding grant attempts. Additionally, if you are in an Institution that doesn't have a cultural expectation of external funding, if you go after funding and get it, that will set you apart and be an additional positive factor in your P/T portfolio. I have no doubt one of the factors that played into my favor when I went up for P/T early was the fact I had been active and successful in landing external funding as a junior faculty even though I was in an Institution where external funding was not an expectation. Understand that the cultural expectations of your home unit can provide additional information about the necessity of you pursuing external funding.

The advantages and disadvantages of getting funding

If you are going to spend time working to develop external funding, you should have a good sense of both the advantages and disadvantages of working to get funding. Since I'm a 'good news first' type of guy, we'll tackle the advantages first.

We've already covered some of the advantages of getting funding; you'll have money to support your research efforts, your students, and even provide salary support. Those advantages are fairly clear-cut and obvious to most. However, there are some more indirect advantages to having funding and frankly these are advantages I had no clue about until I landed funding.

Table 4.1 – The Advantages and Disadvantages of Working on External Fund Development
(see the text for elaboration on these points)

Advantages	Disadvantages
• You'll have money to support your research efforts, your students, and provide salary support for yourself.	• External fund development is hard, especially in the current 'hypercompetive' times.
• You don't have to ask anyone for money to support your research.	• There are higher rates of failure with attempts to get external funding than you've probably experienced in the past.
• Funding will give you leverage within your University.	• External funding efforts take a lot of time.
• Funding is the first step toward national/international impact in science.	

Having Your Own Money: One of the first indirect advantages of having external funding, is you do not have to ask anyone for research money. If you don't have your own research money, you'll have to ask your Department Chair, your Dean, or others in the University for money to support your research. With your own funding, suddenly, you don't have to ask anyone and if you are spending your funding like you said you would in your proposal, you'll be good to go. This may seem like a small deal, but think about it this way: Do you remember being a teenager and having to ask your parents for money? Do you remember the freedom there was when you were working and had your own money? Suddenly you could buy the things you wanted or needed without asking anyone. That same freedom is what you'll experience when you have your own funding as a faculty member.

Leverage: Developing your own external funding will give you leverage within your University. When you are bringing in money to the University, you are also bringing in those precious IDCs. The University doesn't want to lose those IDCs which puts you in a position where you have leverage. There are few times as a faculty member you'll have leverage within your University; one time was when you were negotiating your initial contract with your University[36] - they wanted you and whether you knew it or not, you had leverage in that negotiation. But once you signed your contract, your leverage within the University decreased as you became a faculty member. Once you have your own external funding though, you become more valuable to the University, especially if it is possible for you to transfer external funding to other Universities. In a nutshell, external funding gives you leverage.

You may be hesitant to use that leverage, and generally, hesitation is a good thing. But there may be times your funding leverage can help. For example, when I landed my first NIH R01 award (total direct cost ≈ $2.5 million, with ≈$600,000 IDC), I realized other faculty in the University with similar funding levels were teaching much less than I was. I took that information to the Department Chair (and Dean) and used that information to justify a decrease in my teaching load so it was equivalent with others in the University. Without funding, I would not have had the leverage to justify my request for a reduced teaching load. Again, I would be careful with using this type of leverage; you always run the risk of the University saying "okay – take your funding and leave". But don't feel bad about thinking about this aspect of funding; the University does the same thing. The more external funding the University receives, the more it has leverage with the state in budgeting.

---

[36] There's a whole chapter dedicated to that in Book 1 – check out Chapter 7 there!

Establishing Your Reputation As A Scholar: The last, and maybe more important advantage that comes with external funding, especially funding from the federal government, is your establishment as a national leader in your area of research. That may not seem important, but it is. Not only is it great for P/T purposes, but when you have funding, other high-level scientists will start to notice your work and you will then be asked to serve on national grant review committees and national science policy discussions. It has always been an honor when I have been invited to Washington DC for roundtable discussions and reviews at NIH about the future of my field; those invitations were almost singly the result of external funding efforts and my publications. You will notice that the prestige that you build with your funding efforts is one of the major points mentioned in Info to Know 4.3 by Dean Reid! So, building your scientific reputation through external funding can be a critical advantage of developing funding.

Overall, not only will you be able to fund your research with grant money, but you'll have great benefits by developing and getting funding. You'll have freedom, leverage, and will get to play a role in national science discussions. Talk about having an impact on science!

Now we turn to the 'bad news' side of the story. There are certainly disadvantages of going after funding; in my experience, it is these disadvantages that keep most faculty from even pursuing funding. If these disadvantages seem overwhelming to you, then you need to think seriously about whether a job at an institution that wants you to develop external funding will be the right job for you. There's nothing worse than being in a university where you and the University have different expectations. Probably the greatest faculty misery I've seen over the years is when the University starts to ratchet up the external funding pressure; if the faculty member doesn't want to pursue funding, it becomes very difficult for them to enjoy their job.

There are three primary disadvantages to developing funding: 1) It is extremely competitive; 2) You will fail much of the time; and 3) It takes a lot of time. Let's unpack those disadvantages to get some perspective.

Hypercompetition: It is generally agreed we are in a 'hypercompetitive' time in regards to external funding (a term used by Dr. Sally Rock, the former director of Extramural Funding at NIH). Funding agencies are seeing more and more grant applications, but the funds available to give out are less than what they've been in the past. For example, Figure 4.2 is from the 2017 NIH Data Book[37]. Notice the number of applications NIH has received since 1997 has

---

[37] Here's the link if you want to dig through the data. http://bit.ly/NIH_data

over doubled, while the number of awards NIH has made has stayed steady at approximately 10,000/year. And while this is NIH, every other funding agency has seen the same increase in applications, without a corresponding increase in funding. In fact, it has been observed that federal funding for research has fallen from about 10% of the federal budget in the 1960s to less than 4% today[38]. So, funding has become hypercompetitive because on one hand we have an increase in applications primarily due to the pressure on faculty to apply, and on the other hand, federal budgeting for research has continued to be cut (or not keep up with inflation). You can quickly see why there is a lot of competition for research dollars today: we've gone from an NIH funding rate of about 30%, to less than 15% today[39]. However, a truism that applies in every case is *'you certainly will not get funded if you don't apply'*. So being afraid of competition and not applying will automatically eliminate any chance of funding.

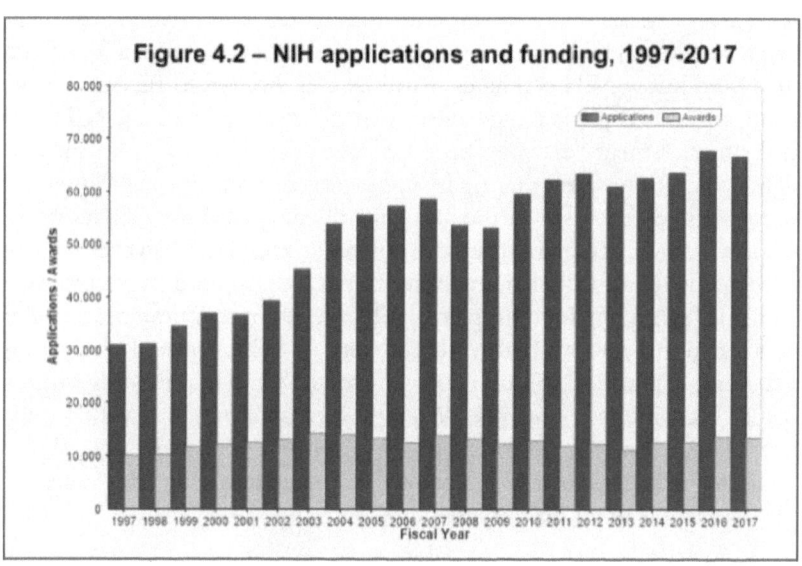

You will often fail: The second disadvantage to going after funding is that you will rarely be successful. It is probable that to this point in your life and in your career, you have rarely failed. You probably have never failed a class,

---

[38] American Association of the Advance of Science, "Historical Trends in Federal R&D", June 2016, http://bit.ly/History_RD.
[39] These percentages are based on the NIH overall numbers and vary by program and research institute. While not indicative of all funding entities, watching how NIH performs gives you a good sense of how external funding on a whole is going since NIH is the largest funder of life science research in the United States.

flunked an exam, or had a manuscript not eventually get published. In fact, your life and your career have probably been a long string of successes gained through a lot of hard work, thought, and study. Unfortunately, grant funding is the one aspect of your professional career where you will most likely fail more often than you succeed. In fact, in my experience and in talking to other colleagues who write grants, a success rate of only 10% is not unusual (yes, only 1 in every 10 proposals submitted is funded). Most academics are not used to this level of non-success and are not prepared for how to handle the continued lack of success. You may think at this point, "no big deal, I can handle it"' but, continuing rejection of your scientific ideas and proposals can be a difficult drain on your psyche and motivation. So, understand if you are going to work to develop external funding, you'll need to work on how to handle the low success rates that come from grant applications (more on that later).

It takes time to develop good grant proposals: No matter what anyone says, developing a good external funding application and program, takes a lot of time. You should know NIH estimates it will take 22 hours[40] to fill out the NIH funding forms. There is a big caveat with this estimate because NIH notes that their assessment "excludes time for development of the scientific plan" which is the core of any grant. In my experience and through interacting with many investigators over the years, it will take you at least six months to develop a well-written grant if you are doing nothing else. However, as a new faculty member you will be doing other things, so you need to plan for more time to develop your funding plans. This development time must include time for external reviews before submission, as well as several weeks to get the funding application through your University's external funding proposal process. Yes, the time you take developing external funding will take away from the time you can do research. You can overcome this time shift by developing processes in your lab so others handle items like data collection, while you handle grant development.

While I'll talk about lab processes more in the chapter on Research, you need to start thinking about your role in your research lab at a higher level; you must have others do tasks and jobs they can do (e.g., run samples through an analyzer), while you do jobs others in your lab can't do, like write grants.

Lastly, be aware that you will rarely ever waste grant verbiage. Since grants are not published, you can use the verbiage you develop for those grants over and over and that includes the 'meaty' portions of the grant – significance,

---

[40] These estimates are required as part of the federal government paperwork burden requirements: https://grants.nih.gov/grants/paperwork-burden.htm

innovation, and methods sections. In fact, I've found that after a portion of the grant becomes well developed, I will often wind-up using that portion in a published paper. So, I didn't waste the effort even if the grant didn't get funded; I was just developing verbiage I was able to use later.

In conclusion, there are real advantages and disadvantages to developing external funding proposals to support your research. In many cases, you will find developing external funding is a requirement of your position; however, with a clear understanding of the benefits and risks that are involved in that requirement, you hopefully can be smarter about how you go about getting funding.

Types of funding

So far, I've been focusing on 'external fund development' generically, with some conversation regarding NIH grants. However, there is a wide variety of funding you can pursue, each with their own pros and cons and each with their appropriate time and place in your career. The below sections are an overview of each of these types of funding, but just understand there are also other variants of these basic types.

Internal funding: This type of funding usually comes from within your Institution and is the reason for the 'internal' funding name. Internal funding is the type of funding most junior faculty start with so they can begin to build for external grants. In general, that is the purpose of internal funding; to provide you with enough money to develop pilot data, methodology, or pay for data collection so you can eventually go after external funding. Most Universities have internal funding mechanisms meant to support faculty in this way and you should look around your University to see what programs are available. Most of these programs will arise out of your University's Office of Research, but also can come out of your College, your Department, and even some specialty Institutes. Another internal source of funding for initial pilot data generation may be from any of the large NIH-funded research centers you may have on campus. So, talk to your Department Chair and colleagues, and pay attention to announcements from the University about these types of funds.

The general advantage to internal funding programs is they are usually easier to apply for, often with little requirement for supporting data and fewer forms to fill out. If you are a junior faculty member or even an older faculty member switching research programs, these types of programs can help you easily receive money to start your research. Conversely, one of the biggest disadvantages is that these internal programs do not pay IDC and so you are not paying back into the University to offset the indirect costs of your research (and some Departments may require you to come up with some money to at least partially pay the IDC). Again, for most junior faculty, the priority for the University is to help you get your research up and running as quickly as possible, and that will usually entail the University giving you some financial support through internal funding.

External grant applications: As I've already mentioned, there are several different external agencies that award grant funds to support research in a variety of areas. These granting agencies include both governmental and non-profit foundations that provide funding for research. Governmental agencies include the National Institutes of Health (NIH), the National Science Foundation (NSF), NASA, the Department of Education (DOE), and others. Your state may also have research supporting institutions as well (e.g., in Texas, we have the Cancer Prevention Research Initiative of Texas – or CPRIT). Non-profit foundations to which you might apply for funding include organizations like the American Heart Association, the Muscular Dystrophy Association, and the Robert Woods Johnson Foundation.

One advantage of going after funding from these organizations, both governmental and non-profit, is most have very well-structured grant programs with clear proposal requirements and clear review processes. Additionally, most allow IDC – both full and partial – which will make your University happy. Also, many times, the grants these organizations award are multi-year grants that will give you funding over several years (usually five or less). Lastly, one of the big advantages of getting a 'grant' versus a 'contract' is the grant is usually awarded to investigate a general topic using the best science available. This gives you the flexibility to change your scientific approach if better methods or new knowledge becomes available after the grant has started.

Because getting grants from external funding organizations is usually difficult, if you do land a grant from one of these organizations, there is some prestige that accompanies these grants. In most cases, your grant application had to undergo serious scrutiny by a scientific review panel made up of nationally-known scientists, and so, getting funding after that type of review is an indirect, but no less prestigious stamp of approval on your science which will also help you with P/T!

Contracts: Contracts are most often associated with research from for-profit institutions such as corporations. Unlike grants (usually), contracts have specific lists of items you are going to do; therefore, what you are contracted to do, you do, regardless of whether a better approach becomes available. Additionally, contracts are often for a shorter period than a grant. On the positive side, contracts are sometimes easier to get, with a less formalized process and review than grant applications. It is rare that a junior faculty member comes into the University with the network needed to propose and land corporate contracts. Contracts are often initiated through a network of acquaintances and the more established you become in research, the more contracts you may receive.

One last concern with contracts revolves around the independence of the researcher to publish the results of the contract. A contract may put stipulations in place regarding what data you can publish and the venue for those publications. Given the corporation is paying for the research, they may feel it is better if your research findings are not published, especially if your results did not support their product or processes as being effective. Many Universities will not accept contracts having these types of prohibitions in place, but you must be very careful as to the contracts you sign. You want to make sure you'll be comfortable abiding by the terms of the contracts; your University office that handles these types of contracts can provide great guidance for you in these matters.

I have had several colleagues over the years that preferred working to land contracts versus grants. One reason for this preference is they perceived they had better chances of obtaining contracts versus grants, especially after they were established researchers. Additionally, some disciplines focus more on contracts versus grants; an example I used earlier were my colleagues in Sport Management. Their discipline primarily uses corporate contracts as a funding mechanism. So, given your discipline and the norms you work under, contracts may be the right funding mechanism for you. However, you should be careful in what you agree to in the contract because it is very difficult to change the contract once signed.

Endowments: One last type of research funding I'll cover are endowments. Endowments are usually large funds that have been set aside by a philanthropist or foundation, where the interest that is made off the endowment each year supports research. To give you a sense of how this works, pretend a benefactor gave your University $1 million to set up an endowment to fund your research program (these types of endowments are managed by separate entities – usually called Foundations – that are associated with the University). While setting up endowments is complicated and there are many factors in determining how much you'll be able to use from the endowment proceeds, a good conservative guide is to assume the University Foundation will allow you to use an amount equivalent to approximately 4% of the endowment yearly. Thus, with that $1 million endowment, you'll have about

$40,000 every year to spend on research[41]. University-managed endowments are by far the most numerous types of scientific support endowments available, but there are several large-scale research foundations that are supported by interest off their endowments. For example, one of the largest independent research support endowments is the Howard Hughes Medical Institute (HHMI.org). The Howard Hughes endowments have many different types of research support programs, even some for junior faculty. I would encourage you to investigate Howard Hughes endowments especially if you are at a university that has Howard Hughes Fellows.

As noted above, Universities as a whole, diligently build endowments to support research as well as other activities on campus; if someone has money to give, Universities are generally willing to set up an endowment to support what the donor wants to support.[42] Building a large endowment is another way to augment the budget of the University. For example, Harvard University is reported to have the largest university-led endowment which exceeds $36 billion (yes, that's billions); if they can access just 4% interest yearly from their endowment, it will *add* $1.4 billion to their yearly budget forever. According to reports in the *Chronicle of Higher Education*[43], there are 185 Universities in the United States that have endowments larger than $500 million. That amount of endowment would be $20 million per year more for your budget if you had that endowment.

These types of financial impacts of endowments have led to two recent developments: 1) It's one of the reasons that Congress – for the first time – just passed a tax on Universities that have large endowments[44]; and 2) It's the reason so many Universities at so many levels are now working to develop endowments. While it takes a rather large endowment to bring substantially large dollars into the University, the endowments will pay out forever and

---

[41] Foundation endowment earnings were much more generous before 2008; after 2008 when many university Foundations lost billions of dollars, Foundations became very conservative and reduced the amount that is allowed to be spent from endowments.

[42] However, some Universities are getting flack because some of the endowments they've set up appear to be driven by certain political and ideological agendas, so there is starting to be some caution about setting up some endowments. Here's an article from the Chronicle of Higher Education about one of these examples: http://bit.ly/Endow1

[43] If you want to see if your Institution made the list, here's the whole 2018 list. Thanks Chronicle! http://bit.ly/Endow2

[44] Actually, it's a tax based on the value of the endowment standardized by the number of students. If the University's endowment is larger than $500,000/student, then the endowment is taxed 1.4%.

continue to grow if managed correctly. In a very real sense, if your University has donors that are willing to help support the University, then endowments are certainly a way to offset the declining dollars from other sources.

Hopefully, the above discussion gives you perspective on what endowments can provide for university resources. While grants and contracts are short-term, putting effort into building an endowment can provide additional research support in perpetuity. The most tangible way you'll see this type of endowment support is through the creation of 'endowed chair' positions in academic units. An endowed chair position indicates there is an endowment supporting the research of the faculty member who holds that chair. One of more famous endowed Chair positions is the Lucasian Professor of Mathematics at Cambridge University, first established in 1663 by the will of Henry Lucas who was a member of Parliament. Scientific luminaries such as Isaac Newton and Stephen Hawking have held that Chair over the years[45] showing the long-lasting effect an endowed Chair can have.

Depending on the size of an endowment, it may provide a lot or little research funding support. Also, while these types of endowments are becoming more prevalent, they are usually given to senior faculty members that have well-established research programs. However, if nothing else, the availability of these types of research support programs should be a good reason for you to work toward establishing a solid, well-focused research program so that by the time you are a senior faculty member, you can work to develop (or find) these endowments.

In conclusion, research funding can take several forms ranging from internal grants to endowments, with grants and contracts in between. While knowing about these different avenues of funding is important, it is more important for junior faculty members to understand which avenues of funding are important and available for their current academic rank. As such, you will find the types of research funding you pursue will necessarily change over your career (Figure 4.3). At the beginning of your career (even as a doctoral student or post-doctoral fellow) you'll be going after training grants and small internal grants to develop the pilot data and build the foundation you'll need for larger grants. As a junior faculty member, you'll focus on internal grants, but then move toward foundation and smaller federal grants. As you approach P/T, you should be applying for more independent research grants/contracts (such as an NIH R01) that will establish you as an

---

[45] To my knowledge, the Lucasian Endowed Chair is the only real-life endowed chair that has been mentioned in the popular media – most specifically as being held by the character Data in the *Star Trek: Next Generation* TV series!

independent investigator. After P/T or after receiving an R01-level grant, you'll continue to develop R01 level grants, but you'll also start to work on larger multi-PI grants at the Consortium/Program Project level. Lastly, about this same time, you should start investigating and pursing endowment research funding to support your lab. As you can tell, this external funding 'arc' takes you from smaller projects in the beginning of your career to larger projects as you go through P/T and become a senior faculty member. This type of funding arc allows you to develop both your research and funding base across most of the types of funding so when you do become a senior faculty member, you will be well established and well placed for endowment funds and larger multi-investigator grants.

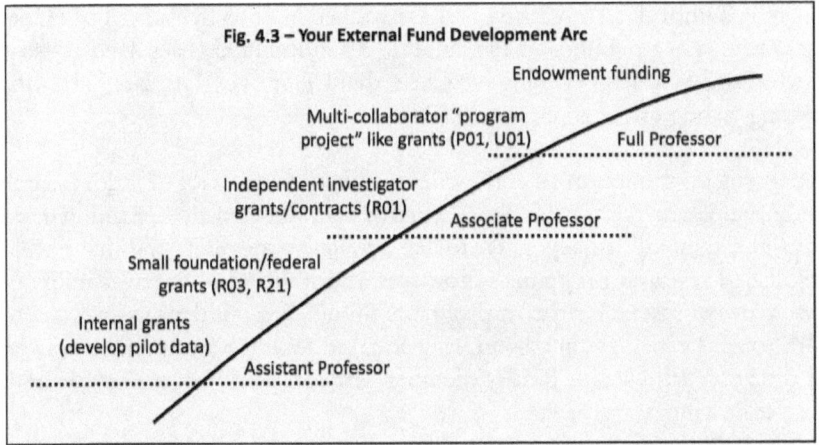

How to Apply for Funding

How to apply for funding is a much bigger topic than can be covered in a portion of a chapter, and indeed, there are whole books devoted to this subject. However, let me recommend a few starting spots for you. If you are going to develop federal funding (and most of you will want or need to do this), take advantage of any workshops or grant development courses your University offers. Also, I would highly recommend the books published by Grant Writers Seminars and Workshops (GrantCentral.com). Grant Writers has several different books based on the agency to which you are applying (e.g., NIH, NSF, USDA, etc.). These are the best grant-writing books I've read and I continue to use these as the recommended textbooks in my grant writing classes. Also, Grant Writers does seminars and workshops that can be invaluable in honing your grants to be their best. If your University or Department doesn't offer these types of workshops, ask to have them offered; a workshop is a great way many of your colleagues can also gain benefit from your efforts.

Over the years I have observed many junior faculty members that don't seem to grasp how to write successful grants. To that point, I'd like to share several tips that seem to elude many junior faculty members (see Table 4.2 for the short version).

Table 4.2 – Tips on Writing Grants and Being Successful	
• Take advantage of any university/college/department resources to develop your grantsmanship	• Read all the instructions and follow all directions when writing and applying for your grants
• You must work hard consistently on your grant writing	• Get to know the individuals in your sponsored research services office
• Collaborations – especially with senior faculty – is key	• Figure out how to handle failure when your grant doesn't get funded.

First, you've got to really work hard on grantsmanship. The competition for funding is so high you have got to submit your best effort each time you submit a proposal. Grants, especially those to foundations, federal agencies, and corporations, are not documents you can write at the last minute. Grant proposals have fewer page allowances and require succinct and concise writing, with the verbiage even more sparse and succinct than general scientific writing.

Secondly, collaborations are key. As a junior faculty member, you must show you are interacting and supported by senior researchers that have experience with grant funding. Meaningful collaborations show you have access to resources that can multiply the approaches you take to answer your question.

Third, the tip that seems to be the hardest for most folks, is to take the time to read and follow **_all_** the instructions for each grant you are applying for. It is amazing the number of grants I've seen under review that did not go forward simply because the investigator did not follow the directions. Grant reviewers will think "if they can't do something as easy as following directions, how can they do complicated science?" That's a fair question and one you need to eliminate by following all the directions and building the best grant application you can.

Fourth, it will also help your grant writing efforts if you get to know the large group of individuals at your University whose job it is to help you get your grant submitted. Most of the time, these individuals are in your College/University Research Support Services offices. It is worth your time to get to know the individuals in the research support services aspect of your institution because writing grants is stressful enough so why not get to know the folks who can help you get the grant out? Also, you may find in getting to know these folks, you'll hear early on about programs the University is offering to help with grant writing. Getting to know these incredibly important support staff are another way of increasing your network on campus so you can do your job more efficiently.

Lastly, a key in maintaining your sanity and putting out great grants is to figure out how to handle the inevitable failure that is prevalent in the pursuit of external funding. As I noted before, you probably haven't been exposed to the level of failure you'll be exposed to when you write grants. Here are just a few ideas that seem to work:

1) Don't look at grant review results on the weekend. Grant review results – especially if your grant is not funded – will ruin your weekend, trust me on this. Besides, everything (and I mean everything) in that review can wait until Monday.

2) When you do look at your grant review outcome, read the reviews and then put the reviews away for a few days. It will do no good to stew on what the reviewers said. Take a couple of days and get rid of the inevitable frustration that comes with grant reviews. Let your subconscious handle the review, and you'll find in a couple of days, you'll have a much healthier outlook on your review.

3) In the end, you have to accept that the ultimate reason your grant failed was your writing. You will probably read your reviews and disagree with much of what was written in your review. That's okay, but remember you were responsible for writing the grant, so any problems with the grant review are, in the end, your responsibility. It doesn't matter whether you think the reviewers were capable, qualified, or nice; those are things you can't control. The only thing you can control is the quality of the grant you wrote, so evaluate the reviews, consider the comments that are pertinent and useful in your review, and use them to improve your grant in the future.

How your department sees your grant efforts

At the beginning of the chapter, there was an extensive review of why you should pursue funding from the *flip side* perspective. Now, I want to end the chapter with how your grant writing efforts will likely be perceived by your institution as you move toward P/T review. It is important for you to understand the Institutional perspective of your efforts because understanding that perspective will help you put your efforts into the appropriate light. Most people who write grants are extremely critical of their own efforts, and the reviews you get back, may increase your criticism of your efforts. In short, because you did not get funding, you'll feel like a failure. But, you should be relieved to know the University doesn't necessarily look at your unfunded efforts as a failure.

As disappointed as you may be if your first grants are not funded, you should understand your University doesn't expect you will be successful right away; they are hopeful you'll be funded right away, but they probably don't expect it. In most cases, your department will expect as a junior faculty member you will build your grantsmanship skills, and the building process will necessarily involve failures. Your department will expect you to learn from those failures and subsequent grants will become better and better. In fact, when you come up for review at either three or five years, what the department will likely be interested in seeing is how your grant efforts have improved and gotten better over time. For example, perhaps you will show your early grants were not scored and now you are regularly getting scores on your grant (that is huge progress). Perhaps you will show you've not been scored, but have also received some smaller grants that are allowing you to build toward bigger grants. The key is continued development (remember *kaizen?*); every grant you submit should be better than the last one with your scientific plans clearer, better supported by data, with efforts to eliminate and resolve comments from earlier grant reviews. The key is to keep working on making your grants better and you'll make your University happy.

One way to be sure your University/College/Department is not happy with your external funding efforts is to not even try. If you are at an R1 institution, you should be making the effort to put in 2-3 grants per year to a variety of funding agencies based on where you are at in your career (see Fig. 4.3). I had a colleague once that believed (probably rightly) he had to get an NIH grant to get promoted. He submitted 13 (yes, thirteen) grants to NIH

> **Info to Know – 4.3**
> **Your Department's View of Your Funding Efforts**
>
> Funded grants are difficult to get and will be the source of your greatest failure and frustration as a faculty member. However, your Department (and University) is not disappointed in your continued efforts because they see these efforts as necessary for you to build your 'funding-chops'. The only way you fail with grant funding efforts is if you don't try to get funding and/or if you don't learn from the grants that don't get funded.

in one year and hit on one of those grants. You might think "wow, that's not a very good percentage of success", but probably the best way to think of it was with one year of super intense effort, he got five years of funding worth over $1.2 million (plus, he did get promoted). Most faculty would take that outcome. No one could question this individual's commitment to getting funding and I suspect, even if he hadn't gotten funding, he still would have received promotion because this was the type of effort he normally put forward. So, if there is any take home message for you from this section of the chapter it should be "the real path to failure is to *not* try; the real path to funding success is littered with unfunded grants."

The Take Home Message

At many universities, external fund development is now considered a fourth part of a faculty member's job and a critical part of your career 'furniture' you are assembling. In fact, without funding, it may be very difficult to do the research portion of your job. As a junior faculty member, especially if you are in an R-Institution, you must accept your responsibility for external fund development. Today, external fund development is critical in the functioning of Universities, and will have many benefits for you. External fund development is also difficult and filled with failure. However, you must keep your eye on the prize and continue to move forward. Many great scientists[46] have been met with rejection when it comes to funding. Just remember that if great scientists have had failure, then what you experience should not be a roadblock to you developing external funding and a great scientific career.

---

[46] Here is a hilarious clip of Dr. Carol Greider, winner of 2009 Nobel Prize in Medicine/Physiology, describing how she won the Nobel prize and on the same day, one of her grants was triaged by NIH. Heck, if it happens to a Nobel prize winner, you shouldn't feel bad about it happening to you! http://bit.ly/nobelNF

5

SCHOLARSHIP AS A FACULTY MEMBER: ALL YOU NEED TO KNOW, BUT DIDN'T KNOW YOU NEEDED TO KNOW

Scholarship is one of the three 'classical' pieces of a faculty member's job – one of those parts of your career 'furniture' - and most students, faculty, and administrators think they know what scholarship and research is. However, changing mores' in research as well as differing types of research publication, challenge many of the traditional thoughts about research. Given this book is directed at professionals in Life Sciences fields, I'm using the term 'research' to generally indicate the expansion of the knowledge base in your area with the clear understanding that research will basically entail answering questions and disseminating those results. This is unlike 'research' in the Humanities or in many of the social sciences where there are different ways of disseminating scholarly work; ways that are fascinating in and of themselves, but aren't germane to the primary audience of this book.

This chapter focuses on the aspects of research you may not know much about, but aspects that could trip you up as you work to establish yourself and your research production as being worthy of P/T[47]. With a focus on what many would see as 'traditional' approaches to research and dissemination, topics such as the appropriate products of your research work (i.e., what will be evaluated at P/T time), some tips for multiplying and handling your research production, and metrics that will likely be used to evaluate your research production will be covered.

For many reasons, the products of your research, primarily your published papers and the funding you develop, are the 'coin of the realm' in academia. While most

This Chapter:

Your scholarly products 86

Where to publish your research? 91

Getting your research done 98

Finding people to work with you 102

Supervising your research team 107

Evaluation of your research (the flip side) 110

The Take Home Message (finally!) 119

---

[47] As in past chapters, P/T stands for Promotion and Tenure and includes those up for contract renewals as well!

academics can teach – notice I'm not saying how well they teach – the defining line most Carnegie R- and many M-Universities use to determine who they want to keep is the research production of a faculty member. Because most Universities have a dual mission of both educating *and* expanding knowledge, a faculty member must do both well. Those that do research well will be of value in the eyes of their administration, which will help them keep their academic jobs.

Most of us, when we were junior academics – just as you are now – would have read that last statement and said "yeah, yeah – that'll be easy". What you may not anticipate – or maybe you're finding out now – is a faculty job suddenly puts a lot of items on your plate that have very specific due dates. You must teach classes several times a week, you have committee duties that have deadlines, heck, even your grants often have deadlines. Because research is something you direct and often doesn't have hard-deadlines, it is easy to put off 'until you have more time'. As such, one of the more difficult factors a junior faculty member faces – and probably one of the most surprising – is you've gone from a situation as a doctoral student or post-doc where research was your *only* priority, to a situation where research is just one of several priorities that all jostle for your attention. That's why one of the aims of this chapter is to not only review factors in research dissemination, but also strategies for making sure your research efforts don't get eliminated by your other faculty duties. It is an unpleasant surprise to work on your P/T portfolio and realize you have very few scholarly products to show for your time as a faculty member. So, buckle-up and let's go!

Your scholarly products

The primary scholarly product you will be judged on is the dissemination of your research results. To expand the knowledge base in your area, you must publish your results. I have known many academics who loved being in the lab and collecting data, but hated writing. As a result, those scholars know a lot, but no one else knew what they knew, and thus, they received no credit for any new knowledge they had discovered. You can do all the lab experiments you want and discover wonderful things, but as one of my former professors used to put it, very succinctly I might add, "If it ain't published, it ain't worth shit!"[48]. Another way to think of this would be to ask yourself, "if Einstein had not published his results – even though at the time he was a patent clerk – would Einstein have been given credit for the huge advances he caused in physics?" Thus, you must disseminate your results in accepted scholarly outlets so you can add to the base of knowledge in your area.

---

[48] My apologies if you were offended. But I chose to keep the whole quote because frankly it makes the point clearly. And, most importantly, it is true.

Publication is your overriding task as an academic scholar.

Disseminating your results means you must go through the accepted process to get your work into scientific outlets and that means going through 'peer-review'. Most of us understand peer-review as the system whereby other scientists that are familiar and knowledgeable about our area, review our work and determine whether it should be published or not. All good scientific journals use peer-review and peer-review is considered the gold standard of scientific publishing. Are there issues with peer-review? Absolutely. Peer-review can take a long time, often several months if not longer. Additionally, there are documented cases of negative bias and the halo-effect that can either hinder or help a paper get accepted, and unkind comments tend to occur due to the blinded nature of the reviews. However, even given the disadvantages, there are no better methods known at this time of determining the scientific validity of research findings. Remember the function of peer-review, at its very base level, is to ensure as much as possible, the results you are reporting and the interpretation of those results are as truthful and as factual as possible at that time. So, while no one denies peer-review has problems, it has been used for hundreds of years, and in most cases, peer-review gets it right.[49] It is important to remember that as you work to disseminate your research results, while you may have issues with peer-review and you may accumulate rejections, there is literally a journal home for every paper; you just have to keep looking.

Given you must publish your research results, we need to talk about what are acceptable forms of dissemination or publications in the eyes of most P/T committees. At its root, dissemination means putting your results into the public sphere where others can see them and hopefully, accept them into the recognized body of knowledge. As such, you might believe many forms of dissemination would be acceptable, especially given publication is so easy these days. However, you must remember that those judging your scholarly products during the P/T process are other academics. And academics are strict about appropriate dissemination venues. The key to remember is that to add to the accepted body of knowledge, which is what you are supposed to be doing, you must publish in outlets that are read and are used in furthering your area of knowledge. By and large, these outlets are scientific journals because to publish your results in them, you must go through peer review.

---

[49] There is copious literature, books, and reports out regarding peer-review, and especially the problems with peer-review. It seems most scientific outlets become very interested in this topic every 10 years or so (maybe when they forget they've already covered the same topic previously). If you are interested in this topic, do a PubMed.org search – you'll find there are almost 32,000 papers you can choose from! Enjoy!

Certainly, you can put your results in a blog post online, publish them 280 characters at a time on Twitter, or print them in the newspaper. However, while these forms of dissemination may get your results out for people to read, these outlets will not add your results to the body of knowledge because they haven't undergone any type of validity screening which is the purpose peer review. Just so we are clear, while you may be able to publish your results in a wide-variety of forums, you will not get any 'academic credit' from your peers until you publish in peer reviewed scientific journals. However, before we jump off into how you can determine appropriate scientific journals for publication, let's detour into abstracts.

In the process of presenting your results at a scientific conference, you probably will submit an abstract. Besides using an abstract to signal you have some results you want to present, often the organizers of the conference will publish these abstracts in a book, online, or in an issue of a journal. Rightly so, you should list these abstracts in a separate section as publications on your CV[50], but you should be under no illusion these abstracts will be taken as indications of appropriate dissemination of your research results. Yes, abstracts show you are presenting, but abstracts in most cases do not show you are adding to the body of knowledge in your field because most abstracts undergo only minimal peer review at best. However, I'm not saying you shouldn't present abstracts (or list them on your CV) because abstracts do show you are interacting in a professional manner with your peers at scientific meetings. Because of this, everyone should have abstracts listed on their CV. But it is a red flag if you've got many abstracts listed on your CV, yet have very few published, peer-reviewed articles. This tells the P/T Committee you can collect data and present data at meetings, but you cannot finish the research process and publish your results. Even worse, having a lot of abstracts with few publications could be interpreted as a sign your results are not being accepted into the body of knowledge by your peers which could indicate your research is not very strong.

A productive scholar will have abstracts on their CVs and will have a proportionate number of published journal articles as well. The proportion of abstracts to manuscripts will vary based on the area and how many ways you split up your data for presentation, but just be aware P/T Committees can be sensitive to this issue, especially if you have many abstracts, but few papers. I was on a P/T Committee once that reviewed a candidate's CV where that candidate had presented on average, at five different conferences per year for four years. In contrast, that candidate only had one published paper despite

---

[50] See Chapter 5 in Book 1 (*Finding The Best Faculty Job For You*) for all you want to know about formatting your CV!

having 20 conference abstracts. What would you think about that candidate's scholarly output? We weren't sure how the candidate was affording to do that much travel, much less whether they were having any impact on their field. So, while abstracts are great and easy to get, don't ever forget you must disseminate your findings in peer reviewed journals to show your impact.

Info to Know – 5.1
Establishing your scientific 'stage name'

Today, making sure you use the same name in your publications <u>over your whole career</u> and that your name is easily digitally searchable is incredibly important. This is an issue especially for female scholars who may change their name with a change in their marital status. If you change your name on your publications, you must understand with digital searching, all your citations may not be presented to whomever is searching (and see later in the chapter for why that is incredibly important). I have always advised junior scholars to pick one name as their scientific 'stage name' and only use that name for authorships. For example, I worked with a junior faculty member that to this point, has used four different last names. So, if you try to search for the research production of that faculty member, you'll find what looks like a very paltry research record, instead of their full robust research record. So, using one name across your career will facilitate more accurate results when someone searches for your research production.

You also want to make sure your publication name is easily found when a digital search is done. The first tip is to <u>always</u> use your middle name initial in your name. Secondly, run a Google Scholar or Web of Science search on your name and find out how many other scientists with that same name come up. If there are a lot of other scientists with your same name, you may want to think of using a different middle initial. A doctoral student I worked with had a very common scientific name and so started using 'Z' as his middle name. None of the other scientists had the same combination of first name, middle initial, and last name, so when you put in his name, only his publications come up. That searchability is critically important when your scientific portfolio is being evaluated.

When Life Scientists think about publication, often, we are thinking about publishing original data papers in scientific journals. In the life sciences, scientific papers presenting original data that test a hypothesis is how the body of knowledge moves forward. Original data papers are the papers that will establish your place in the discipline and will be the foundation of your career. After you have published several original data papers, you may be asked to write a 'review' paper. Review papers, in contrast to original data papers, are those where you integrate findings from papers in your area of expertise to synthesize new concepts and hypotheses regarding your field of study. Review papers are often more broad than original data papers, since the latter focus on one hypothesis, while the former focus on a larger area of study. Review papers, while serving as an overview and a way of putting new concepts forward, often will not be accepted if written by junior faculty alone. In my area (Exercise Physiology) our best journals will not even consider a review paper written by someone unless they have several original data papers published on the same topic. As such, as a junior faculty member, you are probably going to focus on writing and publishing original data papers as opposed to review articles.

One question that is dealt with often in P/T is the value of junior faculty writing books or book chapters. In the Life Sciences, the predominant scholarly output P/T Committees are looking for are original data papers that test specific hypotheses. With this type of focus, junior faculty are often not encouraged to work on either books or book chapters; again, the point being that as a junior faculty member in the discipline, you will be perceived to have neither the knowledge base or experience to write a book or book chapter, much like a review paper. However, this is primarily the case in science-based fields; I have many friends in other fields like Sociology, History, and English where the book is the preferred scholarly output, even for junior academics. So, while I've written this book for those academics in Life Sciences, if you are in another field, make sure you talk to your mentors about the appropriate form of dissemination your scholarly products should take.

If you do decide to write either a book or a book chapter, also understand it can take a long time for those scholarly products to be published. For example, several years ago I was asked to contribute a book chapter for a resource manual in my field; even though it took me about nine months to write the chapter, it was almost three and a half years before that chapter was published and I could put it on my CV and annual report. If I had been a junior faculty member, most of my pre-tenure time would have passed before that scholarly piece came out. That is a long time to wait to be able to claim a scientific product and as a junior faculty member, you often don't have that much time.

Lastly, one other disadvantage with writing books or book chapters as a young faculty member is they are generally not digitally referenced. While we'll talk about digital archiving a bit further down, understand that even with all the online scientific databases available, most of those science databases do not index scientific books or chapters. So, it is harder for your output, if it is books or book chapters, to be found by other scientists. In fact, in putting together a large edited volume recently on Exercise Genetics, I had a long-time friend decline to write a chapter because he said the chapter would not be discovered and his efforts to add to the body of knowledge would be wasted. To an extent, he has a point. Some publishers are working on this, but as of this writing, you should understand your scholarly output, if contained in a book or book chapter, will not be as easily discovered as if it were published as a journal article.

Where to publish your research?

You might think after the last section the easy answer as to where to publish your research is in peer-reviewed journals, and you would be correct. However, more complexity lies under the surface of that answer because there are literally thousands of scientific journals from which to choose. When I was going through my doctoral program, I was a bit of a pest to my advisor (Dr. Howley) with questions about knowing where to publish your results. His response was often some form of "we'll train you to know where to submit", which is a variation of "you'll know a good journal when you see it". As a result, my early publications were in journals my mentors and peers thought were good journals, and they were mostly correct. However, over time with the development of many online reference databases and in discussing this topic with doctoral students and junior faculty, I've developed some guidelines on what journals you should work to publish in.

The first question you should answer, is what journal do the scientists read that you want to reach? You can publish articles all you like, but if the other individuals that work in your field don't read those journals, then your efforts to impact your field are lost. As a quick example, I have worked for many years in Exercise Genetics. Early on, we published several articles in a variety of genetics-related journals with little in the way of comments or citations. However, about 10 years into our work, I bucked the trend and published one of our larger papers in a more applied physiology journal I knew had a large readership of the exercise scientists I thought needed to see our results. Surprisingly, about a week after the article was published, I was at a large conference and happened to be sitting a couple of chairs down from one of the leaders in Exercise Science. He made a point to lean out and talk across two people to tell me how great the article was and how he did not know we were doing that type of work. While validation was great, it pointed out to me it is incredibly important to publish your scientific articles where other scientists in your field will be exposed to them. To this point, I would bet you can develop very quickly a list of the 10 most read journals in your area; again, focus on those journals your colleagues read and not just on big name journals. Those 10 journals should be your targets for your research.

If you ask other scientists where to publish your science, you'll often hear you should publish in 'good' journals; of course, this is a derivation of the earlier career advice I was given about you'll know what a good journal is with proper training. However, this subjective question has become a bit less subjective over the years due to the development of several metrics that have arisen; I don't think any of these metrics are perfect, but they do give quantitative scores you can use to *start* to judge the quality of a journal. It is also important for you to understand these metrics because some departments use these measures as an additional factor to determine the quality of your research. The leading journal quality metric you'll hear about is the 'journal impact factor'.

> **Info to Know – 5.2**
> **Factors to Determine Where You Publish**
> 1. What journal do the readers you want to impact read?
> 2. Does the journal have impact using some metric of impact?
> 3. Does the journal meet the publishing requirements your funding has (open-access vs. traditional vs. hybrid)?
> 4. Will the journal you publish in be accepted as appropriate by your peers and supervisors?

Journal Impact Factor: To understand the journal impact factor (JIF), we've got to go backwards – if for nothing else to recognize the brilliance and difficulty of what it took to come up with journal impact factors. The JIF was originally developed by the Institute for Scientific Information (or ISI). ISI, led by Dr. Eugene Garfield, had the brilliant idea back in the early 1960's of tracking every paper cited in every scientific paper. Think about the enormity of that task back in the pre-computer days - tracking every paper cited in every scientific paper. Wow! To put an example with the task, if you published a scientific article that referenced 30 other scientific papers, ISI made a list of the 30 other scientific papers and noted your paper cited them. ISI started doing this in 1964 for *every life science scientific paper published* and not only kept going when new papers were published, but also went backwards to 1900. The result was an incredibly useful tool called the Scientific Citation Index (or SCI) that came in big printed volumes four times a year (and ISI later did the same thing with social sciences – called the Social Science Citation Index).

The usefulness of the SCI was as a scientist, if you had one article on a particular topic, you could go to the SCI and find out all the other articles that had quoted that one particular article. With an SCI search, there was a high likelihood you could find many other papers on the same topic in which you were interested. With the advent of the internet in the mid-90's and the massive increase in computing infrastructure, SCI moved to being an online resource. With the move to the digital realm, ISI started developing other metrics they could calculate using the data in the SCI. One of these metrics was the previously mentioned JIF (or 'Impact Factor' for short). The idea behind the JIF was simple; journals that published articles that are cited by other papers are more likely to have more overall impact than journals that publish papers not cited. So, the JIF is a measure of how many times a journal's papers are cited in other papers. There are several different forms of the JIF, like the 5-year JIF which some journal editors prefer because they contend it is a measure of long-term impact, but the straight JIF is now often used as a surrogate measure for the quality of a journal. JIFs are updated every year, and many journals, especially those at the top of the rankings of their fields, often announce with great fanfare their new JIF when they are released in the summer. While the ownership of SCI and JIF has changed over the last 10 years (now both are owned by Clarivate Analytics and are easily found in the Web of Science you can probably access through your university library), the core concepts of both SCI and JIF have remained and, in many cases, are now used as a measure to judge scholarly performance (more on that practice later). In fact, my home department at Texas A&M uses the JIF of the journals I publish in as part of my annual evaluation and you may find your Department/College/University does the same. So, in general you want to publish your articles in journals that have the highest JIF.

We need to unpack the last statement a bit, because while it sounds simple, it is fraught with complexity. There are some journals, e.g., The New England Journal of Medicine, that have a high JIF because they serve a huge swath of life sciences (2017 JIF for NEJM = 79.26). On the other hand, journals serving small areas in life sciences, may have very small JIF (e.g., Operative Techniques in Sports Medicine, 2017 JIF = 0.337). Therefore, if there wasn't some correction for these disparities, especially if you are publishing in Operative Techniques in Sports Medicine, the JIF for your journals might not impress your P/T Committee at all. Luckily, the JIF can be subdivided by field, with a ranking for each field. For example, in the category of Sports Sciences – where Exercise Physiology journals are indexed – the highest ranked original data journal is *British Journal of Sports Medicine* with a JIF=7.867 (2017 data).

Sometimes, your journals may also be listed in other categories; for example, some Exercise Physiology journals are also listed in the category of Physiology. So, be aware of where you will be publishing and where those journals are listed within the JIF listing. Where possible, you want to publish in a journal having a high JIF in your field. When you access the JIF rankings within the Web of Science, which is usually available through your library, you can filter the list by just the categories in your specific area, so you can see all the journals in your area that have a JIF. Use that knowledge and pick a great journal for your publications.

One of the drawbacks of using JIF is not all journals have a JIF, and there are some journals that claim fake JIF (yes, really). There are a variety of reasons journals may not have a JIF including that it is a new journal. Usually a journal must publish papers for at least two years before being given a JIF. Another valid reason a journal may not have a JIF is the journal has not gone through the process of applying to be included in the listing. Additionally, the journal may not have a JIF because they are what is called a 'predatory journal' (see below). Regardless of the reason, in general, as a junior faculty member, it does you little good to publish in a journal that does not have a JIF. You want to be able to show you are publishing your results in journals that have impact on your field and if you publish in a journal that doesn't have a JIF, you've just removed one way P/T Committees can evaluate the quality of your scientific production. Besides, with 12,200 journals[51] included in the JIF rankings, surely you can find one in your area having an impact factor.

Before we leave the discussion of JIF, you should be aware there are many people that don't like impact factors, for a wide variety of reasons, most of which center around the validity of the JIF. While I would agree a JIF should not be a sole measurement of a journal's quality, the JIF has been embraced by P/T Committees and Administrators because it does provide a single quantitative estimate of a journal's quality. Instead of a candidate saying "this is a great journal because I think it is", the JIF (and some similar metrics) provide a quantitative number to either support or refute that rationale. Given your goal is to get P/T, as a junior faculty member your time is better spent working to publish in journals with a better JIF than arguing about whether the JIF is appropriate or not. Save that argument for when you are tenured.

Open Access Journals: One of the newer publication venues that has arisen with the internet has been the availability of 'open-access' journals. The traditional publication model for journals has been you could not access articles published in journals unless you (or your Institution) had a subscription to that journal. The rise of the internet and the belief 'all information should be free' led many to believe that scientific data should also be free and open to everyone. However, this open-access belief puts journal publishers in a difficult spot because most of them use subscription fees to support the journal operations. No subscriptions, no revenue, no journals. So, a new type of scientific journal has arisen over the past 20 years and that type of journal is called an 'open-access' journal, which has a different payment model.

Most open-access journals do not charge subscription fees and make articles freely available to everyone. They can take this approach because in most

---

[51] This was the number of journals in the Journal Impact Factor Master List for 2017.

situations, the open-access journal charges the author directly for the publication costs of the article. These publication costs can be quite expensive, usually costing at least $2000 and going up from there. Even traditional journals are getting in on the action: many open their articles for open-access after the articles have been published for one year, or they will give you an option to pay an open-access fee, which is usually quite high, when your article is accepted for publication, which allows your article to be open-access from day one.

In either model, the idea is that studies are available to the public immediately, but the charges are paid by the authors. One of the more successful examples of the open-access model are the series of Public Library of Science (PLoS) Journals, which includes the flagship *PLoS One*. These journals operate the same as traditional journals, with a JIF as well as well-founded peer-review models, but just with a different public distribution and funding model. So, if you have the funds to pay the open-access fees, certainly open-access journals might be a good option for your publications. If you decide to publish in an open-access journal, talk to your department chair about whether there are funds available on campus to pay the open-access fees. In many cases, your library may have a fund just for this purpose.

Predatory Journals: With the ease of publishing documents on the internet and the general acceptance of open-access scientific publishing, there has also been the emergence of a new issue in scientific publications – predatory journals. These journals are called 'predatory' because they prey on scientists needing to publish results. Unfortunately, these journals tend to approach junior faculty and faculty in tenuous job conditions that desperately need to show publications. These predatory journals exist solely to make money and as such, if you can pay, they'll publish anything. To appear valid, predatory journals will try things like having a name very similar to a real journal, but with just an 's' added to one of the journal title words. Often these predatory journals have few quality controls: they'll claim to have peer-review processes when in fact, there is no or a minimal peer-review process. Also, these predatory journals may claim to have a JIF, but they really don't have one because their JIF will be fake.

There are a few easy ways to distinguish predatory journals from valid science journals. First, if you receive an email soliciting an article from you for a journal you've never heard of, it's likely a predatory journal. Secondly, if the journal claims to have a JIF, but when you look at the Master List of the Journal Impact Factors the journal is not listed, it's likely a predatory journal. Thirdly, if the journal guarantees they do quick publication, it's likely a predatory journal. Lastly, you can also check the Directory of Open Access

Journals (DOAJ.org) which maintains a list of established open access journals. Additionally, various folks on the internet have worked to maintain lists of known predatory journals[52] but unfortunately, these lists are out-of-date almost as soon as they are published. So, be extremely careful about where you publish; check out the journal thoroughly and make sure they have a JIF that is legitimate.

Pre-Review Archives: Easy publication on the internet has also brought a different type of publishing venue: the lure of 'pre-review archives'. These pre-review archives are online sites where you can 'deposit' your manuscript before it is reviewed and published by a scientific journal; it's often as simple as establishing an account and loading up your manuscript. These pre-review sites have been labeled as 'pre-print' archives, but I hesitate to use that term because the phrase 'pre-print' is often used by traditional journals for articles that have been accepted for publication (i.e., have gone through peer-review) but are not yet printed (hence, 'pre-print'). Since articles on pre-review websites have not gone through peer-review, it is uncertain whether they will ever be in print, and thus, 'pre-print' is used incorrectly when applied to pre-review servers.

Pre-review servers were first established in science fields such as physics and astronomy. These pre-review servers were considered to have two purposes: 1) To establish who discovered something first (i.e., establish primacy); and 2) To allow for comments by other scientists in the field so the authors could make their papers better before they were sent in for review. With the launch of pre-review servers such as BioRxiv.org, some are trying to bring the pre-review model to biology and the life sciences. As you might expect, an avenue where scientific publication occurs without peer-review would be controversial.

As I write this chapter, many professional organizations are working on policies to deal with pre-review servers. Much of these policies deal with the question of whether putting a manuscript on a pre-review server really constitutes publication. Even though the pre-review archives say their role is to make manuscripts better before submission to a journal, many scientific journals clearly note a paper published online is considered published and

---

[52] Dr. Jeffrey Beall was a leader in this area and maintained a list for many years of alleged predatory journals (https://beallslist.weebly.com/). However, this is a controversial topic and Dr. Beall has been accused of bias in this debate. As a result, much of his work has ceased. However, others have picked up his work and used his previous lists as the basis for the continuing identification of predatory journals (e.g., https://predatoryjournals.com/journals/#H).

therefore will not be considered for their journals. Thus, if you put a paper on a pre-review archive, you may not be able to publish in many journals. However, some journals don't have a problem with reviewing a paper that has been on a pre-review archive, *if you denote the paper is on a pre-review archive in your initial submission letter.* Therefore, you should carefully check the 'Information for Authors' section of any journal you plan to submit to and make sure you will not be narrowing your journal submission options if you place an article on a pre-review archive.

Before we leave pre-review archives, let's consider one example, and then consider how a P/T committee might consider a pre-review archive publication. I was asked by a prominent journal to review a paper in my research area; I initially said "yes" because the paper was of tremendous interest to me and right in my area of expertise. As I read the paper – which had as one defining characteristic 377,000 subjects(!) - I got a feeling of déjà vu; I kept thinking, "wow, haven't I seen this somewhere before?" Then I searched my files on the first author's name and found I had read the article a couple of months before. The article initially had been sent to me by a colleague of mine; at the time, I thought the paper was great and very interesting. I also thought the paper had been published because it was listed as being from a journal I didn't recognize; at that time, I had just shrugged my shoulders and figured this was a journal I hadn't heard of (there are so many journals, it's usual not to hear of a few). As I dug a bit deeper, I realized the paper I had been asked to review was the one that had already been disseminated on a pre-review archive. Interestingly, there were some major differences in the paper – on the pre-review version, there were 277,000 subjects; in the journal version, there were 377,000 subjects. Also, the conclusions were different – especially the genetic pathways highlighted. Which version was the correct version? It's seems to be more than an editing error when you suddenly have 100,000 more subjects. When I inquired with the journal that had asked me to review the manuscript, they noted they didn't have a problem with the pre-review archive. However, given the wide-spread circulation of the article I knew had already taken place, I did have a problem with the paper and refused to review it. In the end, my take-home-question was "which was the real paper – the pre-review or the submitted paper"? Eventually that paper was published and my question still holds because now both versions of the paper are available. Which are the real sets of findings?

Given your focus should be on getting P/T, you need to ask yourself a further question when you think about pre-review servers: how will your P/T committee regard any publications you put on a pre-review server? As you can imagine, I've been asking my colleagues that question over the past year, and to this point, only one (out of about 30 I've asked) has said it wouldn't be a big deal. The other 29 are all shocked an academic would consider putting scientific research on a pre-review server, *especially* if it may limit where you can publish the article. At this time, I would advise you not publish your findings on a pre-review server, no matter how tempting it might be. Many scientific organizations are working on this issue; hopefully, there will be some consensus in the next few years. But until 'science' in your discipline has decided whether these new venues are appropriate, as a junior faculty member, you do not need to be experimenting with new publication methods. This is another area where you need to wait until you are tenured to explore.

> **Info to Know – 5.3**
> **Dissemination Venues You Should Be Wary Of**
> 1) Predatory journals
> 2) Pre-review archives
> 3) Dependence only on abstracts for dissemination of your research.

Getting your research done

We've spent a lot of time talking about publication, without spending much time on actually doing research. One of the things you'll find as a junior faculty member is that research will be the one task you'll find easiest to put off. I'll repeat: "you'll find research the easiest thing to put off when you are a junior faculty member". You may be shocked at that statement, especially because your love of research and your research production is probably why you have your current job. However, you'll also find as a new faculty member that most everything you deal with will have hard deadlines. When you teach, you'll have to meet your class certain times every week for a certain length of time and you'll have to prepare to meet those deadlines. Your service obligations will come with deadlines, you will have committee meetings and reports will be due. In fact, the only thing that will not have many hard deadlines will be your research. Sure, you'll have deadlines for abstract submission, but those are easy to meet. The time you need for doing data collection, writing, and publishing have no deadlines, and if there are any, you must set them yourself.

In one sense it is utterly crazy we are so willing to put off our research agenda because of other deadlines; it is crazy because the primary factor that will help you keep your job is your research production. Most all faculty members are adequate teachers and most do service well. However, the distinguishing feature of those faculty getting P/T and those that don't is their research production. Research has shown quite clearly up to 2/3rds of new faculty produce 'virtually nothing' in their first 1-2 years that counts as research scholarship[53]. So, you must be diligent and disciplined to make sure your research gets done and you don't put it off. To this end, there are three primary tips that will make a difference in your research production: 1) schedule time daily for writing; 2) develop and get into 'the cycle'; and 3) learn to delegate.

Schedule time to write and work at it: You are in a writing business. If you are not writing, you will not advance. Period. The sooner you engrave this into your soul, the sooner you will start to move forward with your research. You may already have this attitude; if so, great. If not, you must remind yourself daily that an academic that doesn't write is someone that won't be an academic very long.

One of the best practices I've seen to increase your writing output, and one I've used for years, is an easy one. Schedule yourself to write 30 minutes each day. That's it - 30 minutes. Dr. Robert Boice, author of *Advice for New Faculty Members* - which is an amazing book on faculty development - studied this daily approach to writing by following 16 junior faculty members for six years. Dr. Boice noted those faculty that waited until they had a large block of time to write, or waited until "their *muse* struck" uniformly produced little in the way of scholarship. However, those faculty that scheduled to write in brief sessions every day, produced significantly more research output yearly than those that didn't. As Boice relates[54], those faculty that wrote daily for a short period of time, submitted over 8-fold more manuscripts per year, totaled almost twice as much writing per week, and had over 8-fold more manuscripts accepted per year. There is no other writing tip I've found that has had such an impact on my scholarly production as does scheduling and writing at least 30 minutes per day.

You may be thinking "wow, this is too easy" and you're right, it is easy. The question is whether you have the discipline to do it. As Dr. Boice notes, "Those [faculty] that succeed are 'mindful' about their work of writing." So, you must think about it and have the discipline to take this approach. But if you do, you'll find there are some advantages to writing daily versus waiting until you have a big block of time:
    1) 30 minutes is a short enough time frame that you should be able to work this into your daily schedule every day;
    2) If you do it daily, you'll find you won't have to review what

---

[53] Boice, R. Combined treatments for writing blocks. Behaviour Research and Therapy 30, pg. 107-116, 1992.
[54] Check out Fig. 11.1, on pg. 144 of *Advice for New Faculty Members*; that's where Dr. Boice shows this data!

you wrote previously before you start writing new verbiage because it'll be fresh in your mind;

3) You may find once you start writing on your 30 mins, that time may stretch; your goal may be 30 mins, but because you've started, you'll find you squeeze in extra time;

4) Lastly, if you schedule yourself to write 30 mins every day, when you've written daily, you can mark that task off your daily to-do list; you'll know you're working on your writing versus letting anxiety build up because you're not writing at all.

In the end, scheduling 30 mins a day to write is simple, easy, but most importantly, it is effective. You must write because that's part of your job and a part you'll be evaluated on. It only makes sense for you to do what has been shown to work, so get out your calendar and schedule your writing.

Even if you schedule 30 mins a day to write, it doesn't help if you just sit there and stare at a blank page. Sometimes the hardest part of writing is getting started. A great resource to get over this hump, as well as to strengthen your writing is the writing approach developed by Dr. Pat Goodson.[55] With Dr. Goodson's approach, you'll go through a guided series of exercises specific to not only academic writing in general, but exercises that also focus on specific types of academic products. These writing exercises are based on the latest literature in both psychology and neuroscience and will take you from helping to see yourself as a writer all the way specific exercises to strengthen each part of your research papers. Most scientists would never consider publishing a paper without a methods section; Dr. Goodson has given us all the 'methods section' for how to write your research papers.

In the end, if you schedule your writing, have the discipline to do it, and follow the wonderful resources that are available to help you with your writing, you should be able to produce the writing you'll need for P/T.

Get in 'the cycle': There is what I call a research cycle, through which most research projects go through (see Figure 5.1). This research cycle encompasses all the various phases of a research project, from idea to final publication. Too often, junior faculty focus on only one project at a time as it goes through the cycle; i.e., they don't start another project cycle until one is complete. I would encourage you to look at the cycle holistically and work to

---

[55] Find this process fully covered in Dr. Goodson's book *"Becoming An Academic Writer: 50 Exercise for Paced, Productive, and Powerful Writing"*. I can vouch for this book since all my students take Dr. Goodson's writing class – her book is the closest you'll get to her class, so it's worth the money and the time!

have a project going at every phase of the cycle. If you constantly have multiple projects moving through the research cycle, your production will be greater. In my own lab, I'm constantly mindful of the part of the cycle our various projects are in; if we get projects building up in one part of the cycle, I'll focus on that part to remove the blockade and get back to moving projects through the cycle. Again, if you've got a project at every part of the cycle, this will mean you've got at least five projects at some phase of the cycle (they should be all related topic-wise because you are sticking to your research focus – right?), and you'll then be easily able to describe what your near-term productivity should be. Get in 'the cycle' and be productive.

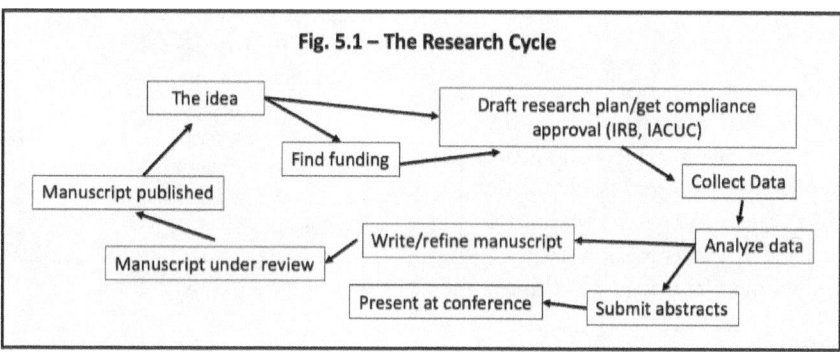

Learn to delegate: Other than writing, one of the most difficult tasks faced by junior faculty member is learning how to delegate, especially when it comes to research. A key to delegating is to understand what *others* in your lab can do and what *you* must do. Regarding your research, you may be hesitant to delegate any of that; I certainly was. My attitude was if I was going to publish the data, then the only way I could be assured the data was correct was if I was the one that did everything; recruited the subjects, oriented the subjects, collected all the data, analyzed all the data, wrote it all up, etc. As a junior faculty member, doing everything in my research, on top of teaching my four courses per term, participating in my assigned committees, writing grants, and working to provide service for my professional organization quickly exhausted me and took a huge toll on my personality, my relationships, and the quality of my job. That's when I realized I needed help.

As I pondered this situation, words from my post-doctoral supervisor came back to me: I had asked her one-day if she missed being in the lab. Her reply was "Yes, I love being in the lab. But if I'm in the lab, then there is no one to write the manuscripts and find funding. So, you get to collect data while I get to do the things you can't do." She was delegating data collection to her lab staff while she was doing the things we couldn't do. My research production didn't increase until I understood that to do research, I had to delegate tasks I could train others to do, while I focused on tasks others couldn't do.

With that approach in mind ask yourself, "what are tasks only you can do, and what are tasks you can train others to do?" I would bet in most cases, you can train others to collect data and to recruit subjects. You might even have collaborators that are working with you that are better at data analysis than you are. Of course, this delegation is all predicated on those you recruit to work with you being competent at these jobs. However, once you start to think about how you can delegate, you'll find your research production will exponentially increase.

There is a reason top scientists have labs full of people; the more people involved, the more work that can get done. But, you've got to first be willing to delegate. And one key to your willingness to delegate is finding the right people to work with you.

> **Info to Know – 5.4**
> **Keys to Getting Your Research Done**
> 1) Schedule time to write;
> 2) Get in the cycle of having projects in various stages of completion;
> 3) Learn to delegate.

Finding people to work with you

There is no doubt research is a team sport; you will find few, if any, lone researchers that are very productive. The above discussion about delegation should provide support for the contention that to be productive, you have to develop a research team. Additionally, most exciting new discoveries and most funding now occurs as the intersections of different fields, which means you need to work with other individuals that have expertise. As a result, you should work to develop collaborations above you in expertise and experience and you should also work to develop a lab team below you to help research the area you are working in. Figure 5.2 is a convenient way of envisioning a research team organization. Each level of individual in your team will be capable of doing different tasks; their capabilities are often dependent upon their knowledge level and their expertise, but in the end, all of them answer to you. You are responsible for your team and for all the research that comes out of your lab.

In most cases, you've already been a part of a research team, so you have a sense of how it is all supposed to work. However, you probably are having to put together your own research team for the first time and that can be a daunting task. Where do you find the people? How do you pay them? How do you train them? To this point, you've only been responsible for yourself, so the questions arise quickly as you start to build your team.

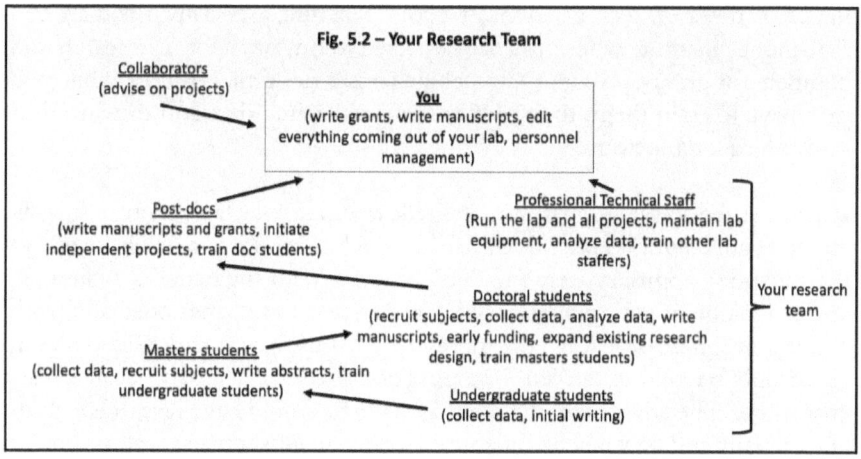

Fig. 5.2 – Your Research Team

The first question you need to answer as you think about building your team, is how will you support your research team members? This means, do you have money to pay people? If the answer is "no", don't despair; there are some great ways to build a research team without support money, but more on those later. Let's start off with what you *can* do if you've got money to support people.

I'm not going to make the distinction of where the money you will use to support lab staff is coming from (e.g., internally vs. externally), but you do need to pay attention to any specific regulations that come from paying people off the different sources of funds you have. The key here is that you have money; now, how much do you have and for how long?

In most cases, your University will have a set pay scale for professional research technicians, post-doc fellows, and perhaps even graduate students (doctoral and masters students). The amount of money you have will somewhat dictate which type of personnel you'll be able to hire. For example, let's say your department is very generous and you've got $75,000 per year for personnel for three years. In general, a beginning professional research technician will cost about $30,000/year with another 25% tacked on for benefits. So, to hire a lab technician, you're looking at about $37,500/year. With your hypothetical budget, you can afford to hire two technicians! The lab technician will be great for running your lab on a day-to-day basis, but with a beginning lab technician, you'll have to teach them everything they'll need to know (much like if you hired a student) so that will cost you time to get them up to speed. Also, you'll only have technicians if you can afford to pay them, so, you'll need to think about finding money to support them after your three-year personnel funding time is up. Despite this disadvantage, as some have noted[56], a lab technician may be your best hire, especially if you are in a soft-money institute where you are expected to put out a lot of research and compete for grants. Given a lab technician is a full-time position, while you may have to train them, their only focus is collecting data and moving your research agenda forward.

If you wanted to hire a post-doctoral fellow and if your University is following NIH guidelines on post-doc salaries, which most do, you will have to pay that post-doc approximately $48,000 per year. With the benefits tacked on, you're looking at approximately $60,000 per year to pay that post-doc (with about a 5% increase every year thereafter). Thus, if you had $75,000/year, you'd only be able to 'afford' one post-doc for your lab, just because they cost more. The advantage of a post-doc is they should have research experience already and they will be capable of writing manuscripts as well as writing for funding. However, keep in mind post-docs will only be with you 2-4 years, depending on the post-doc's career goals. So, there's a chance, that you'll train them and they'll leave quickly. But the normal time-frame for a post-doc is three years, so that would fit in nicely within your hypothetical three-year personnel budget.

As you balance whether to hire a lab technician or post-doc, in general, to get the most research bang for your buck, in most situations you can't go wrong with hiring a lab technician (preferred) or post-doc. In both instances, these staff's attention will be on carrying-out and generating research full-time, and as such, your lab's research production should soar.

However, in some academic settings, you will be judged at P/T on whether you've had a consistent record of training graduate students (usually PhD students). In fact, most of the research labs in the United States are predominantly staffed by graduate students, followed by post-docs and then professional technicians[57]. The predominance of graduate students in labs reflects the general training mission and the cost efficiency of graduate students. Related to P/T, the training mission of your lab can be critical; I can remember a case where a junior faculty member came up for a third-year review at an institution that was an R1-institution that had a clear educational/graduate

---

[56] One great source – albeit a little dated – for more info is the free manual *Making the Right Moves* from the Howard Hughes Medical Institute and the Burroughs Wellcome Fund. While it focuses primarily on soft-money institutions, it is a wealth of knowledge. And it's free! http://bit.ly/HHMIRightMoves

[57] This data, as well as a full economic analysis of the cost efficiency of using different levels of individuals in your lab is provided in an interesting book by Paula Stephan *How Economics Shapes Science* (in particular, Chapter 4), 2012.

student training mission. Over three years, this junior faculty member had not been on any graduate committees or had any graduate students in the lab and this lack of student training almost resulted in not having their contract renewed. So, you need to be clear as to whether the number of graduate students you've trained will factor in your P/T evaluation (either at the third year or fifth year).

If you are in an institution that looks favorably upon training doctoral students, it may be a wise choice for you to hire doctoral students in your lab. While there are certainly pros/cons to hiring doctoral students, let's work through what that hiring package may look like (again, assuming you have a $75,000/year personnel budget for three years). We'll assume the normal doctoral student stipend at your institution is $25,000; you'll also have to pay tuition – let's say $15,000/year – as well as a small benefits package at some Universities (usually just 5% or less) for these students. So, if you hire a doctoral student, you're looking at paying about $42,000 per year, so for your $75,000, you may only be able to hire one doc student.

The drawback to hiring doctoral students is you must train them, and if you have them writing manuscripts (which you should have), you'll have to spend time working with them on their writing. However, one of the advantages of hiring doctoral students is they are normally with you for at least four years, and so, once trained, your lab staff can be stable for several years. You will have to figure out how to support the doctoral students you have after your personnel budget runs out, but often there are teaching assistantships available that will help you bridge the gap between the personnel budget you have and personnel budgets you hope to get from grants. The availability of teaching assistantships may be a way that you can completely have your doctoral students paid by other funds, thus, not touching your personnel funds. Additionally, doctoral students are great mentors for masters and undergraduate students you'll have in your lab (and if you don't have masters and undergrads in your lab, you're missing a big opportunity). Lastly, if your department evaluates you based on the number of graduate students you are training, having doctoral students will work in your favor.

In our example scenario, you've got a lot of different hiring options for your $75,000. You could hire technicians, post-docs, or doctoral students, depending on what you foresee needing in your lab. Or you could try to mix and match to get the biggest bang for your money. To a large extent, the type of individual you hire to be the cornerstone in your lab will depend upon your previous experience, the requirements your Department has for graduate training, and your Institution's funding situation and their expectations for your funding. Personnel possibilities are only limited by your imagination and the funding available, so you'll see you have a lot of options of how to build your team if you have money.

But what if you don't have money? I've known many junior faculty that work by themselves because they don't have any personnel support money and they think they can't build a research team otherwise. As an academic, you may not have money, but you also have something very valuable to students – academic credit! Every University I've been in has had course work, usually titled something like 'Directed Independent Research Studies', for both undergraduates and graduate students. Your department may even require your students to complete these types of research studies before they graduate. You can easily build a research team with undergraduate and Masters students using those independent research studies as the 'currency' to pay them. It is a bit more difficult to build a cohesive team this way, but if you work hard to train the students and make sure they are putting the time in required by the number of credit hours they are getting, you can make it work.

The first University I was at was primarily an undergraduate institution, with just a few Master's students and a small undergraduate program. Directed research studies were the way I built my research team and I found many of my students came back semester after semester, even if they didn't need the academic credit. For most of my six years at that institution, I always had 2-3 Master's students and 5-6 undergraduates working in the lab. Certainly, my scholarly production was not as large as if I had been at a research university with post-docs and doctoral students, but for where I was, the Administration was really pleased with my scholarly production. So, if you don't have personnel support money,

> **Info to Know – 5.5**
> **Potential Lab Staff**
> The people you'll have in your lab are key to your production as a faculty member, both in teaching and research. As such, you'll have choices as to what level of individual to hire; often the primary determinant will be the budget you have. Lab staff can be made up of any of the following types of people:
> 1) Laboratory Technician
> 2) Post-doctoral Fellow
> 3) Doctoral Student
> 4) Masters Student
> 5) Undergraduate Students

don't despair. Use what you have available; you'll be pleased to find out you'll have many students that want to do research just for the experience. Most students don't do research just to get paid – I'm sure you didn't start research just for the money. I've found that most students are really interested in research and want experience. If you build your research team with those type of motivated, curious, and passionate students, you'll find that research becomes even more enjoyable.

Overall, building your research team is a critical move toward getting your research program rolling and productive. While the type of individual you have in the lab helping you will depend greatly on the funding you have available, consider the expectations your University has of your research program (i.e., is your priority research *and* training or just research?), as well as the personnel available.

Supervising your research team

One of the critical aspects of building a research team is proper supervision. Supervision of personnel may be new to you, so you may have a learning curve, but there are a few keys I found to be critical during my 30 years of getting people to work together to produce research. The two biggest keys are to make sure you know everything you can know about your University's hiring and supervisory policies and to maintain a strong connection and cohesiveness within your team.

Human Resources: First, since you will be the supervisor of record for the members of your research team, you will be responsible for all the facets of the hiring process, the evaluation process, and eventually, the termination processes. All these processes are inevitable when you supervise individuals, and every university has established policies that govern every one of these processes. In most Universities, most of these processes are handled through web-based services, and it is critical you learn how to use all these services, as well as learning the processes. There are three big issues in the University environment that will get you into trouble quickly: financial mismanagement, sexual harassment, and personnel process violations. Hiring and supervising individuals cuts across all three of these areas and so, if you are wise, you will learn as much as you can about your University's processes and policies in regards to hiring, evaluating, and terminating personnel. Your best resource in this is to work closely with your Human Resource (HR) representative. You may have a HR representative in your Department or in your College; seek that person out and work with them on all your hires.

Stay Connected: The second key is to make sure you stay connected with your research team. You will very quickly become isolated from your research team if you let your team run amok in the lab and you just go into your office and write every day (and yes, that is more common than you think). Certainly, you are supposed to be writing while your research team collects data, but it is critical for you to go to the lab regularly to interact with your team and to monitor what is going on. With these types of regular visits, you can observe how the team is interacting with each other, how the data are being collected, and whether there are any issues you need to change immediately. My post-doctoral supervisor was great at this; we knew she would wander in at least a

> **Info to Know – 5.6**
> **Scientific Authorship**
>
> A question I get often from both junior faculty and doctoral students, is how do you determine authorship on papers, especially if you had several people working on the project? Most professional organizations and journals provide guidelines on this topic (a quick look at the Information for Authors page on most journal's websites will give you some insight). However, as the leader of the research group, you need to have some clear ideas about how you will assign authorship and you should be willing to share these criteria with your team. Authorship disputes are probably the number one reason for hard-feelings amongst scientists.
>
> The guidelines I use are similar to those from one of my professional organizations (the American Physiological Society). I think of any publication having at least five phases – very similar to those outlined in Fig. 5.1 – Idea, Funding, Data Collection, Analysis, and Dissemination. In my author decision scheme, if an individual has participated in at least three of those phases, they will go on the paper as an author. Usually, the primary author (first in the author list) will be the individual who has spearheaded the project in the lab, with me being the senior-author (last in the author list). All the other authors will be listed according to their contributions. Other individuals that helped but are not authors are <u>always</u> are recognized in the paper's acknowledgements section. The only exception I've ever made for these criteria is if an author has a contribution that was key to the project being completed, even if that author only contributed in one area. For example, early in my career, I published a paper that had cardiac transplant patients as subjects. The cardiac surgeon who was an author on the paper, was certainly involved in the idea stage, but most importantly, provided us access to the patients. Without that contribution, the project would not have been completed. So, I had no problem having that individual on the paper as an author.
>
> You also need to be clear about the meaning of the authorship order on your papers. Some fields – especially in the Life Sciences – designate the first author as the one that guided and did the most work on the project, with the last author designated as the 'senior author' – usually the person responsible for the oversight and funding of the project. If your Department Chair / Dean are from another discipline, they may not understand these distinctions so it is critical that you indicate your role on all manuscripts!
>
> The take home message here is to be open and transparent at the beginning of a project about how you assign authorship and you'll have a lot less trouble!

couple times every day and that was our chance to bounce ideas off her, discuss issues that were coming up, etc. Her efforts to maintain connection with the research team daily were key to the cohesiveness of the group.

Another key to developing and maintaining a cohesive and productive research team is to have regular group meetings. These type of lab meetings serve the purpose of keeping everyone on the same page and will give you a chance to conduct additional training or to discuss new findings. One of my approaches to lab meetings has been to mix the lab meeting with a journal club, especially if there is a new article that has come out regarding our field, with one of my team leading the discussion on the article. However, I would encourage you to make sure you have an agenda for each meeting. Doing something as simple as having an agenda will help your team understand you have a linear process not only for the meeting, but also for the research.

As you develop the personnel on your research team, you'll learn who on your team can handle which tasks. Maybe you have someone very good at biochemistry, while another team member is better with data organization. The constant monitoring of who is good at what tasks will allow you to delegate tasks to the team member best suited for each task. Don't be disappointed when team members fail in their tasks; it is rare you will have a team member that can do all the tasks as well as *you* can on their first (and sometimes, second-third) efforts, especially when they are new in the lab. It is critical you don't overreact to an individual's attempts to learn a new skill. If you give your team members a chance to learn and grow you'll find your research team grows and gets better when they see that every opportunity to learn something in the lab is just that, an opportunity for learning, not failure. I will often give members of my lab team tasks that are bit harder than what they've done in the past; I want to continue to challenge them which helps them to continue to grow and increase their skillset.

As much fun as it is to develop a research team and work to develop young scientists in your lab, you should understand there will be times you may have someone in the lab that is a poor fit. Perhaps an individual doesn't have the ability to perform and carry out the required tasks, doesn't show up consistently, doesn't work well with the other team members, or shows some other behavior that is detrimental to your research team. If this is the case, *as soon as you recognize the issue*, you need to deal with it. Personnel issues never go away by ignoring them, believe me! Dealing with the situation could mean that you need to have a difficult conversation with the individual or realizing you need to terminate their participation in your lab. What you do will be largely dependent upon the situation and the individual involved. It will be difficult for you, but remember to talk to your HR professional before you do anything, and then resolve the issue. Having a difficult individual in your lab can wreck the cohesiveness of your lab group and can bring your research production to a halt.[58]

As a last note about your research team, remember it is 'your' research team. You are the head of the group and as such, you have the responsibility to make sure the team is productive and your team members learn, grow, and are respected. Additionally, any scholarly products coming out of your research team need to reflect the quality and rigor that is expected in science. Making sure your team is productive, while maintaining a professionally graceful environment so your team can learn and grow, can be a big challenge at times. There are times when you'll have to remove people from your team and there are times you'll have to be facilitative. But remember, if you don't set the example and run your team, word will get out and you'll have fewer people wanting to join your team and you'll be less productive in the end.

Evaluation of your research (the flip side)

Everything said previously is all well and good, but maybe the most critical item regarding research for a junior faculty member is how the P/T committees and all the decision makers will evaluate your research. So, we are going to close this chapter by discussing the flip side; just how will your research efforts evaluated?

Quantitative Factors: The old joke regarding the P/T evaluation of your research record was that quantity was all P/T committees looked for. When I was beginning I was told jokingly the P/T committee put all your papers on a scale and if they weighed more than 5 pounds, you got promotion and tenure! Even if that were the case, which it wasn't, in the current academic circles, evaluation of research is a bit more complicated than just weighing your papers. The current buzz word in evaluation of research production is 'impact'; the P/T committee and your administrators want to know your research is having impact on your field.

How 'impact' is defined is somewhat up to how you craft your P/T documents, but in general, research impact is defined as showing your scholarly products are resulting in international and national recognition, as well as being published in quality journals and being cited by other investigators as evidence you are having a positive effect on your disciplinary area. With this

---

[58] To see how destructive a disruptive research team member can be, listen to this fascinating podcast from Malcolm Gladwell - http://bit.ly/LabStaffDispute. Hear how a disruptive lab technician created false charges that led to investigations by the NIH and U.S. Congress!

type of definition of impact, the P/T committee generally will look at metrics related to 1) the impact of your publications in quality national/international scientific journals, and 2) the impact of your research on how other scientists in your area judge you. These areas are *in addition* to your external funding efforts which can be viewed as another avenue through which you have impact.

Building a research program in a relatively short period of time where you can claim to meet both criteria for impact depends primarily on your ability to have a cogent and succinct research focus. You must be focused while you are a junior faculty member; in fact, every project you do, you should be able to tie back to your one primary, central research question (see Fig. 5.1). This is not to mean you can't have side projects or collaborations with other investigators, but you should be very careful with these side projects and be able to tie everything you do back to your central research focus.

Having one research focus, with all your project efforts in one area, will increase the chance you'll have impact on your research area. For example, let's assume your research focus was on how exercise altered the metabolism of carbohydrate. For every study you do, you should be able to link back to that focus. However, if you were also interested in other topics, perhaps the effects of weightlessness on eye shape (that's a real research topic by the way), your efforts would be split between doing research in two completely different areas. Since you are halving your research efforts on each topic, you've also decreased the chance by 50% you will be able to show you've had impact on your research area. My exhortations for you to have a single research focus is not an indication you *can't* have more than one research focus, it's just an acknowledgment your task of having significant impact on your area of research during your first five years as a faculty member will be much more difficult if your research efforts are subdivided amongst different foci.

What if you decide to change your research focus? As a junior faculty member, if you are going to change your research focus from what you indicated in your job interview[59], you need to do it early in your career so you have plenty of time to establish yourself in the new area. Otherwise, I would strongly encourage you to stick to the research focus you brought with you when you were hired throughout your first five years as a faculty member. Reestablishing your research program with a different focus is very difficult; I changed my research focus from studying how the human body copes with

---

[59] At least you should have shown a research focus during your job interview. If necessary, review Chapters 5 and 7 in Book 1. If you got a job without having to state a research focus, then you're probably not at a research-intensive university.

blood loss to the genetics of exercise about midway through my time as an Associate Professor. I didn't have tenure on the line, but it still took me several years to reestablish myself as a credible scientist in the new research area. So, in general, pick your research focus, and stick with it diligently during your first five years until you get P/T.

Assuming you have had a singular research focus, how is the impact of your research program determined? As noted above, there are several criteria that can be used. The first is the impact you are having at a national/international level. This type of impact is easy to determine; usually the

> **Info to Know – 5.7**
> **Quantitative Metrics That May Be Used to Evaluate Research**
> 1) Amount/source of external funding;
> 2) Number of citations;
> 3) H-index;
> 4) Journal impact factors;
> 5) Number of papers.

P/T committee will look at your publication outlets. The journals you publish in should be national/international journals and your scientific talks should be at national/international meetings. If your science talks don't go past the state or regional level, then you will not be deemed to have much of a national/international impact. However, if you are presenting at large national/international conferences, this can be one index of your national/international impact. Another factor that can be considered here is your external funding; if you are getting funding from national organizations, or even international organizations, this funding shows your research having national/international impact. As you think about your national/international impact, make sure you emphasize these types of factors as indices of your impact.

The other two criteria listed in the evaluation of your research impact (besides external funding) involve your publications; are you publishing in quality journals and is your work being recognized by other scientists? You'll note I didn't mention quantity of papers you publish as being a criterion of impact. There are certainly minimal expectations for number of publications you must have in most departments and you need to make sure that you have discussed these expectations with your Department Chair before you start your job. Additionally, while you should build your research portfolio based on solid scholarly activity that is accepted in your discipline, you may want to keep in the back of your mind specific smaller projects, both data and writing, that will allow you to generate publications fairly quickly if needed, especially if you start hearing that you aren't publishing 'enough' papers. However, while number of publications may be used for basic expectations of your position, the use of the number of publications you have as a measure of your scholarly impact is problematic because the number of publications can be dependent upon several factors, some of which are out of your control.

Some faculty members perceive the number of publications is a badge of honor, with more meaning better. In a former College, our Dean kept lauding a faculty member who regularly published 25-30 papers per year. In my field, that type of production is unheard of, so out of curiosity, I started looking up this faculty member's papers, especially since the Dean kept using this faculty member's production as indicative of good research. It turned out what the faculty member was reporting as publications were usually just poems relating to his field (and short poems as well) – these publications certainly did not require compliance approval (human subjects can slow down data collection), data collection, or analysis. While these publications evidently counted in this faculty member's field, those types of publications would not have counted in my field. My point to this example is not to criticize other fields, it is that quantity of publication is often a bad descriptor of an individual's research production, and now with pre-review archives and predatory journals, just raw number of publications is certainly not an indication of either quality or impact.

So, if raw number of publications is not an adequate measure of scholarly impact, what is? Today, most P/T Committees will use a blend of quantitative (objective) measures and qualitative (subjective) measures. It is always a good idea to talk to your Department Chair and the Chair of the P/T Committee about what measures are used most frequently in your University. I would do this early in your job so you've got time to make sure your research is reflected well in those measures.

First, the quality of the journals you publish in, as measured by the JIF which we discussed earlier, is seen as a surrogate measure of the quality of your work. The rationale for application of the JIF (or any other journal quality metric) as a surrogate of the impact of your work is the reasoning that if a high-quality journal chooses to publish your work, then necessarily, your work is of high quality because high-quality journals don't normally publish low-quality research. If they published low-quality work, the reasoning continues, then their JIF would not stay high long. So, as stated earlier, it's important for you to publish in the journals with the highest JIF in your field for just this reason.

A second measure of the impact of your publications is how often they are recognized by other scientists. The easiest measure of this criterion is the number of times your publications are cited by other scientists in their papers. The citation rates of your articles are easily determined through services like the Web of Science who derive that data through the Scientific Citation Index described earlier (also, Google Scholar provides citation rate data as well). Citation rates are merely how many times your work is cited, with the thought being the more citations you get, the more impact your work is having on other scientists. Some P/T Committees may differentiate the number of self-citations (how many times you cite your own work) from your overall citations to find out how many other scientists are citing your work, but again, that data is easy to get. To my knowledge, there are no 'standards' for how many citations you should have; the number of citations you have depend somewhat upon the size of your field. For example, Dr. Paul M Ridker, a physician who has published 710 articles and reviews primarily dealing with markers of inflammation (such as C-reactive protein) which has many clinical and medical applications, has had over 122,000 citations. In contrast, my articles deal primarily with molecular pathways controlling genetic regulation of physical activity (a much narrower field without clinical application yet) and have only been cited a little more than 1,100 times. While I'm happy with my citation rate, to compare my citation rate with Dr. Ridkers' would make me look like a slacker. So, while citation rates are a useful measure of impact, you must help your P/T Committee understand the context of your citation rate, by helping them understand the size of your field, a topic called 'citation context'.

This issue of citation context is one that led to the development of a metric – derived from citation rates – called the 'H-index'[60]. Simply put, the H-index is the number of papers you have published that have been cited that many times. Descriptions of the H-index don't seem to make much sense without an example. Thus, let's return to Dr. Ridker (from above); his H-index is 166 which means he has at least 166 papers that have *each* been cited at least 166 times. Thus, you can calculate an H-index for all scientists that have published (both Web of Science and Google Scholar will do it for you).

But once we understand what the H-index is, the question becomes what is a 'good' H-index? There are not any hard and fast guidelines as to what is an appropriate H-index, so often subjective experience guides P/T committee expectations. For example, in my experience, most Full Professors that have had a successful research program, have an H-index of at least 20 (i.e., at least 20 of their papers have been cited at least 20 times by other papers). The H-index is somewhat dependent on how long the scientist has been publishing (i.e., the longer they've been publishing, the more time for others to cite their work and their papers to build citations), but in all, it gives a type of insight as to the impact of a scientist.

---

[60] The H-index was developed and first proposed by Dr. Jorge Hirsch in 2005. You can either blame or credit him, depend on your view of the H-index!

The concept of the H-index has also been applied to a variety of other publishing characteristics, including journal quality, with the thought that journals having higher H-indexes have greater impact than those that don't. While neither citation rates or calculations such as the H-index are perfect, they do provide a more quantitative measure of the impact and quality of your research and many departments and P/T Committees are using these types of measures to judge the quality of faculty members' research output.

There are at least three drawbacks to the use of citation rates and the H-index as a measure of research impact. First, it takes time for other scientists to read your work and then cite it. There is at least a one to two-year lag time from when you publish until citations to your published work start showing up in the literature. As a junior faculty member, using a citation rate measure can be difficult because it will probably take you 1-3 years to have any significant amount of research published. Thus, you may not start seeing citation rates increase until right before you go up for promotion and tenure (4-5 years). So, anything you publish as a junior faculty member may not show up in these indexes until you are going up for P/T. This is another reason to start publishing as quickly as you can as a junior faculty member.

Another drawback of citation rates – besides being influenced by time - is they are also affected by the number of publications you have. If you have 200 scientific papers, it is more likely another scientist will read your work and ultimately cite it, versus just having a small number of papers in print. Thus, citation rates (and the H-index) are heavily influenced not only by *how long* you've been publishing, but also by *how many* papers you have published.[61]

Another significant drawback of using citation rates, that may act to offset the first two drawbacks, is your citation rates (and H-index) can vary dramatically depending on what source you get the citation rates and H-index from. Up to now, I've primarily talked about the Scientific Citation Index (i.e., Web of Science) estimation of these numbers, primarily because SCI has been around the longest and is the most well established. However, Google

---

[61] A useful way of correcting for this issue is to standardize (i.e., divide) a scientist's H-index by their number of publications to get a relative index of citation rates versus the number of publications. You get a better sense if a scientist's H-index is driven by just the number of publications they have vs. relative impact per paper. For example, if you take Dr. Ridker's Web of Science numbers – 710 papers and H-index = 166 – you have a ratio of 0.23 meaning each paper has an average H-index of 0.23. Compare that to my numbers: 100 papers and H-index = 22. At first it doesn't look like much of a comparison, but if you do the ratio (0.22), each of my papers has almost the same average H-index as Dr. Ridker's.

Scholar has also gotten into the game and one of the caveats with Google Scholar is they also consider published abstracts, not just published papers (like SCI does). Also, because digital indexing is never perfect, there are often differences between the estimated citation rates and H-indexes from Web of Science and Google Scholar. For example, if we use Dr. Ridker again, Web of Science says he has over 122,000 citations and an H-index of 166. Google Scholar shows Dr. Ridker as having over 266,000 citations and an H-index of 218. Most scholars that are listed in both Web of Science and Google Scholar have higher rates in Google Scholar; just be aware of the difference and use the number that is most appropriate or the number dictated by your University[62].

External Sources of Evaluation: Any evaluation of your research production will have external reviewer evaluations attached to it; some of these external reviews will be quantitative and some will be qualitative. In most cases, external reviews are accorded greater validity by the P/T Committee and your University administrators because it is assumed external reviewers will not have a conflict of interest or other biases affecting their evaluation. Whether this assumption is true or not, it doesn't matter; external evaluations of your research tend to hold greater weight in P/T than do internal evaluations of your research. These external reviews can encompass several different forms, ranging from the number of external grants you've received (quantitative) to external letters of review (qualitative). Let's take a few minutes to unpack the common external sources of research evaluation.

It is assumed the number and amount of external research funding you've received is a good evaluator of your research because funding agencies are usually not willing to give money to scientists with bad ideas or less than productive research records. Additionally, to be funded by an external organization means your research plans have been thoroughly scrutinized and evaluated by a panel of scientists that have some familiarity with the topic of your work. Thus, the thinking goes, "if an external panel of scientists approve and a funding agency gives you money, then your science must be good." That's another reason to work to develop your external funding; it shows external scientists value your science.

In conjunction with examining your external funding record, another quantitative metric of the impact of your science is how many grant review panels you've been invited to be on. These review panels are the groups that handle

---

[62] Another source of these numbers is a paid-service called *Scopus*. Be sure and talk to your Chair as to which source of citation rates and H-index is considered appropriate by your University.

the scientific, peer-reviews of grants submitted to different funding agencies; usually, if you've developed a record of external funding, you'll eventually be asked to be on these panels. As a result, your participation in these types of review panels, while they are a lot of work, will also show that your research program is having national and international impact.

Another couple of indices that can be used as a surrogate for external reviews are the number of external research awards and the number of external invited lectureships you've been asked to do. Both metrics are easy to count for your review committee, are quantitative, and they indicate how scientists outside your University value your science enough to either give you awards or to ask you to come speak. In most cases, the external speaking invitations do not include professional conferences; most scientists going to professional conferences will speak in some form or fashion, even if it is standing in front of a poster presentation for three hours. External invited lectureships that count as an external source of evaluation are those talks you don't necessarily pursue, but are ones where other Universities or organizations specifically ask you to come speak.

One of the drawbacks of the previous three metrics of external research evaluation – funding, reviewing, and speaking - is that as a junior faculty member, these types of external invitations, while quantitative, don't often happen early in your career. However, when they do, make sure you put them on your CV and in your P/T evaluation materials. Because junior faculty often don't have time to accumulate other external sources of research valuation, to provide another external evaluation, a junior faculty member's P/T portfolio will be sent to external reviewers as part of the review process.[63]

Having external evaluators look at your research portfolio during P/T evaluation, is an established process in academia. I cover this process extensively in Chapter 8, including how these external reviewers are picked, but because usually the major item an external reviewer will review is your research portfolio, a few words regarding external reviews is appropriate here.

Rarely will the external reviewers conduct much of a review of either your teaching and/or service activities; rather the focus of external reviewers will be on your research portfolio. You may be thinking "wait, he was covering objective/quantitative evaluations, but now, he's talking about subjective evaluation". In actuality, you should understand the best external evaluations

---

[63] While external reviews always happen during P/T consideration, I've also seen them occur at the three-year review mark. So, don't be surprised if your research portfolio gets externally reviewed at multiple times during your first five years.

are based on quantifiable data. As an external evaluator, you want to be able to show proof for your evaluation, so, in my experience, while external evaluations would technically be considered subjective/qualitative, the best external evaluations are based on the most quantifiable data available (much of which we've already talked about).

The external review letters, a citation analysis of your work, and other quantitative metrics, will comprise most of the evaluative material to judge your research production. Certainly, there are many aspects you can't control, but, all these factors hinge on you publishing your work in good journals, being involved in your professional society so you get a national reputation, and working to develop external funding. In short, your evaluation will stem directly from your publishing and fund development efforts.

Qualitative factors: Quantitative, objective criteria is often easier to deal with because it is...well...quantifiable. That's why it is often hard for junior faculty to address the qualitative aspects of their research impact. However, if you can't or won't address the qualitative aspects of your research impact, you will have a difficult time during your evaluation process.

> **Info to Know – 5.7**
> **Key Items for Qualitative Evaluation of a Research Program**
> 1) Why you research what you do;
> 2) Why your research topic is important;
> 3) What gaps in knowledge are you addressing?

In essence, the qualitative aspect of your research is your description of how your research makes an impact and is usually reflected in the impact statement you provide in your P/T portfolio. As difficult as it may be to describe and verbalize, your impact statement will be about how your research positively affects society and our world. Another reason this type of qualitative impact statement is tough to write is because we are all often hesitant to toot our own horn, but in this aspect, you must be willing to talk about the importance of *your work*. And if you can't communicate the importance and impact of your work, who can?

As you develop the impact statement about your research[64], in general, you want to cover three aspects regarding your research: why you do the research you do, why is that topic important to society and knowledge, and what gaps is your work filling within your field. In general, a qualitative assessment of your research will consider these three points which you should start formulating so you are prepared to compose that all important impact statement when it comes time for you to develop your P/T portfolio[64].

---

[64] This topic is covered extensively, with an example, in Chapter 8.

Other factors used to evaluate scholarly production: While the above sections cover the vast majority of metrics that may be used to evaluate your scholarly production, there are some new metrics that are being talked about and used. The most common 'new' metric being used attempts to measure the impact of your research on the public sphere. Most often this metric is based on social media mentions, likes, and references to your research. One company that is leading this discussion is Altmetric.com who claims to be able to determine who is talking about your research on social media. Whether a measurement like Altmetric is an appropriate index of scholarly production in your field depends somewhat on the focus of your discipline, with fields that deal with social issues probably more dependent upon social media as a judgement of relevancy. However, the point for you is not whether such a metric is appropriate, but understanding whether this type of metric will be used in your evaluation. As I've said earlier regarding other controversial topics in academia, while the use of social media to judge research may be a topic you have opinions about, your focus needs to be on fulfilling the expectations your University places on you. If your University counts Altmetric data as an indicator of research production, then you need to figure out how to use it to show your research in the best light possible.[65]

As we wrap up this section, remember both external and internal reviewers will use a combination of objective and subjective measures. You must show you've been productive from a quantitative stand point, but you also must be able to explain the qualitative impact of your work.

The Take Home Message (finally!)

This has been a long chapter, but rightfully so because in almost every case, especially if you are at an institution that places a high priority on research, your research production will be the *defining* portion of your academic record. In most cases, your research production will get you promoted and tenured. Teaching and service will help, but your research will define your academic record and will allow you to establish a national and international reputation, as well as having an impact on knowledge. All of this may seem overwhelming right now, but remember that research - finding and reporting new,

---

[65] Interestingly enough, there's been an intriguing suggestion by Dr. Neil Hall (Genome Biology, 15:424, 2014) to establish a 'Kardashian Index' (K-index) which is a "measure of discrepancy between a scientist's social media profile and publication record". In short, the higher the K-index, the less likely the scientist has a substantial scientific record.

unknown knowledge - is hard. If it were easy, everyone would do it. You've been given an opportunity to do research; prove that the search committee were right to hire you!

6

TEACHING:
HOW TO GIVE YOUR STUDENTS THEIR MONEY'S WORTH

Teaching is another critical 'piece' of your academic career and your eventual P/T evaluation, so, you have to determine how it fits in with the other pieces of fund development, research, and service to build your academic piece of furniture. Teaching is important because it is where most of your students will 'touch the University'; in the classroom is where the students interact with their Professors which is usually their most tangible direct interaction(s) with a representative of the University. Teaching is often where a student will first judge whether their University is doing a good job and if they are getting their money's worth when it comes to their education.

Unfortunately, teaching, while a cornerstone of most academic environments, is often outshone by the importance put on research, especially during P/T deliberations. Teaching is outshone by research because it's assumed 'everyone can teach' and it takes no special skill to do so, unlike research. However, the public doesn't often appreciate that the classroom environment can be a difficult place for faculty members and even more so for new faculty. Even though a new faculty member may have had some experience with teaching as a teaching assistant, most of the time, the *process* of teaching (i.e., pedagogy) has been given little attention during the doctoral training period, unless you were lucky enough to have an undergraduate and master's background that offered you significant pedagogical or andragogical[66] training. Unfortunately,

This Chapter:
What is Teaching? 122
Your class and classroom 123
Preparing for your teaching 128
Delivering material and interpretation 138
Evaluation of your students' learning 146
How Others Will Evaluate Your Teaching 157
Student Issues 166
Improving your teaching 172
The Take Home Message 174

---

[66] While I'm not one usually in favor of using complex words (or jargon), these two terms – pedagogical and andragogical – you should know since you will be in the education business. Andragogical pertains to the techniques of educating adults and pedagogical pertains to the theories of teaching and learning.

in the case of most life scientists, they haven't been exposed to the necessary training. Many times, it is assumed that the new faculty member has learned how to be a college teacher because they've had to sit in numerous classes. While this faulty assumption is being challenged at many Universities and junior faculty are being provided with ways to improve their teaching, it is critical junior faculty get basic training in simple techniques and thoughts in conducting classes. The aim of this chapter is to provide thoughts and ideas about what teaching is today, how to set up your class, how to deliver your class, how to evaluate your students without losing control of your classroom and your sanity at the same time, as well as how to deal with the inevitable student problems. In the end, my goal is to help you be truly inspiring in the classroom; you never know when your teaching will inspire a student to do great things and certainly, you want to be the best representative of the University you can be to truly give each student their money's worth.

There is no doubt I love teaching; while research is the reason why I've had the positions I've had, I initially went to College to be a teacher and a coach. With both a B.S. and M.S. in Education (in Physical Education/Math and Physical Education/Counseling, respectively), I was fortunate to have the benefit of great Professors who also loved teaching and who helped me gain tips and tricks that helped make me a better teacher. On top of my education, teaching 7th grade math in a public school for a year taught me lessons I still use every day. Later, getting to help doctoral students and junior faculty hone their teaching skills has been some of the most impactful moments of my career. Truly I was born to be a teacher. That's why this chapter is so important to me; I've seen too many junior faculty members struggle in the classroom unnecessarily and as a result, I've seen their students not get the education they deserved. My hope is this chapter will not only give you techniques that will improve your teaching and reduce your anxiety in the classroom, but will encourage you to continue to work to improve your classroom skills so every one of your students can claim to have had the best professor ever.

What is Teaching?

With the advent of technology and the easy access to information, I believe the purpose of university teaching is different than what it was just 30 years ago. In the 'old days', the Professor at the front of the classroom, in combination with the textbook, was the deliverer of information. The Professor and the Textbook were the authority on the course content. Sure, you could find more information, but you had to go to the library and who was going to go to the library to read another textbook? So, the Professor was the sage that delivered information, often referred to as the 'sage on stage'; whatever the Professor said, it was assumed to be fact.

With easy access to information through the internet (and Wikipedia), the Professor stopped being the sole authority on any topic many years ago (about 1998 by my observations). At that time, unbeknownst to many Professors (even today), the role of the Professor at the front of the classroom began to shift from being the sole source of information, to being a guide and translator of the available information. Instead of pontificating on what knowledge is out there, the role of a university Professor has transformed into an individual who points out the important items in the base knowledge and helps the student build a scaffolding of knowledge they can use to evaluate the other information they come across. Besides, most scientific fields have way too much knowledge to think you can cover everything in a 15-week semester. Over the past 30 years there has been such an explosion of information, there is literally no way to cover everything that is known about a specific discipline in one semester. Therefore, you must shift your thinking and appreciate that your job is to guide and help your students interpret the information they can readily access. If you start to see your role as guide and interpreter, this will help ease some of your anxiety about having to know everything before you walk into class, a problem for many junior faculty. You are a university Professor because you have shown you have skills in scientific reasoning; there's no reason those same linear thinking skills and your core content knowledge abandon you when you walk into the classroom. So, start thinking about being a guide and interpreter.

> **Info to Know - 6.1**
> **What is teaching now?**
> As a Professor (teacher), you are the guide and translator of the available information for your students.

Your class and classroom

As you shift your thinking toward being a guide and interpreter, and not just a 'fount of knowledge', you also need to consider the learning environment you set in your class. How you plan and organize your class can either hinder or help the learning that takes place in your class. Therefore, you need to understand this is *your class and your classroom* and you should plan, organize, and manage your class so the learning environment is optimal for all your students. Whether your students learn or not is up to them, but your job is to do the best you can in delivering the material as well as organizing and promoting a learning environment conducive to learning.

A side note while we're here. I've never agreed with the argument the Professor/teacher is ultimately responsible for how much their students learn. I believe the Professor's job is to be prepared and to provide the best learning environment possible regarding the content of the course. However, how much a student learns is completely the student's responsibility. The old adage about 'you can lead a horse to water but you can't make him/her drink' is appropriate here. By providing a good learning environment and being prepared for class, you've led the horse to water; whether the horse drinks is completely up to the horse (student). So, be prepared to push back if someone tells you are responsible for how much your students learn; that's not your responsibility, that's the student's responsibility. Regardless of whether the student decides to learn or not, you still have a big responsibility in providing a great learning environment and being prepared. It truly comes down to what you can and cannot control. And one component that you can control is providing a great learning environment.

The critical first part of setting up a great learning environment is understanding a classroom is not a democracy; what happens in your classroom and how your class is run is your responsibility and your academic right. As a faculty member, you do have academic freedom to conduct the class as you see fit, within the boundaries of ethical, moral, and socially-aware parameters of the course. Given you are the guide and interpreter, it is not the students' privilege to set how the course is conducted. Think about it; if you had hired a guide to climb Mt. Everest, you wouldn't second-guess the guide or try to guide yourself as you climbed the mountain. The same thought applies to your class; the students are scaling a mountain, you've been hired to guide them and as such, it is up to you to choose the best route to take.

Sometimes faculty believe that to relate to students, they must try to become their students' friend. However, as the guide and interpreter (i.e., teacher) of your class, you *cannot* be the students' friend. Being 'friends' with someone implies an informality that is not appropriate for the classroom, especially since you oversee the learning environment. Given you have to set the boundaries for your class and evaluate your students, these responsibilities will necessarily be conflicts of interests if you are also 'friends' with the students. Now don't misunderstand me; certainly, you should be concerned about your students, you should engage with your students, and in short, you should do everything you can to provide the best learning environment. However, your role is to be their teacher and not their friend. You have responsibilities in class and those responsibilities give you authority. If you mix the dynamics of friendship with your teaching responsibility and authority over those 'friends', you will have many difficult situations arise. Thus, it is best to maintain a professional distance from your students. Again, that doesn't mean you can't engage with them, care for them, and be concerned for their welfare. But it does mean you must engage and care for your students in the role of a responsible professional educator.

Before we leave this aspect of teacher vs. friend, there are two issues that can develop out of this topic. The first issue is the potential of deeper relationships with students. In most universities today, consensual relationships with undergraduates is strictly forbidden and as a faculty member, you could be subject to immediate dismissal. As a faculty member, there is a power differential between you and your students and no matter how consensual a relationship may seem to be, since you have power over the student, primarily through their grades, this makes consensual relationships not advisable and frankly, inappropriate. Again, maintaining a professional distance between yourself and your students will help you avoid these types of relationships.[67]

The second issue is how students should address you; how should your students address you in class? What you allow students to call you in class can either increase or weaken the professional boundaries between you and your students. For example, calling someone by their first name often implies an informality and familiarity that may not be appropriate for the faculty-student relationship. Allowing your students to call you by your first name may decrease the appropriate professional distance between you and your students. The alternative is to have your students call you by your title (Dr. XXX or Professor XXX). While it may seem formal, using your title reinforces the professional distance between you and your students and is another sign you are not their friend, but rather their mentor, teacher, and guide. You may feel uneasy about doing this because the likelihood is you may be only a few years older than your students. Further, how do you deal with this in class? How do you tell your students to call you Dr. XXX? It seems awkward to say "Class, you can call me Dr. XXX, but not by my first name." In my experience, I don't make a big deal of it; I just introduce myself the first day of class as "Dr. Lightfoot". My syllabi do not have my first name (just my initial), so the students really don't have an opportunity to easily learn my first name and I don't provide it. Most of professors I had, I still think of as "Dr. XXX"; in fact, my doctoral advisor – Dr. Howley – is still 'Dr. Howley' to me to this day!

In the end, you are responsible for setting up the learning environment in your classroom. As a part of that responsibility, you must set up the proper relationships with your students. Mixing the 'authority' responsibilities you have with friendship will only make your job and your life more difficult, and may put you in violation of university policies.

---

[67] Consensual relationship policies vary great between Institutions; it is advisable if you read the policy at your University carefully. Sometimes these also apply to relationships with graduate students and staff members, so read these policies carefully!

The second part of setting up a great learning environment is you need to set appropriate expectations for your students and convey those expectations to your students early and often. The expectations you set up apply to both learning the material and to the behavior of the students in the classroom. Setting expectations may seem daunting to you, but after having taught hundreds of classes over the years, I've found when you set realistic expectations, your students will know what their goals should be and will work, sometimes ridiculously hard, to meet those expectations. When I've set expectations for my classes and have verbalized those expectations, my students have always met my expectations. The only exception to this was when I taught a class for public school teachers (a continuing education class); I assumed I didn't need to set expectations since this was a class with teachers as the students. I figured these 'students' would know what they needed to do. In over 30 years in the classroom, I've never had such trouble as I did with that class. After many years of reflection, I truly believe I had trouble because I didn't set and share my expectations for the class with the 'students'.

> **Info to Know - 6.2**
> **It's your Class**
> Your class will run smoother when you set a great learning environment. To do that, remember that:
>
> 1) You are responsible for everything in the class;
>
> 2) Don't be afraid to set expectations for your students.

How do you set expectations for your class? One of the easiest ways to set expectations for your class is to be clear on the syllabus what you expect and then stick to the syllabus during the semester. In particular, the syllabus can be used to set behavioral expectations for your class. For example, if you don't want students using their cell phones, checking social media, or talking during class, put that in your syllabus. If you expect your students to have respectful dialog with other students, put that in the syllabus.

But be forewarned; if you are going to put these expectations in your syllabus, you need to have a plan for how you'll enforce your expectation. For example, I expect my students will not use digital technology for non-class items during class (e.g., checking their social media). To enforce that expectation, I walk around the classroom quite a bit during my classes. I've often sat in the back row of the class and lectured from there. Just the simple act of walking around during class allows me to see what students are doing on their phones and on their computers. It's amazing how powerful it is to stop talking for a moment and quietly tell a student to turn off or put away a device that is being used inappropriately in class. You won't have to do that many times before you'll find the problem ceases. Setting expectations is great, but those expectations are predicated on you enforcing the behaviors you want or students will ignore you.

Another expectation I share with my students, and I think you should as well, is I don't let students 'hide' in class. We all have students that would prefer to remain anonymous in class and 'hide'. Students try to hide in class for a variety of reasons; they may be shy, they may not like attention from the instructor, they may not have studied, or any number of other reasons. For example, I had a young woman in one of my Exercise Physiology classes who not only sat in the back row of the classroom, but right up against the brick wall; I think her preference would have been to crawl into the wall if possible.

Regardless of their reason for wanting anonymity in class, if you allow students to hide in class, you'll find it very challenging to get the whole class engaged. One solution to this issue is to learn all your students' names as quickly as possible. I take the time during my first class to have students fill out index cards with their name and ask them to jot down a fact about themselves that can be shared during class. Not only does that activity make all students introduce themselves to the whole class, but the cards become a prop I use to interact with the students until I have learned all their names. Over the first few meetings of the class, I don't hesitate to randomly call on students from the card stack to engage them in class. If I see someone trying to hide, not only do I walk around in the class toward them, but I will engage them in class, and learn their name at the same time. Let me assure you that it will be difficult for you to engage with your students if you don't work to learn their names.

Unfortunately, I've had colleagues that have claimed they can't learn students' names. I don't buy that excuse because most Professors are where they are because they've been able to assimilate and remember large amounts of material. Unless you have 300 students in your class, not learning your students' names is unacceptable. Just as you want someone to remember your name, your students are no different. When you make it a priority to learn their names, the students will notice and appreciate it.[68]

Remember, that with every class you teach, you will need to set and enforce class expectations. As such, it is important to engage with your students during class, and not merely by just lecturing at them. If you work to engage with your students by learning their names, walking around class, asking them questions, and not allowing them to hide in class, you'll find the students will

---

[68] And of course, there is an app that will help. I've used the app 'WhosWho' to memorize names of large numbers of students.

be responsive and will appreciate your efforts. You'll find they may be surprised at first, because unfortunately, their College experience has probably been filled with professors who don't and won't engage with them. If you work to engage with your students during class, you'll find not only will the students give you the respect you deserve as their professor, but they'll also reciprocate and become more engaged in class. And when the students are engaged and involved in class, it makes teaching much more fun.

So, set expectations for your students; you are working to help young adults master knowledge they'll use. If you set up your class with that expectation and goal, your students may be surprised at first, but they will rapidly get on board.

Preparing for your teaching

One of the first situations where you as a junior faculty member may have been a bit overwhelmed was when you were assigned your class schedule for your first semester; that was the time when I knew I was a real faculty member. The Department Chair said "Here are your Fall classes; they meet at these specific days and times. Have fun." And I was thinking "Gulp, how do I do this?". One of the keys to a successful class is adequately preparing for your class(es), but not overpreparing.

Your Syllabus: The first thing you need to do in preparing for your class is to develop the syllabus for your class. You may have the luxury of having a syllabus used previously by another instructor, but unless your class is just one section of multiple sections of the same class that require coordination, you have complete freedom to design and conduct your class as you think is best (welcome to academic freedom!). It is helpful to remember your syllabus fulfills two goals for your class:

    1) It is an outline or plan for how your will conduct your class; and
    2) The syllabus can serve as a type of contract with your students.

At minimum, your syllabus tells your students what you are going to cover in class, how they will be evaluated, and how their grade will be calculated. Most Universities have some specific verbiage that must be put in your syllabus and these are items you need to ask your Department Chair about to find out what needs to be included. Your University may also designate the format of your syllabus; again, that is something you'll need to discuss with your Department Chair. The example syllabus (Example 6.1) is one from one of my undergraduate courses and has some things that may or may not apply to your situation, but it does provide an example of a well-developed syllabus that will guide both you and your students through the course.

Given the syllabus serves as an outline/plan for the course, you'll need to put in your syllabus a summary schedule for your class. However, I would encourage you to put in a more detailed schedule that at least designates what days you'll give exams, the topics you'll cover on other days in class, and any materials the students need to turn in on each class day. In all my classes, I've always told the students the only thing on the class schedule that was set in stone were the exam dates; regardless what else happened during the semester, the exam dates would not change. However, the content planned on each day of the schedule – as well as potential assignments – were flexible and were largely dependent upon our coverage of the course material.

Info to Know - 6.3
A quick checklist of things that should be included on your syllabus*

- Your name, university contact information, office hours
- Start / stop times for class
- Schedule for the course
- Dates of exams
- Flexible dates of content coverage
- When are other course materials due
- Evaluation plan (how they will get their grade)
- What will be the graded items
- How will those items be evaluated
- Bonus points / quizzes
- Grading scale
- Behavioral Expectations
- Respectful conduct and discussion
- Electronic device usage
- How you'll handle instance of academic dishonesty

*Also make sure you've got everything in your syllabus your University requires!

Keeping the exam dates firm and the content coverage dynamic gives you the flexibility to adjust what course material is being covered to account for the varying pace of different classes. This approach to the course material and exam scheduling gives the students solid dates for when exams will be so they can plan studying and attendance, but takes the pressure off you of having to cover specific material on specific days, especially if you find some material didn't 'teach' as easily as you thought. For example, while I've taught Exercise Physiology for 30 years and have a good idea how long it takes me to cover specific concepts, there are still semesters when a class will really catch on quick or be slow in catching a concept.

Having flexibility in my content coverage schedule allows me to adjust the class so I can give the students the time they need to master the material. Having this flexibility in content delivery, but rigidity when exams are offered will mean you may have to change the content covered on your exams, but

Example 6.1

 SYLLABUS

Course title and number: Physiology of Exercise – KINE 433 - 502
Term (e.g., Fall 200X): Spring XXX
Meeting times and location: Day/time, Classroom number

← Required info

Course Description and Prerequisites

Physiological bases of exercise and physical conditioning; measurement of metabolic efficiency during exercise, neuromuscular efficiency and body composition. Prerequisites: Junior or senior classification; admission to the professional phase of program or approval of instructor for non-kinesiology majors. (*Interpretation*): This course provides an introduction to the physiology of exercise. **The course builds** on the students' knowledge of human anatomy and physiology, and describes the acute effects of exercise and the influence of chronic exercise training on the various functional systems in different populations and under different environmental conditions. Ergogenic factors and the contributions of exercise to health and wellness are considered from a physiological perspective.)

Required info →

Learning Outcomes or Course Objectives

1 - To promote understanding of the perturbations to homeostasis that occur in energy utilization, neuromuscular function, and the cardio-respiratory and other systems during exercise;
2 - To learn the adaptations that occur in the various systems during exercise training;
3 - To understand the differences in acute and chronic responses to exercise in different populations, including youth, the aged, and the two sexes;
4 - To appreciate the influences of different environmental conditions and ergogenic factors on exercise physiology;
5 - To understand the physiological bases for the health benefits of exercise.

Instructor Information

Name: Dr. J. Timothy Lightfoot
Telephone number: xxx-xxx-xxxx
Email address: xxxx@xxxxxxxxxx
Office hours: Days/times
Office location: Location

← Your information should be here (of course)

Textbook and/or Resource Material

(required) Powers, SK and Howley ET. *Exercise Physiology: Theory and Application to Fitness and Performance*. 8th Edition. McGraw Hill, 2012 ISBN: 978-0-07-802253-1. Online resources: http://www.mhhe.com/powers8e

Class Requirements (i.e. what you have to do in this class to get a grade)

1. **Exams** (n=2 regular and 1 final) - Primarily short answer and essay questions. Very few multiple guess questions. The questions require you to answer "why" and "how" questions and I strictly grade

What students are really interested in: ↑   *What type of tests and how I grade.* ↑

Example 6.1 (continued) — *notice detail on what happens with exams.*

on your ability to answer the questions. I attempt to grade and return the exams by the next class period. The exams are then yours to keep and study with. The final exam is comprehensive. (The exams = 86.6% of your grade)

Clarity is important!

2. Make-up Tests - Do not exist (No excuses). You have the schedule. Plan accordingly.

3. Quizzes - May occur virtually daily. The quizzes will be very short answer and will cover material from the previous class. Therefore, keep up with your material. (The quizzes = 13.3% of your grade.)

4. Extra credit opportunities - May occur (no guarantees) throughout the semester and may consist of attendance at selected speakers, participation in lab projects, etc. The instructor will announce extra credit opportunities in advance. Each student can accumulate no more than 10% of the total class points (45 pts) in extra credit points. There will be no extra credit opportunities the last two weeks of the semester. ***NOTE: If you can't make/attend an extra credit opportunity, do not ask for an 'alternative' opportunity. That's why it's called 'extra credit opportunity' and not a 'required opportunity'.

Clarity is important!

Your final grade will be determined using a 10% scale based on the total possible points of 450. Thus, "A" = 405-450 points, "B" = 360-404 points, "C" = 315-359 points, "D"=270-314 points, and "F"= 0-269 points.

There is no attendance policy in this class (more on that later).

Course Topics, Calendar of Activities, Major Assignment Dates

Week	Topic	Chapter
Date of Class	Introduction	0
Date of Class	Homeostasis & Energy Sources	2, 3
Date of Class	Energy Sources (cont)	
Date of Class	Energy Sources (cont)	
Date of Class	Exercise Metabolism	4
Date of Class	Exercise Metabolism	
Date of Class	Exercise Metabolism; Hormonal Resp	5
Date of Class	Hormonal Responses **(EEM)***	
Date of Class	**EXAM**	
Date of Class	Nervous System	7
Date of Class	Skeletal Muscle	8
Date of Class	Skeletal Muscle	
Date of Class	Lactic Acid	
Date of Class	Circulation & Exercise	9
Date of Class	Circulation & Exercise	
Date of Class	Blood Pressure Control	
Date of Class	**Spring Break (enjoy)**	
Date of Class	Respiration	10
Date of Class	Respiration **(EEM)**	
Date of Class	**EXAM**	
Date of Class	Acid-Base Balance	11
Date of Class	Thermoregulation	12
Date of Class	Physiol of Aerob Training	13, 21

Example 6.1 continued

Date of Class	Physiol of Aerob Training
Date of Class	Physiol of Strength Training
Date of Class	Physiol of Strength Training
Date of Class	You Pick The Topic
Date of Class	You Pick The Topic
Date of Class	You Pick The Topic **(EEM)**
Date of Class	Final Exam – 12:30 pm (NOTE Day/Time)

These are put in for flexibility to cover other topics the students request.

*EEM = End of Exam Material

Expectations section here

About this Class – Studying & Miscellaneous:

I have found over the years that the students that are successful in LEARNING exercise physiology are those that study consistently. You should read the material before we go over it in class, and then study your notes and book at least one hour per day. Additionally, you should feel free to tape class (either audio or video) and use the tapes for study help (but be forewarned that I own the copyright to all my class notes, stuff on the web, the audio, and video portion of the class).

You'll note that there is no attendance policy for this class. You are adults and fully capable of determining if you should come to class. IF YOU come to class, you should be prepared to be alert and engaged in the class. That means that you should be prepared to stay awake during the whole class, participate in class discussion, and stay off of social media while you're in class. If you can not make those commitments, then I ask that you stay home.

The use of electronic devices in class is welcomed. Feel free to record, look up stuff, type notes, etc. – *as long as it is about class*. I have a tendency to walk around during class and if I find you using your electronics for non-class related items, I'll ask for your device for the remainder of class (or ask you to leave).

You will note that I will not use digital presentations (much) during class. Class is a discussion and meant for you to get clarification and guidance on the things you don't understand (related to Exercise Physiology). You'll find that this class will be a richer experience if I don't use digital presentations (and so be prepared to take notes).

You should be prepared to have respectful discussion during class. While disagreement is sometimes part of discussion, I require you to be respectful toward all individuals in class, regardless of their opinions and/or statements.

Required (you'll have something like this)

(the legal stuff)

Americans with Disabilities Act (ADA)

The Americans with Disabilities Act (ADA) is a federal anti-discrimination statute that provides comprehensive civil rights protection for persons with disabilities. Among other things, this legislation requires that all students with disabilities be guaranteed a learning environment that provides for reasonable accommodation of their disabilities. If you believe you have a disability requiring an accommodation, please contact Disability Services, xxx-xxx-xxxx. For additional information visit http://disability.tamu.edu

> **Example 6.1 continued**
>
> *Again, required.*
>
> **Academic Integrity**
> For additional information please visit: http://aggiehonor.tamu.edu
>
> "An Aggie does not lie, cheat, or steal, or tolerate those who do." I will enforce the honor code to the fullest if you are caught cheating (or plagiarizing) in class. For any written work you turn in, I reserve the right to submit it to "TurnItIn.com" to check for plagiarism.

that is a small price to pay for making sure the students know when they'll be evaluated, as well as the students having enough time to master concepts.

Another item to cover in detail on your syllabus is how the students' will be evaluated and how you will determine their grade. Frankly, at the beginning of a class, those two items, how the students will be evaluated and how you will determine their grade, are foremost in every student's mind. The only thing they really care about on the first day is what they are going to have to do to get a specific grade. Don't worry; they'll fall in love with the content and the course later! The biggest issues I've seen with classes has arisen when there is ambiguity in grading. Not knowing how their grade will be determined or what they'll be graded on will lead to confusion, frustration, and sometimes, grade grievances. While most Universities require that you specify how you will determine grades, it is still interesting that some syllabi have very little, or confusing information on how grades will be determined. Make sure you are clear how you are going to assign class grades and this will ease many problems you may have.

How you grade in your class, again, is largely up to you. What items you are going to include, what percentage system you'll use for the final grade, and how you'll grade the evaluated items are usually up to you[69]. While various professors and the literature suggest grades have differing functions, remember the primary purpose of a grade should be to serve as an indication of the student's mastery of the material. You should be able to relate the items you are grading your students on directly back to an evaluation of their content mastery. If an item you're considering using as a component of the grade does not relate back to content mastery, do not use it as a grading factor. One of the reasons accreditation agencies (these are the organizations that certify your University is doing what it is supposed to do) frown on using course grades as metrics of student learning is because often, faculty put in

---

[69] I have heard comments from colleagues that their University required a certain percentage grading scale or some other aspect of grading, so make sure you speak to your Department Chair about class grading so you are compliant with your University's policies.

grading factors that have nothing to do with content mastery. While you are free to include whatever you wish in your grading scheme, assuming these items meet ethical, moral, and appropriate standards, you should really hesitate from including items in grade determination that do not directly evaluate content exposure or mastery[70].

As mentioned earlier, you also want to use the syllabus to set the parameters for student behavior during your classes. These student behaviors can run the gamut from whether you allow the use of electronic devices in class to what you do if someone is late for class. Student behavior has become such a big issue, that some universities now have behavioral codes of conduct that you must include in your syllabus. Along this line, there are a wide variety of student behaviors you may want to emphasize in your syllabus in the pursuit of creating the best learning environment possible, but I'm going to touch on just a few I've found to be critical, especially in the last several years.

One point of emphasis I've always made is the time the class starts and ends. Emphasizing the time class starts and ends will help the students understand your class is bounded by some time parameters. I've always found students appreciated it when you stick to your starting and stopping times; often students have classes that are back to back and if you keep them late, they are then late to their next class. I'm sure you're not happy if students come to your class late, so keep that in mind especially when you are tempted to make class run a 'few extra minutes'. Your schedule may have flexibility in it after class, but it is likely your students don't have the same flexibility.

Another item you should emphasize in your syllabus is your philosophy about the use of electronic devices in class. Today, it is often difficult to get students to disengage with their electronic devices for a whole class period. As mentioned earlier, you need to be clear in your syllabus that class-time is the time to focus on the content at hand. Because electronic devices are so ingrained in our lives, it is very difficult to put a staunch 'No electronics in class' ban in place (and there has been much dialog in the literature about whether that is feasible or not). I've also seen more and more students using electronic devices for notes and class recordings, so those students would be hurt by a total classroom electronics ban. But, if you allow technology in class, you must figure out how to make sure the students are using them

---

[70] Some items may be appropriate to use in some classes but not others, such as class attendance. I think a case can be made that class attendance can be a 'gradable' factor if the student's learning or exposure to the material would be harmed by not being present in class. The same argument goes for class participation and other 'non-exam' type factors. If you use 'it' for a grade, just know why you use it!

appropriately by enforcing your policy.

One last item about the use of technology in class. U.S. copyright law has held that Professors' notes and class materials, unless they are derived from other sources, are the property of the Professor. This means that students cannot record, copy, and/or distribute your class materials, videos from class, or other items from class without your consent. It is worth pointing this out in your syllabus to help keep your students from providing class notes and materials to students that aren't attending or to tutoring companies known for scraping Professors' notes off the web and then using them to make money through tutoring services.

Lastly, one other behavioral expectation I put in my syllabus is I expect and demand respectful conversation/discussion in my classes. If you – as the Professor - treat your students with respect, then you should expect they'll treat each other and you with respect. You can have difficult conversations in class, but you need to make sure the foundation of respect is in place. With that foundation clearly laid out in the syllabus, you then have the basis to correct students who are disrespectful, and if necessary, pursue further action against those students that disregard respect. I've found if you are up-front with your students regarding your expectations, in 99.99% of the cases, they'll exceed those expectations!

Class Preparation: Almost every junior faculty member I've known – including me – wanted to make sure when they walked into the classroom, they knew as much about the material as possible. One of my anxieties early on was it would make me look bad in the students' eyes if I didn't know the answer to every question asked of me. As a result, I spent huge amounts of time preparing for class to make sure I could answer *every* question. And most every junior faculty member I've ever known has felt the same way.

In his work with new faculty, Dr. Boice[71] noted junior faculty were often afraid of losing face or not being considered the authority if they didn't know it all. However, there are several issues for you as a teacher that result from this desire to at least appear as if you know everything. First, you wind up spending far too much time on preparing for your class. Second, you kill the students with detail that often they don't need or even know exists. Thirdly, because you know so much, you try to cram it all in during your class, which

---

[71] You may remember Dr. Robert Boice from chapter 5 and writing 30 mins/day. All of this comes out of his book, *Advice for New Faculty Members*. If there was ever another book (other than this one) you should read as a junior faculty member, Dr. Boice's is it. I'm sure it is in your University's library!

leads to fast-talking on your part, the attempt to take copious notes on the students' part, and a lack of general comprehension on everyone's part. All three of these issues resulting from over-preparation not only results in a terrible classroom environment, but will eat up your time which means that you have less time for your research, your work/life balance, and for your students.

The attempt to 'know it all' is one of the main keys Dr. Boice found that separated successful junior faculty from those that struggled. The faculty that thought they had to know it all often struggled because they spent so much time preparing their classes, they didn't have time to write, didn't have an appropriate work/life balance, and couldn't participate in other necessary events in their lives. Boice noted (many times in fact) the key for junior faculty was to be prepared 'just enough'; in fact, he called his approach to class preparation "*Nihil Nimus*[72]" which is loosely translated to mean nothing in excess and everything in moderation. Through his studies, Dr. Boice observed teachers that used the *nihil nimus* techniques had higher student comprehension and ratings of teaching than those that didn't (based on a sample of 40 junior faculty). As such, as you prepare for your class, you must work to focus on being prepared only 'just enough'.

How do you determine what is 'just enough'? That is a tough question and one that will get easier with the more experience you have in your classes. To get you started here are some tips I've found that have helped me determine what is 'just enough', which when coupled with the delivery techniques coming in the next section, can help you minimize preparation while maximizing your class effectiveness and your students' learning.

Step one is to think about the material you want to cover in your class and think about what are the big conceptual points you want the students to understand in each topic area. Once you have those points, jot them down and then add these to your syllabus. For example, if I'm planning for my undergraduate Exercise Physiology class, and I plan to cover energy sources for exercise, I certainly want my students to understand the primary sources of energy during different types of exercise, how these sources are influenced by different dietary substrates, and how these energy sources are regulated during exercise. That's the three main conceptual points I want my students to get. You'll note these points aren't too detailed; in fact, each of them is rather broad and I could probably teach a whole course on just those three points. In fact, if I tried to know everything about those three points, I would

---

[72] *Nihil Nimus* is actually the subtitle to Dr. Boice's book – that's how strongly he believed in the concept!

certainly over-prepare for my class of undergraduates.

Step two is to take your broad points and for each point ask yourself what is the minimum set of facts needed to help your students understand the basic broad concepts of each of the points you set out earlier. Notice I've been very deliberate to use the term 'concepts' (and often tagged them with the term 'broad'). If you believe your students will remember every little detail of each concept you teach them, you need to reconsider your expectations. I doubt you remembered every detail of each concept when you first heard it in class; in fact, I would wager the big concepts were what you remembered and what really planted themselves in your head. Therefore, drill down on your large broad points and ask yourself, what do your students really need to know? If we go back to my example from above, one of topics was the primary sources of energy during different types of exercise. In particular, in this area, I want students to have an understanding of which energy sources are called on during short-duration exercise, moderate-duration exercise, and longer-duration exercise. These three divisions help me plan the details I need to give these students and help me focus on what information I need to deliver and what I can leave to the students to find out. And that is the key; what are the critical points you *know* you must expose them to and what are the details they can learn on their own if they have got the foundation? You're really helping them develop their foundation that everything else will be built on.

In developing what you will cover in your class, you repeat Step 2 until you've got a manageable set of concepts you know your students need and ones that will be a springboard for their further learning. Differentiating what concepts your students need versus which details can be left out can be tricky, but does get easier with experience. If you find you teach a class and the students have lots of questions about a certain aspect, that's a sign you didn't teach enough detail there. But if you teach a class and the students are too busy writing to ask questions, that's a sign you're probably giving them too much detail.

As I've worked on my own teaching over the years, I've always been concerned I'm cutting out too much information and only giving my students an outline of the material. In one sense, that is true. But what you are really doing is giving your students a framework – just the basic skeleton – they can use to hang facts on later. In my case, it is not critical my students memorize all the names of the enzymes involved in energy production during exercise but it is critical they know the circumstances under which energy production process is invoked. In summary, is it critical you give them all the facts? No. However, what is critical is you help them build a solid framework they can use for facts they'll get in the future.

So, as you prepare for your classes, constantly ask yourself "what do I need to help the students understand so they can have a strong conceptual framework?" If you constantly focus on that question you'll find your students do better, comprehend more, and are able to use the framework you give them to build amazing and sometimes unexpected concepts and ideas.

Preparing in this 'just enough' manner, also means you are preparing to walk into class not necessarily knowing every little nuance of the topic at hand. However, you must remember, the students you are teaching probably know very little about the topic and so you are way ahead of where they are (after all, that's why you have an advanced degree in the topic). As such, you already have a foundation on which you can base any answers you may not know. Also, since you have a much more advanced 'framework' than your students, your framework will allow you to seek out answers to the questions you are asked that you may not know. Believe me, students respect you so much more if you act human and admit you don't know something but will find out and share with the class later, versus being a walking computer with all the factoids spouting from your lips.

Just remember, teaching a successful course is rooted in two things: 1) having a solid plan and syllabus for the course; and 2) preparing appropriately, but not overpreparing, so you can help the students establish a solid framework of concepts in your content area. But no matter your preparation, if you can't deliver the course, you'll have problems. So, we turn now to delivering material in your class.

Delivering material and interpretation

After preparing for your class, eventually you do have to deliver the material. Unfortunately, many faculty don't think about how to deliver their course material and it's not as easy as just walking into the classroom and reading your notes. There are several facets to how you deliver your class materials that are incredibly important and can help learning. This section talks about the aspects of delivering your materials that are many times forgotten, but are no less important in determining whether your students learn or not.

Your appearance: As we talked about extensively in Book 1 regarding your job interview, it is an unfortunate human trait that we are all judged by our appearances[73]. The literature has shown you are judged as either trustworthy

---

[73] There's a whole section about the importance of appearance and how to have a professional appearance in your interview in Chapter 6 of Book 1.

or untrustworthy in as little as *30 milliseconds*.[74] As important as your appearance was during your job interview, your appearance is just as important when you are in class. Given it is your class and appearance can influence whether you are trusted or not, you should always dress in a professional manner for your classes. If I am forced to characterize the level of professorial attire for class, business professional should be the level of attire you should strive for in your classroom. For males, that means at minimum clean and ironed dress slacks, dress shirt, and tie. A woman's options are a dress, skirt, or slacks with appropriate blouse. Much like during your job interview, you want your attire to not be distracting but to add to your appearance. At this point, you may be thinking to yourself "yeah, but I had a professor who wore jeans and t-shirts and I always took s/he seriously." It is probable you've had a professor like that, but it is also probable the professor you are thinking of already had tenure. You don't have tenure yet and your goal should be to do everything you can to tilt the P/T[75] decision in your favor. Taking care to have an appropriate professional appearance when you are teaching will show your students you care enough about class to make the effort to dress appropriately for class (again, this is another way you can set an example for your class).

Your classroom attitude/behavior: Another aspect of your class delivery is your attitude during class – performers call it 'stage affect'. People judge you by your stage affect and this affect is based on the non-verbal clues you provide; do you smile, do you make eye-contact when someone else is speaking, do you appear engaged? As a teacher, you have got to project a warm, caring, and engaged attitude, otherwise you run the risk of being perceived as aloof, non-caring, and dismissive. Your chances of being perceived as aloof, non-caring, or dismissive can be the natural result of constantly thinking in class about the content, thinking about what you are going to say next, and/or hurrying to get through the material. That's a reason you must intentionally work to relax in class and show the students you do care and you are engaged. As noted earlier, there's an old saying that applies directly to your classroom attitude: "They don't care how much you know, until they know how much you care." And that is so true.

As a Department Chair, I worked with a junior faculty member who I knew to be kind, sensitive, and really concerned about her students' learning. That's why she and I were both puzzled when her teaching evaluations

---

[74] Of course, I have a reference! Freeman, JB et al. Journal of Neuroscience, 10573-10581, 34(32), 2014.
[75] As in past chapters, P/T stands for Promotion and Tenure and includes those up for contract renewals as well.

continued to slam her for being disengaged, aloof, and dismissive in class. When I went to observe her class, it was apparent she was getting this 'in-class' rap because she didn't show she was kind and caring. Instead, this junior faculty member had fallen into the trap of being so concerned about covering a certain amount of material during each class, she came into class, immediately started lecturing, and rarely stopped to find out if the students were keeping up or even understood the material. She was so concerned about not covering all the material she thought she had to cover, she would get quite anxious and nervous about class, which made her appear to be disengaged, aloof, and uncaring. Once I shared my observations with her and some potential techniques to offset these problems, her class evaluations quickly turned around. The point of this whole example is to emphasize that your appearance and the attitude you project (even unconsciously) can affect your students and their learning.

Another attitude that can be seen and felt by students is whether you are respectful toward them. Being respectful doesn't mean you always agree with what they say or how they say it. Being respectful means you listen and you are pleasant and polite. In other words, you are 'professionally graceful'. If a student asks a question or makes a comment, dismissing it out of hand can completely eliminate student engagement in your class. As an example, I was observing a class for a colleague who had been receiving poor class evaluations. When discussing a topic with the class, he encouraged them to participate, even using the phrase "nothing is too silly to consider". Several brave students started speaking up and as they spoke up and weren't immediately rebuffed, other students started to engage and the discussion became lively. At one point, a student made a suggestion that was, well, frankly out in left-field. My colleague, despite his earlier "no comment is too silly" proclamation, immediately looked at the student and snapped "no, that's not worth talking about". The room instantly went quiet with all participation coming to an end. With that snap reaction, my colleague immediately lost his class and this was the 'clue' about why he'd been having trouble engaging his students. This example shows so well that all it takes is a small comment, put-down, or bit of hypocrisy to completely turn off students. So, you have to constantly be aware that no matter how ridiculous, silly, or otherwise out in left field your students' comments are, you have to be professionally graceful and respectful of your students. You must project that caring, engaged, and warm attitude.

Conversely, you need to remember that as much as you should respect students, you should never allow student disrespect toward you, or other students in your classroom. It is up to you to establish and maintain a good learning environment in your class. If you have a student(s) who will not act in a civil manner, you are the first line in taking care of the issue. Unfortunately, there will likely always be students that grumble about your teaching, your grading, or their grade. Some of my former students have told me with delight the number of times they met in the parking lot to have a group bitch session after exams; these types of sessions allowed them to let off steam and frustration and there is nothing wrong with that sort of behavior. You probably engaged in the same behavior. (I did – Dr. Smith in calculus got us all riled up all the time). What is not permissible is for disrespectful behavior to spill out in the classroom. As soon as it occurs, you need to immediately stop it – phrases like "that's not appropriate for class" or "how would you put that in a more respectful manner?" will often bring the student's attention to the fact they've crossed a boundary. If the student continues, I would stop class and ask the student to chat with you outside of the class *immediately*. Once outside of the class, you should clearly explain to the student how their behavior was inappropriate and explain how you will not allow it to continue. I would then reenter the classroom and pick up as nothing had happened; yes, all the students will know something happened, but the fact you handled it will be a great example to all of them that there are boundaries. If these types of situations occur, document the situation the same day that it occurred. Be sure to document what you did, who was involved, and the resolution. If you had to call a student out of the class, you should make sure you let your Department Chair know what happened.

In my experience, those two simple steps - once in class, once out of class – will stop the majority of the disrespect and misbehavior in class by all your students. However, if you have a student that continues to disrespect or misbehave and you have done both previous items, you need to immediately leave the classroom and get your Department Chair, explain the situation, and they will handle it from there. If the situation continues to escalate, University security needs to be called as soon as possible.

As a Department Chair, I got called to a class where a student was being verbally abusive to the instructor and many of other students. I got the student out of the class because there was a lot of shouting going on, but no physicality, which was a miracle. I sent for security, who then escorted the student out of the building. This student was ultimately barred from coming into our building. Interestingly enough, about every five years, I and the University where this happened get legal requests to expunge this former student's disciplinary record, none of which have been successful to this point. This example is extreme, but, thankfully rare. However, if these situations happen, you need to be clear about what you will do and who you will notify.

Delivering the material: To guard against either over-preparation and/or rushing through the material, about 12 years ago, I decided to experiment and give up using either detailed notes or digital presentations (e.g., PowerPoint, Keynote, etc.) in my classes. I'll give you a moment to ponder that suggestion...

As you've thought about my suggestion to ditch digital presentations and detailed notes in your classes, you've probably just gasped or quietly thought I am out of my mind! After all, all of us, especially in scientific circles, religiously use digital presentations to illustrate and guide their presentations (I bet you used a digital presentation in your job interview talk). I'm not suggesting you drop digital presentations in your scientific or more formal presentations, in fact, I still use digital presentations extensively in these settings. What I am suggesting is you drop detailed notes and digital presentations in your classroom teaching. If you do this, I will guarantee your classes will be more interesting for the students, will engage the students more, will increase your students' learning, and will make classes more terrifying for you, but ultimately more rewarding. As you ponder whether I'm out of my mind or not, let me make the case for using 'real-time' class presentations.

In a learning environment, the key is to guide and interpret material for your students *at their pace*. Have you ever been in a talk where the speaker moved through the material so fast you couldn't keep up or take notes fast enough? Using digital presentations makes it easy to move through a talk very quickly; after all, the material is all in the presentation file and you can just zip through the material. But from the students' perspective, they are trying to understand the material as it is presented and they know they'll be evaluated on their comprehension of the material. So, trying to write notes while a speaker zips through slides is a frustrating experience. From a teaching perspective, if you use digital presentations, you have to constantly focus on going slow enough so your students can keep up with you. They are having to write and all you're doing is clicking a button.

Another drawback is that a digital presentation makes it difficult for you to go 'off-script'. Because your digital presentation is in a certain order you pre-arranged, it is difficult to skip around to help illustrate points. Given students in each class are different, you'll find a slide order that worked for one class may not work for another. The ongoing example I have of this is the role of the hemoglobin oxygen saturation/desaturation curve during exercise. It seems every time I teach this topic (probably over 50 times in my career) I have to approach it from a different angle with every class. It is this example that made me initially start thinking about how to deliver the information better, which led me to dropping digital presentations from my classrooms.

Another issue with digital presentations is far too often it is easy for the students to 'zone out' during class. Digital presentations are close to being a video format and students often get in the same state of 'zombie-like' staring during digital presentations, especially if you are going too fast through the presentation, as they do while watching videos and movies. You may be thinking, "yeah, but I can give them the slide deck later". If you are thinking this, I would ask you "then what was the purpose of class? To put them in a zombie-like state? To keep them non-engaged? Or just so you can give them your slide deck later?" Dropping digital presentations from your classes solves all these problems.

Before we get into the mechanics of how you can teach without digital presentations in class, you should know I'm not the only one that advocates for dropping digital presentations. Steve Jobs (co-founder of Apple Computer) was famous for hating digital presentations because they didn't allow spontaneous conversation.[76] Some military generals – such as the former Secretary of Defense Jim Mattis - banned the use of digital presentations because, in his words, "The reason I didn't use PowerPoint is, I am convinced PowerPoint makes us stupid."[77] In my mind, if corporations, the military, and other branches of our government are actively taking steps to discontinue use of digital presentations during meetings, then as teachers, we should pay attention to what they are trying. After all, our military relies on being able to educate their soldiers and leadership in a variety of different ways.

So, if you drop digital presentations from your classroom, what do you do? How should you deliver the information? There are many different alternatives you may want to try such as student debates, project-based learning, group discussions, and several other approaches – all of which there is ample discussion of in the literature. However, one of the best approaches I've found is to simply use 'old-school' technology – the chalk/whiteboard or a document projector (no, not an overhead projector – that's too 'old-school') and develop your class material 'real-time' as you go through it. Most classrooms now have either whiteboards or a document projector; you will find what works best for you once you make the switch. My favorite approach is with a document projector and blank white paper with a fine-point Sharpie pen. With this approach you can go back to presenting the material and developing the notes *real-time*.

---

[76] This preference of Jobs was mentioned numerous times in the great biography of him by Walter Isaacson.
[77] This and other facets of this argument are presented in *The Atlantic* (http://bit.ly/no_digital_present) and more recently by the *Washington Post* (http://bit.ly/2no_digital_present).

To do a real-time presentation, I take an *outline* of my lecture with me to class (notice I didn't say a detailed outline), and I use that outline (I don't project it) to develop the content and guide the discussion as we go through class. Even if I just write and project the first point of the outline, this gives me the starting spot to start talking about the material. The beauty of the real-time method is students will write down whatever you write down – in essence, your lecture becomes their notes. Students try to do this when you use a digital presentation, but they can never write fast enough. When you are writing the notes in front of your class, they'll follow along. This method keeps you from moving through the material too fast because you are limited by how fast you can write, much like students' notes are always limited by how fast they can write.

Presenting text using real-time methods is easy, but what do you do about figures and illustrations? I draw them real-time as well. I always give the students the reference figure number from their textbook, but then I always draw the figure freehand as well. You'll find students will do the same thing; they'll draw the figure free-hand in their notes. Then, not only do they know where the figure is in the book, but they'll also have a rough approximation of it in their notes.

Don't get me wrong, I'm in favor of using technology in class; for example, I don't hesitate to pull up the internet during class if I need to illustrate a point better. If you supplement your real-time lectures by going to the web real-time, that's also illustrative for your students because it helps them understand how to integrate what they are learning with what they can find online.

A distinct advantage of presenting real-time, other than slowing your presentation, is it will give you freedom to take the discussion anywhere the conversation goes instead of being locked into a set order of slides. You essentially will be walking through the material as a guide and interpreter, at the same time as your students.

One huge drawback of the real-time approach, and the reason I didn't adopt it for my undergraduate courses until I had done it a couple of years with my graduate courses, was that as an instructor, you lose your safety net. As instructors, too many times, we rely on the slides in the digital presentation in case our memory fails us. And while most of us know our content very well, not having that safety net in case of a 'memory failure' can be intimidating and terrifying. But I would contend that teaching without the digital safety net can also be invigorating. You'll find that without your digital presentation and with just your class outline, you'll rely on what you know and what you think the students should know as you present in class.

Yes, the thought of presenting without a digital safety net can terrifying and the students will be uncertain of what to do in the early part of the semester because they are so used to all their courses being digitally presented. In fact, when we go through the syllabus and I indicate class will be done real-time (no digital presentations), mostly I get groans from the students. However, it is interesting that by the time the semester is a few weeks old, most students love the real-time approach. In fact, while my class evaluations have always been good, since I dropped digital presentations and have gone exclusively real-time (in the last 10 years), my student evaluations have gotten even better with many positive glowing comments about that approach. An additional bonus is that I've yet to have a negative comment about not having digital presentations!

Another aspect of delivering the material real-time in class is you have to be cognizant of how long students can focus on material. Neuroscience now indicates that even in the best learning environment, most students have difficulty concentrating for more than 10 mins at a time. Dr. John Medina[78], has suggested that learning is best when the material is broken up into 10-minute segments with a summary and conclusion at the end of each 10-minute segment. I believe you will find the 'real-time' approach to delivering material is conducive to this 'summary every 10 minutes' approach. Because you are

---

Info to Know - 6.4
Things to remember to help engage your students when you present

1) Have a professional appearance;

2) Remember the speed you talk has an inverse relationship to how engaged the students are;

3) Learn and use your students' name as soon as possible;

4) Don't let your students 'hide' in class;

5) Try to directly talk to each student during class as much as possible;

6) Smile and at least act like you enjoy teaching!

7) Try different approaches to delivering class material. The students will like the change of pace!

---

[78] *Brain Rules, 2nd edition* by Dr. John Medina, is an immensely enjoyable book that is easy to read but will give you insight into the current neuroscience literature regarding learning (as well as a lot of other topics regarding brain health). It's well worth the time to read it!

developing your notes (and the students' notes) as you go through class, it is easy for you at the end of a concept to do a short summary and conclusion before you move on to the next concept. While you don't have to do a rigorous 'every 10-minute summary' just keep the 10-minute block idea in your head as you go through class and look to summarize and tie the material together whenever you can.

In summary, while planning your class is critical for your students' success, how you present the material is also a critical part of the success of your class. Having an appropriate appearance, an appropriate attitude, and working to deliver the material in a way and at a pace that engages students, will all play roles in making your class a great learning environment, as well as helping the students see they are indeed getting their money's worth.

Evaluation of your students' learning

One of the great responsibilities, and sometimes an overwhelming responsibility, of being a faculty member is to evaluate your students. It is your task not only to teach your students, but also to provide a fair and objective evaluation of their learning across the semester. You've probably had experiences during your education where you had a professor that was unjust, unfair, and not objective with their grading. So, you should understand how your students will look to you to provide a fair and objective method of determining their learning.

As I noted earlier, one of the advantages I've had was I had a couple of classes on learning measurement and evaluation. Both classes (at the undergraduate and graduate level) made clear impressions on me regarding how I should design and conduct my class evaluations. I am happy to note even though I've had students upset with their grades over my career (that's an occupational certainty), I've never had a grade overturned through a grade grievance. Please don't construe the last few sentences as bragging. I share my teaching experiences because you should understand that if you are clear, transparent, and consistent with your evaluation procedures, you'll have fewer issues throughout your career.

Supporting my experiences as a teacher are my 11 years as a Department Chair and often being the first step on the grade grievance ladder. As such, the majority of grade grievances I've ever dealt with have been due to confusing and changing grading and evaluation processes in class. If you keep your testing and grading schemes clear, transparent, and consistent, you will eliminate a large number of issues regarding the grades your students earn. Also, remember the experiences you've had with your own grades; weren't you better satisfied with a class when you clearly understood how your grade would be assigned?

Toward making your evaluation process clear and transparent, you must be clear in your syllabus how you will test the students' knowledge (including what types of tests you will give) as well as being clear how you will use the results of those tests to determine the student's final grade. All this detail needs to be in the syllabus; see the example in Example 6.1 for how I've handled this in the past.

Notice I'm clear about when the exams will be in the class schedule, I'm clear about what format the exams will take, I'm clear about how I grade and exclude answers, I'm clear about how many points each exam is worth, and I am clear about how the exams results will be summarized to result in the grade. Further, you can also see I am clear how I treat potential bonus opportunities and about the use of quizzes. All elements I use to determine a student's grade are in the syllabus and my promise to my students is these elements will not change during the semester. If you give your students this type of information, they can rest assured that only the factors you've outlined will be used to determine their grade. Your evaluation plan needs to be planned carefully and then stick to it (and yes, you can alter your evaluation plan in the future – just don't change it during the current semester)[79].

The types of student evaluation you will use in your class is solely up to you. The biggest key is to identify what is the best way to determine each student's mastery of the material. If you have larger classes, which I'll define as

> **Info to Know - 6.5**
> **Key to reducing problems centered around grades:**
> "Be as clear, transparent, and consistent as you can about the process you use to evaluate students."

over 20 students, you may be limited to written exams or written papers. If you have smaller classes, you may also use other types of experiential exposures; for example, when I teach graduate courses which are rarely more than 20 students, I will often use 'real-world' (or 'experiential') projects to test the students' content mastery. For example, when I taught an Introduction to Clinical Exercise Physiology course, one project I assigned a group of students was to develop and implement a process to establish state-wide

---

[79] There are always exceptions to this 'don't change it during the semester' policy. It is possible you will find an idea you had for grading/evaluation just doesn't work or puts some students at a disadvantage. If this is the case, you should change that item, but explain to the class why you are changing it (to remove disadvantages) and welcome feedback. You'll find being open about a change will be appreciated and respected by the students.

licensure for Clinical Exercise Physiologists. While that project didn't result in state-wide licensure, it did give the students an opportunity to understand how healthcare professions are regulated as well as giving me another opportunity to evaluate the students' learning. The key to using an experiential exam is to make sure the project will give you an opportunity to judge whether the students have learned the content.

Most of the time, especially if you teach undergraduates, you are going to be limited to using some type of written work, either an exam or papers, to evaluate each student's content mastery. Whether you are going to use short-answer exams, multiple choice, fill in the blank, or full-scale papers, I encourage you to think clearly about *why* you are using that type of evaluation. It is never a good enough reason to say "I'm using this type of exam because that's all I've ever done or seen done". Your students deserve a well-thought out evaluation plan and that includes having good justification for the type of exam you use. Often, if you talk to faculty and ask them why they use the exams they use, they will often base their choices not on effectiveness of evaluation of content mastery, but rather on the amount of time it takes to grade the exam.

If the type of exam you use is just based on how long it takes you to grade the exam, you are missing major factors that impact how long it takes you to do the overall evaluation. In fact, as you consider the time involved in an exam, this consideration will include how long it takes you to develop the exam, how long it takes to administer (usually this is set), and how long it takes you to grade the exam, within the context of maintaining the integrity of your exam. Let's unpack these factors a bit more (and in pieces).

> **Info to Know - 6.6**
> **Factors to balance in determining what type of exam to use**
> 1) What is the best way to determine content mastery? Written test? Practical test? Oral exam?
> 2) If written exam, factors to consider:
>   - How secure will the exam be?
>   - How long will the exam take you to construct?
>   - How long will the exam take you to grade?

When you decide to give an exam to your students - I'm leaving quizzes aside for a moment - you have to make sure the exam you use is secure, meaning that there aren't copies of it floating around that will give some students an advantage. You also need to consider how long it takes you to construct your exam; will it take you 30 mins to build the exam or 3 hours? Certainly, how long it will take you to grade the exam also comes into play and this factor is often dependent upon how many students you have in your class. What I have learned is if I consider these three factors, I begin to get a good sense of what type of exam I should use for my class. Of course, an example is in order.

Let's assume you have a class of 50 undergraduate students and you are going to give them a major exam after four weeks of class. So, you're trying to decide what type of test to give your students.

You may immediately decide to do a multiple-choice exam, because that is the predominant way of testing in today's educational systems. If you use a multiple-choice exam, the grading will be relatively quick and painless. However, developing a good multiple-choice exam, one where the multiple answers are somewhat plausible for each answer so the exam is not too easy, can take several hours and can be quite difficult. Furthermore, once you've written a good multiple-choice question, because it takes so long to develop, instructors are often tempted to use those questions in the future.

After you have graded and given your students their exams back, there is the real and probable chance the exam will make its way into the hands of other students, thus, obviating its use in the future[80]. Besides the time it takes to construct a multiple-choice exam, another drawback of multiple-choice exams is they don't give students the opportunity to show you how they really think. The students are locked into picking from the multiple choices you gave them and none of those choices can show you how the student thinks[81]. So, while multiple choice exams don't take long to grade, they are difficult to develop and can be prone to lack of integrity, especially after you used them once (or more).

Let's run the same example with short answer exams. Short answer exams do not take long to develop, but they take a long time to grade. Since they are different every semester, these tests tend to have better security and integrity than other types of exams unless you use the same exam every semester. One of the reasons I've always used short answer exams is they allow me to really know how the student is thinking about the question and the process by which they arrived at their answer. Plus, it allows me to give students partial credit for their efforts which is incredibly important to students.

---

[80] And if you're not aware of it, you should understand there are tutoring companies, as well as Greek and other student organizations, that build 'books' of professor's exams from certain classes that can be used to study with – or maybe to memorize?

[81] Evaluation and measurement experts would tell you what I just said is false and that you can design answers that will show you how students think. I'll buy that but that argument just made constructing the exam much more difficult and will really make you want to use the same question again in the future.

I 'help' the students keep their answers short by requiring them to only use the amount of space I give them on an exam for each answer, usually about an inch of blank space between questions, so that helps them be succinct and to the point. I never look forward to grading my short answer exams, but I figure that is the price I pay for taking less time to develop the exam, giving the students opportunity to show me how much they know, and for having some measure of confidence in the security of my exams.

Whatever format you use for your exams you should be able to justify why you use the approach you use, especially in the context of the effectiveness of measuring the students' content mastery since that's what it is all about. Think about your choice of exam type in terms of the security of your exam, how long it takes to develop the exam, how long it takes to grade, and if the students can show you how much they know. These factors will help you develop the rationale you need to justify why you evaluate student learning the way you do.

Before we leave the topic of major exams in your class, let's touch on a couple of items you may encounter and ways to deal with these items. Specifically, I'm going to cover three topics:
    1) Whether to have others help you grade your exams;
    2) The use of item analysis of your exams; and
    3) How to give exam results back without losing control of your class.

Getting grading help: You may be tempted to have a assistant help you grade your exams, with this other person often being a graduate assistant. Certainly, if you have someone assist you with grading, it will cut down on the time it takes you to grade the exam. However, when you allow someone to grade your exams (except for multiple choice exams where you provide the key) you have relinquished a very important part of evaluating your students to someone else; the determination of whether they know the material or not. Imagine a student comes to you wondering why you graded a certain item the way 'you' did. What do you say? "I didn't grade your exam?" or "Let me look at this and we'll figure it out?". Either way (or any way you put it) you have lost the ability to evaluate the student fairly because someone else graded their exam.

Some faculty may say having a graduate assistant grade their exams is an important learning activity for the graduate assistant. This is true, but is the purpose of your evaluations to teach your graduate assistants how to grade exams or is the purpose of your evaluations to determine your students' mastery of the material? Unless your exam is a straight, no-complicated multiple-choice exam, it is best if you grade your exams. In fact, some Universities have prohibitions against anyone other than the instructor of record grading exams because it violates the student's right of privacy guaranteed by a federal law known as the Family Educational Rights and Privacy Act (popularly known as 'FERPA'). FERPA basically says a student's grade and the items that make up that grade are only the student's business and cannot be shared with anyone else without the student's approval. In other words, the student has an absolute right of privacy when it comes to grades and the items that make up that grade. If you are the designated teacher of the class, often called the 'Instructor of Record', then you have a legal right to know that student's grade and graded items in your class. Notice that right doesn't carry over to other classes of that same student. No one else, not parents, not spouses, and certainly not graduate assistants have the right to see those grades or the graded items. Again, depending upon how your University views FERPA, and more and more Universities are applying very strict interpretations of FERPA, then you may be violating students' federal rights to privacy if you allow other individuals to grade their exams.

So, while it may be tempting to have others grade your students' exams, it is probably in your best interests not to do so. Further, you'll then be able to honestly answer those student questions about why you graded an item a certain way. Grading can be onerous, tough, time-consuming, and often no fun. However, it is one of those incredibly important responsibilities of being a faculty member that comes with the job.

Item analyses: One of the huge tricks I've used in grading over my career is to do an item analysis on every exam I give. Simply put, an item analysis is a tracking of the frequency of how many students answer each question incorrectly. Doing an item analysis lets me immediately do a couple of things with my exams.

First, and most importantly to me, an item analysis helps me understand which concepts I didn't get across to the students. This understanding allows me to loop back to the troublesome concept and cover it again in class, especially if it is a foundational concept. Without an item analysis, I might have a vague notion of which concepts my students had issues with, but I won't have the substantive data I can use to decide what to recover.

The second reason to do an item analysis, and probably most important to my students, is it gives me a good basis to determine which exam questions were not constructed well. Having this information allows me to decide if I should omit the results of that question from my students' exams. For example, my rule, which I always state in my syllabus and verbally in class when I give back the exams, is that any question 75% (3/4) of the class miss, I omit from the grading (i.e., if the student missed it, I don't take off those points; however, if the student got the question correct, I give them bonus points). In this way, I work to not penalize students' grades if I have written a bad test question (and I do write bad test questions, as will you). Having the item analysis allows me to see what concepts need strengthening *and* what questions I wrote poorly.

Doing an item analysis is as simple as keeping track as you grade exams how many students miss each question. You can also choose to indicate a question was only half missed if you write multiple part questions. If you wish, you can also get much more complicated and track other parameters as well, such as exactly what part of the concept the student missed; it is all up to you.

Whatever you decide to do, I would strongly encourage you to do item analyses on your exams, for one last reason: this gives you quantitative data you can share with anyone that questions the fairness, balance, or appropriateness of your questions. For example, I have had students say to me "well, everyone missed this question and I would like credit for the question since everyone missed it". For a comment like that, I smile, pull out the item analysis and check how many people actually missed the question. Often, only a small number missed the question, and the student's rationale for their request for leniency immediately goes away.

Grade grievances are another example of where an item analysis can be useful. For a grade grievance to succeed, the student usually must prove you unfairly graded their exam in an unbalanced or prejudicial manner. That is a high bar to reach for a grade grievance, but usually students that grieve their grade will attack the fact the Professor usually has no data to show the questioned grade was reached in a fair and impartial manner. However, if you have an item analysis of each exam or contested factor, you can show the distribution of students that missed a question and how you interpret that data. Usually, when you can show you take student evaluations seriously enough to do an item analysis of your exams, it is usually adequate proof of the fairness of your evaluation processes. So, do an item analysis; it's well worth the time.

Maintaining control of your class when giving back exams: Giving back exams can be an interesting experience if you've never been on the teaching side of the desk. As a graduate teaching assistant, I had taught activity classes and had created, administered, and given back exams without much of a big deal. But when I became a full faculty member and started teaching lecture classes, giving back exam results became quite a different experience.

When I gave back the exams, all the students cared about was what grade they made, what they missed, how their grade was calculated, why I marked some questions as incorrect, how it was going to affect their grades, etc. Giving back exam results immediately shifted the classroom environment from learning to "OMG! I'm going to flunk!" This shift in environment quickly took students out of a learning mode and it became very difficult to get them back into a learning mode. Also, you'll find as soon as you release class, you will be mobbed by many of your students wanting answers to the 'how, why, what, impact' types of questions.

With most of your students wanting these answers, their distress feeds on each other and shortly, you have lost control of your class. How do you handle this? How can you keep control of your class, maintain order, respect, and appropriate behavior? I've found it to be fairly easy to keep your class learning oriented if you try a few techniques I've developed over the years.

> **Critical Teaching Point - 6.1**
> *Any class activity that causes the engagement and learning environment to decrease needs to be mitigated as much as possible. One such activity that is common is giving back exams. This activity is often over-looked, but if not handled properly, can lead to not only a decrease in the learning environment, but also the classes respect for the instructor by students who did not do well. Look for ways to handle exam returns so you do not lose the learning environment, but you still allow students the opportunity to discuss their performance with you (see the text for ideas).*

First, never give back exam results at the beginning of your class (quizzes are different; I cover those below). My experience has shown giving back exam results immediately moves the students out of a learning attitude, and there is very little you can do to get that learning attitude back. As a result, I always give back exam results at the end of class. Knowing I'm going to dismiss class immediately after I give out the exams signals to the students that learning of the content has stopped. This alteration in class attitude keeps me from having to regain that learning environment after I give back exams.

Secondly, before I give back any exam, I always tell the students what the average score and the standard deviation were for the exam. Most of my undergraduates have had statistics classes by the time they take my class, so most of them will be able to use the average and standard deviation to understand where their grade lies compared to the whole class. This information helps especially if you have a student that has done poorly on the exam and falls into the bottom portion of the grade distribution. When discussing their test with these students, it is easy for you to counter any arguments of unfairness based on what the class as a whole did, plus, you can also use this type of data in any grade grievances you may experience. So, be transparent with that information and share the average/standard deviation with your class.

Thirdly, before I give back the exam, I will note any questions I omitted from scoring due to my item analysis. Once again, this is a transparency issue and it will help the students understand you too are human and write bad questions, just like they are human and give bad answers at times.

So far, I'm not advocating anything out of the ordinary and I would bet you'd come to the first three by yourself fairly quickly, if you don't already practice them. But here's where I'm going to suggest something a bit radical I've found works tremendously every time: I place a 24-hour moratorium on questions regarding the exam. That may sound a bit ridiculous, especially from someone who has been advocating engaging with the students, but let me tell you the parameters I place on this moratorium and why I started doing this.

I found when I gave back exams, most students did not take time to look at the questions they got incorrect and why those questions were marked incorrect. While I usually give feedback on each wrong answer indicating what is wrong and why it is wrong, I found students would get their exam, look at their grade, and if it wasn't what they expected, they would immediately rush to see me contributing to the mob scenes I experienced. I further found if I pointed the students to what I had written on their exams, they usually understood why the item was wrong. So, I instituted a 24-hour moratorium on questions about the exam to force the students to take time to look at their exam and more importantly, why they got questions incorrect before they came to see me.

I do put some stipulations on this 24-hour moratorium; I'm very clear before and after I announce the moratorium I welcome their questions about their exams any other time during the semester, even up until the final exam. I actually like talking to students and I make it clear that the only time I won't talk to them about their graded items is during that 24-hour time period. Further, I stipulate if they look at their exam and see I've made a mathematical error in calculating their test score, they can come see me immediately about that error so the 24-hour moratorium doesn't apply to grade calculation errors. But if the student tries to use that exception to talk about a test grade item, I politely defer the conversation until the end of the 24-hour moratorium.

The last step I take in handing back exams is I ask the students to be respectful and stay seated until I've given back all the exams. I walk around the classroom and place the exam face down on their desk. In the early part of the semester, this is an excellent way to reinforce your knowledge of your students' names. As soon as the exams are all given out, I release the class.

Again, my goal is always to maintain a respectful learning environment. Allowing chaos to ensue because I've given back an exam does not lend itself to a respectful learning environment. Therefore, don't hesitate to try the above tips to control your class during exam give-backs.[82]

Using quizzes: As a student, you've probably dreaded 'quizzes' especially the sub-species known as 'pop' quizzes. However, as an Instructor, using quizzes, which I define as very short tests with a specific purpose, can help you accomplish the goals of your class.

Any time I think about giving a class an exam (of any type), I consider the points I outlined above:
    1) test integrity/security/validity;
    2) time to prepare;
    3) time to grade; and
    4) application to course context.

Since quizzes are meant to be very short evaluations, I give questions that require very short answers (one or two words) I can grade quickly. In my undergraduate classes, I will give quizzes at the beginning of every class because these quizzes help me accomplish several purposes:

    1) They get the class started on time;
    2) They motivate the students to study; and
    3) They help me to engage with and learn who the students are.

I accomplish the above purposes by giving quizzes when class is supposed to start and covering material we covered in the last class. The quizzes are set up to be short and easy to grade with the semester-total of quizzes equal a letter grade. If the student doesn't show up for the quizzes, their grade, no matter how well they do on everything else, will be one letter grade lower.

It is amazing how effective a quiz is in getting students to class on time. In fact, very quickly they get used to the phrase "Good morning/afternoon. Please take out a blank piece of paper and put your name and date on the top of it".

---

[82] And if you come up with any others, please share them! I'll give you full credit!

Whether you allow people that come in late to take the quiz is up to you, but if you do that, you remove the motivation for the students to be in class on time (I've even gone so far as to lock the classroom door during the quiz, only opening it up after the quiz is over; again, this is up to you).

Further, if you limit your quiz questions to the material from the last class, and the students know where the quiz material is coming from, they are more likely to at least review their material from the last class *before* class. Trust me, this does work! Additionally, I always give back the quizzes from the last class <u>before</u> class starts, so this gives me an opportunity to not only work on knowing all the students' names, but gives me an opportunity to circulate through the classroom and chat with the students before class starts. Yes, all of this means you have to get to class early to set-up and then give out the past quiz before starting, but if you are there early and ready to go, it sets that critical example for the students to be in class on time which seems to be an issue for students everywhere.

In short, using direct and focused quizzes helps the students stay up with the class material, gives insight into potential problematic concepts, can help enforce class starting times, *and* can help you get to know your students.

Bonus Points: Before we leave the evaluation section, we need to cover a topic I believe is too often abused and one which is part of Accrediting Organizations' reluctance to use course grades as indicators of learning: bonus points. Most of us understand the concept of bonus points; these are points awarded for various reasons that fall outside of the normal scope of exams, quizzes, papers, projects, and class assignments.

Because points toward a grade are the 'currency' the Instructor has, Instructors use bonus points for all sorts of reasons. As mentioned earlier, I give bonus points to students who get answers correct to questions I remove from the exam. However, when it comes to bonus points, a great rule of thumb is whenever you are considering bonus points, these points should relate *directly* to the course materials. For example, if you are teaching an exercise physiology class and there is a speaker coming to campus to talk about heart rate and exercise training, using bonus points to award those students that go to the talk would be appropriate since the topic ties back to the course content. However, if the reason for the bonus points does not relate directly to the course, you run the risk of having your whole grading system and grades overturned if you are ever involved in a grade grievance proceeding. So, awarding bonus points in an exercise physiology class for going to a farmer's market would not be appropriate unless you can tie it to the course content!

As a faculty member, you must use bonus points wisely and be clear about their usage because otherwise, students will ask you to give them bonus points for all sorts of reasons. Usually, the end of the semester is when many students will suddenly get 'very interested' in bonus points because they believe it will help their grade. As a result, I clearly put in my syllabus strict limits on how many bonus points a student may get during the semester as well as the period of time during which I'll give bonus points.

In Example 6.1, you can see how I've handled the bonus point issue; I've clearly noted a student cannot accumulate more bonus points as would equal one letter grade (usually 10% of the total points) and I will not give bonus points during the last two weeks of the semester because that's usually when students start *thinking* about their grade.

Bonus points are a useful tool to further the understanding of your course content, and may help you give students exposure to material you didn't know would be available at the beginning of the semester (e.g., a speaker or seminar). However, you need to use bonus points *cautiously* and make sure they are directly related to your course. Bonus points can be useful for you as an Instructor, but can also cause you a lot of grief if not used carefully.

> **Info to Know - 6.7**
> **Using bonus points wisely**
> 1) Use bonus points only to augment the students' exposure to course-related content;
> 2) Limit the number of bonus points you give;
> 3) Don't give bonus points (or bonus activities) the last two-three weeks of the semester;
> 4) Make sure all students have the same opportunity for all bonus points.

How Others Will Evaluate Your Teaching

Most universities mandate each Instructor in each class be 'evaluated for teaching effectiveness'. It is amazing how many different interpretations of those last four words exist, and how many issues can arise from evaluating teachers. How do you evaluate how effective a teacher is? Do you ask the students, many of which have only sat in class? Do you ask other professors, yet adding another duty to their workload? Do you ask supervisors (like your Chair), which adds another duty to their workload? Do you allow crowdsourced outlets (e.g., RateMyProfessor.com) to do the evaluating, despite the fact not all students in the class have an opportunity to use these outlets? Yes, assessing how effective a Professor is in the classroom is very difficult, but it must be done, and so this section deals with things you need to think about when your teaching is evaluated.

First – and I'll repeat this several times - remember to put distance between your self-worth and confidence in regard to your teaching evaluations, wherever those evaluations come from. One of the largest problems most faculty members have with class evaluations is teaching can be an intensely personal activity and thus, any critiques or criticism you get can also strike very close to your personal self-worth. It is not unusual for faculty to focus and dwell on the few negative comments they received in class evaluations and ignore all the positive comments. So, I would encourage you to give some thought to how you can separate your self-worth and confidence from the results of your teaching evaluations.

Student class evaluations: By far and away the most common type of course evaluation is the student class evaluation. Most Universities now require all lecture classes be evaluated and usually prescribe these be student evaluations. All of us are probably familiar with these types of evaluations where students use a pre-approved questionnaire and bubble-in answers on a scantron sheet with space for written comments. Usually these evaluations are done at the end of the semester and some Universities even prescribe exactly when they must be done. The questions on the class evaluation are often determined by committees at either the college or university level, and so you won't have any choice as to what evaluation questions are used. Further, students are asked to rank the Professor based on some linear scale, usually something like 1-4 (or 1-5) where the higher number corresponds to a better ranking. Additionally, there is usually one specific question, something like 'the Instructor taught the course effectively', that is used as a 'summary' question to indicate an overall rating of the instructor. With the advent of newer technologies, some Universities have given the Instructor an option to have their students do the evaluations online, not the best option, or continue to do paper evaluations, which is the better idea. Again, most of us, whether we've been students and/or faculty, are familiar with these types of evaluations.

Student evaluations have been subject to much debate in the literature as to whether they

> ***Critical Teaching Point - 6.2***
> **Student Evaluations**
> *Student evaluations can be devastating especially due to the anonymous nature of the comments. It is critical you focus on using the comments to strengthen your teaching and ignore the comments not relating to your teaching. Pay attention to the comments you know to be fair criticisms and always remember to appreciate – and put as much weight – on the positive comments you'll get. Don't dwell on the negative, and accentuate the positive (at least in your mind). Lastly, your teaching evaluations **do not** define who you are as a person or as a faculty member.*

accomplish what they are supposed to do.[83] Whether student evaluations do what they are supposed to do is an important topic, but in the end, doesn't help you understand or use the evaluations you get. Much like other topics in academia, student evaluations are subject to a lot of debate, but whether student class evaluations are valid or not really is a moot subject for you because you are going to be evaluated with student evaluations whether they are valid or not. Again, leave these types of debates for when you have P/T.

Almost every faculty member you will talk to will have some thoughts about how to get good student evaluations. Before we dive into that discussion, I want to give you some context for my thoughts (and please don't take this as bragging; these events are just the context that has formed my opinions). As a junior faculty member, and probably for the first 15 years of my career, I taught courses that were prerequisites to being able to progress in the degree program; i.e., if the student didn't pass my course, they couldn't take other more advanced courses and were effectively stopped for a year. If there is any type of class that is prone to bad student evaluations, it is these types of prerequisite courses. There is a lot riding on the course for the student and if they don't perform well and pass, their educational progress is put on hold. This type of pressure can breed extensive ill-will toward the Instructor no matter how well the Instructor does. In fact, between 10-25% of the students in my classes regularly made non-passing grades (D or F) and so I was always prepared for poor student evaluations (and perhaps this explains why I am so adamant above about basing your class grades on solid criteria related to the material). Sure, I received some bad evaluations, but overall, at least 95% of my students always evaluated me positively. Again, please don't construe this as bragging, but a real-life example of how student class evaluations don't necessarily follow the grade, which some of the more recent literature insists happens. How could I give so many non-passing grades and still get great evaluations?

In fact, because the belief that grades are linked to course evaluations, many junior faculty are told to grade their classes easy. As you might guess, I think this attitude of giving easy grades to get good evaluations is a cop-out and prevents many faculty from actually taking steps in the classroom that can positively affect their class engagement and environment without cheapening the grading process.

Earlier I talked about an Instructor who got poor evaluations with the students thinking the Instructor was disengaged, aloof, and uncaring. As I noted

---

[83] Here's a recent 'gateway' article that will lead you into the labyrinth that is the student class evaluation literature: http://bit.ly/eval_con1. Enjoy!

at that time, and the critical issue for student evaluations, is whether the students think you care about them and their education. Truly, this was a case of 'they didn't care how much the Instructor knew because they didn't know how much the Instructor cared'. If your classroom demeanor is one of engagement, patience, and support, I think you'll find your student evaluations overall will be very positive. Does this mean all your evaluations will be positive? No; there will be things pointed out on the evaluation you'll need to work on and you'll always have a few students who are just upset because they are getting a bad grade even though it is really their fault. But overall, your evaluations will be positive. *Every* junior faculty I've worked on this issue with has had similar results. If the students know you care about them, they'll rate you positively (overall). Coming back to points made earlier, simple items like knowing each of your students' name, respecting your students, valuing their input and questions, and setting up a positive learning environment will contribute to each of your students knowing you care about them. This whole paragraph may sound nebulous and ambiguous, and to some extent, figuring out how to make students know you care about them is difficult. But developing an attitude of caring is made up of many small behaviors, none of which are difficult, but each of which are critical to the overall attitude.

Info to Know - 6.8
Ways to get better student evaluations:
While these items are not guaranteed to give you great student evaluations, they will go a long way toward making sure the students give you a fair evaluation:

1) Engage your students in class (know their names, talk to them, don't let them hide);

2) Be consistent with **all** your grading processes;

3) Be enthusiastic in class. Bring the passion you feel for the topic into the classroom;

4) Don't make your class easier in the mistaken belief it will make the students like you more;

5) Make your class a fun and engaging experience for every student;

6) Pay constant attention to whether your presentation style is allowing the students to learn and take the notes they feel they need.

Early in my career, I experimented quite a bit with student class evaluations to see if some common factors determined how the evaluations came out. I offer the very anecdotal results from my informal experiments to help you understand how important an attitude of caring for your students is in determining your evaluation.

Your students' attitude and their evaluation about your teaching prowess is set very early in the semester and there is actually some literature to support this idea. For example, one semester I gave the class evaluations to the students after the second week of class before they had had a major exam and then again at the end of course. Interestingly, the evaluations were almost the same regardless of when they were given. Also, different sections of the same class, even though they were at radically different times of the day, 8 am vs. 1 pm, resulted in the same positive evaluations. I've also made up my own 'unofficial' evaluations with what I perceived were more appropriate questions that would help me with the class, and overall, no matter how the class was evaluated, with unofficial or official evaluations, the general tone of the evaluations was the same. The take home message I got from these informal experiments was the easiest way I could positively influence my evaluations was to show I cared about my students.

Earlier, I made some parenthetical value judgments about online student evaluations versus paper evaluations. I judged the online evaluations as a bad idea and the paper evaluations as a better idea. One of the concepts most of us have become familiar with as internet technologies and comment threads have become common-place, is people usually don't comment unless they have a gripe. The same is true for online student evaluations; my colleagues that have tried this approach have found unless they make all the students do the evaluations in class on their electronic devices, they find the number of students participating in the evaluation drop and the proportion of negative comments rise greatly. Paper evaluations certainly are not perfect, they still take a great deal of staff time to compile especially if there are written comments. However, paper evaluations must be done in class and as a result, *all* your students participate. So, just based on my observations of the current use of technology, if you can, use paper evaluations. If you have to use online evaluations in your class, work to implement methods to insure as many of your students participate as possible.

Before we get away from student evaluations, don't underestimate the usefulness of 'unofficial' evaluations you make up. Often, if I want to get a general sense if something I'm trying in class is working, I'll put together a short anonymous questionnaire and ask the students what they think. Students, especially if you've created a great learning environment, are always willing to help you understand if what you're trying is working or not. So, don't be shy about doing an unofficial evaluation; they don't count against you officially, but you can certainly report you're doing these types of evaluations to show you are working to make your classes better.

As a last word, remember student evaluations are not something to be afraid of or dread. In fact, you can use student evaluations to make the class better, which is supposed to be a primary purpose of student evaluations, as well as establishing a track record regarding your teaching capabilities. Further, looking at student class evaluations across the span of your early years of teaching can clearly show how your teaching improves and can be a powerful piece of data testifying to your increasing teaching skill during P/T.

Other types of class evaluations: I have devoted a lot of time on student evaluations because unfortunately, most academic administrators put much stock in these types of evaluations. Interestingly, many who tout the use of student evaluations seem to miss the basic point that the only qualification students must have to evaluate your class is that they've sat through it. And if you believe the suggestion that grades and student evaluations are linked, it is puzzling administrators would put stock in a supposedly independent evaluation metric that is so linked to an outcome.

That being said, if you think this section is about bashing student evaluations, don't get excited; in actuality, I want to make the case that other types of class evaluations can be extremely useful for you as you build your case for P/T. The types of evaluation I'm going to advocate take a bit more time and require your colleagues' participation, but usually without fail, these evaluations can provide a great support or counterpoint to the student class evaluations you receive.

Think about it differently: if you don't actively do any other type of class evaluation, the only evaluation your supervisors will have regarding your teaching ability is your student evaluations. Wouldn't it be better if your supervisors also had evaluations from people that were trained and experienced teachers? It can be invaluable to make the effort to have additional types of class evaluations in your teaching portfolio.

The two types of evaluation I would advocate *every* junior faculty member do are peer- and supervisor-class evaluations. These evaluations are basically the same thing and just differ based on who is doing the evaluation. If you have a peer-evaluation done, one of your fellow faculty members, preferably an established senior faculty member who is recognized as a good teacher, comes in and evaluates your class. Similarly, a supervisor-evaluation is where your immediate supervisor (e.g., Department Chair) comes in and does an evaluation. While these evaluations are similar (and probably will use a similar form (see Example 6.2 for such a form[84]), the person doing the evaluation will be coming at the evaluation from differing perspectives. While both

---

[84] I want to thank a long-time colleague, Dr. Linda Berne, for this peer-evaluation form. It has served me well for many years!

Example 6.2

PEER/SUPERVISOR CLASS EVALUATION

Instructor evaluated_____ Class_____ Date_____ Time_____

Evaluator_____

Directions:
Review the course syllabus or class objectives prior to observing the instructor. After observing the class, check the number across from each statement that most closely agrees with your observations of this instructor.

Code: NA = Not applicable/unable to evaluate. Please explain under comments.

1	2	3	4	5
Strongly Disagree	Disagree	Neutral	Agree	Strongly Agree

Easy, but thorough, checklists

CONTENT	1	2	3	4	5
1. Material presented is current and scholarly					
2. Examples are relevant to students' experience					
3. Different viewpoints are presented if appropriate					
4. Amount of material presented is adequate					
5. Concepts and principles are defined					
6. Relationship of theory to clinical practice is apparent					
7. Occasional restatements/summaries are provided					
8. Did not digress from main topic					
9. Teaching method appropriate for content presented					

Comments/Suggestions:

ORGANIZATION	1	2	3	4	5
1. Purpose of class is stated					
2. Relationship between present and previous material is stated.					
3. Content discussed in a systematic manner which coincides to syllabus/objectives					
4. Uses questions occasionally to determine student's understanding					
5. Uses examples to clarify difficult concepts.					
6. Encourages student's questions					
7. Pauses after questions to allow students time for thought					
8. Summarizes important ideas					
9. Addresses problems raised during class					
10. Relates current lecture/discussion to future class					

COMMENTS/SUGGESTIONS:

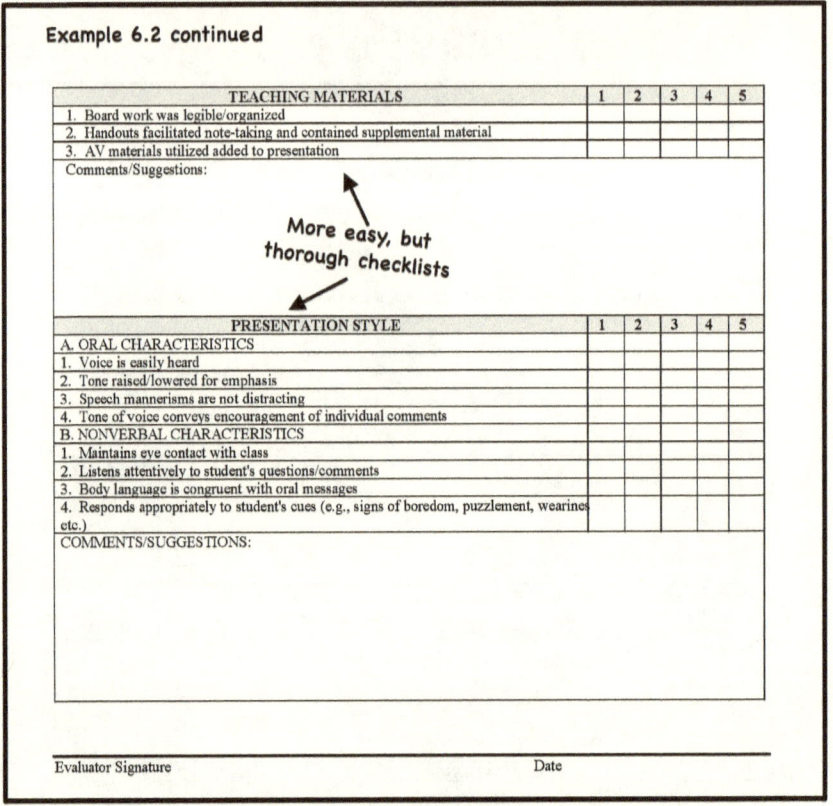

peer- and supervisor-evaluations will basically evaluate your teaching effectiveness and will have significant overlap, your peers will probably come at the evaluation more from a teaching perspective (e.g., is this person connecting with their students?) while your supervisor will certainly take an administrative perspective (e.g., is this person doing well enough in the classroom to keep?).

Remember the faculty member from earlier in the chapter with trouble in their class because of perceived aloofness and disengagement? We were able to solve the issue because I did supervisor-class evaluations for that faculty member; the student evaluations had pointed to a problem, while the supervisor-evaluations helped target the problem and devise solutions. Without the supervisor-evaluation, I'm not sure this faculty member would still be in academia.

Regardless of whether your University requires peer- and/or supervisor-evaluations, they can be very valuable to you and to your case for P/T. Plus, these types of evaluations help you 'show-off' your teaching capabilities to your peers and supervisors. Unfortunately, in too many cases, faculty really don't have a sense about how well other faculty teach in the classroom, and with their myriad duties, supervisors are even more hard-pressed to know how well all their faculty teach. Thus, asking your senior colleagues and your supervisor to do a class evaluation, or even better, multiple evaluations across your first few years of teaching, can help show how good a teacher you are becoming.

If you are unfamiliar with peer- or supervisor-evaluations, here are a couple of guidelines so if you need on of these evaluations, you can be the one to suggest how to do the evaluation.

First, peer- and supervisor-class evaluations need some type of written documentation that is standardized so that way all your evaluators will be using the same set of evaluation points. As you can see, Example 6.2 is a very thorough evaluation and tracks everything that goes on in your class. The detail in the example may seem overwhelming, but this type of detail can help you identify and overcome any potential problems you may not be aware of.

When do you have these evaluations done? I always liked 'surprise' evaluations; I would just give my evaluators a schedule of my exams, because to evaluate those would not be very useful, and asked they come to any other of my class periods. Many faculty prefer to arrange exactly when the evaluators will come in so the faculty member being evaluated can prepare. However, I always figured if I didn't know when the evaluators were coming, I would prepare every class the same and so the evaluator would be more likely to observe me in my 'normal teaching state'. The decision of when to have the evaluation done is up to you, but I would advocate having the evaluation done somewhat early in the semester so you still have time to correct any major issues the evaluator observes before the class is 'too far gone'.

In closing this section, having evaluations of your teaching abilities through class evaluations, whether they be by students, peers, or supervisors, can be a powerful tool you can use to become a better teacher and/or prove you are a good teacher. Many of us are afraid of evaluations; however, I would encourage you to embrace what class evaluations can do for you and use evaluations to bolster your teaching record. You will be evaluated one way or other whether you like it or not, and these evaluations will be part of your P/T portfolio. You might as well figure out how to make class evaluations work for you, rather than against you.

Student Issues

You will find the '90/10' rule applies in teaching: 90% of your students will be thoughtful, respectful, and hard-working and 10% will present you with challenges no matter what you do or how well you prepare. These percentages differ by Instructor and years and sometimes I experience the 100/0 rule and some years, it's more like 80/20. That's just the business of teaching. Whatever percentage you face, there are things you can do to prevent the 10% from consuming your life and your career and that's the topic of this section; common-sense things to keep in mind that will help you keep your head when you are challenged by a 'student-issue'.

> *Critical Teaching Point – 6.3*
> **Students**
> *You must remember most of your students will be diligent, well-behaved, and will work really hard. Don't let the 10% that don't fit the characteristics of most of your students detract you from providing the best learning environment for all your students!*

First, I am going to assume you've followed most, if not all, of the tips and techniques above so your course is well planned, you are engaging in the classroom, the students get a sense you care about their education, and you have valid and consistent grading schemes. Those four items can prevent a lot of issues. Dr. Boice, who I quoted earlier, spends a great deal of his book talking about causes of classroom incivility and ways to prevent this misbehavior. You might be surprised Dr. Boice's research showed "teachers were the most crucial initiators of classroom incivility" – "as a rule, their [faculty] most telling provocations occurred during the first few days of courses"[85]. Table 6.1 lists Boice's observations of the most frequent provocations for classroom incivility showing that many causes originated with the teachers as with the students. In fact, Boice observed students tended to wait about three class periods before beginning to act out and if the teacher showed disdain, disengagement, or other examples of not caring, the level of classroom incivility went up drastically!

From looking at Table 6.1, you can quickly see how working to engage your students, being involved in their learning, working to deliver the class material in an appropriately paced manner, and having a clear grading plan would eliminate four of the most common causes of classroom incivility.

The last four causes of incivility, if not taken care of by your work to plan and have a respectful learning environment, rest solely on the student. However, if you allow any of those four student-caused issues to continue, then

---

[85] R. Boice , pg. 98!

any further issue with the learning environment rests solely on your shoulders because remember the classroom is your domain; it is not a democracy. And if you allow classroom incivility to persist, then while the student may have initiated the issue, you are allowing it to continue and you've become an enabler.

Overall, if you have an issue, it is best to immediately resolve it. Often, these issues can be fixed by quietly talking to the problem student outside of class and noting you are not going to allow the behavior to continue. If that does not solve the problem, then you need to take the issue *immediately* to your Department Chair. Most departments have student conflict resolution processes and you'll need to make sure you closely follow those guidelines. But in most cases, those resolution processes require the faculty to take the first step which usually is to make it clear to the problem student the behavior will not be tolerated. Again, have the quiet discussion with the student outside of the classroom, but not in your office where you and the student are the only ones in the office. If you are in your office when you have the discussion, leave your door open!

> **Table 6.1 - Boice's Most Common Causes for Classroom Incivility**
> - Teachers alienating themselves from students with negative comments
> - Teachers distancing themselves by way of fast-paced, non-involving lectures
> - Teachers surprising students with tests and quizzes
> - Students talking too loudly
> - Students coming late and leaving early
> - Students making sarcastic comments, remarks, and gestures
> - Intimidation and distraction by problem students

Cheating on exams and assignments is the other most common problem you'll have with students, even though I've observed cheating 'instances' are cyclical; once it is clear to students you have processes in place to prevent and prosecute cheating, word spreads even across different class years and tamps down the urge for some students to cheat. I've noticed about once every four years I'll have to deal with one or more instances of cheating and then I won't have to deal with any problems for another four years or so.

When I talk about cheating, I'm going to lump together all behaviors where students work to gain an advantage on graded material, including, but not limited to cheating on exams and plagiarism on assigned work. You must work to stay vigilant for cheating because if a student cheats, it invalidates your grading scheme, the purpose of which is to measure a student's mastery of the content. It goes without saying that if you allow cheating to continue, then the student's grade really won't be indicative of their content mastery.

As you work to put in place processes to prevent cheating, you need to understand your campus policies and procedures regarding cheating; what is the official process you follow if you catch a student cheating? I've been at Universities that had very ambiguous policies (e.g., "Cheating is bad. Don't do it. It's up to the Instructor to deal with it if you are caught.") to Universities that had very specific policies (e.g., "There is a step by step process for how to deal with the issue.").

I would recommend before you write your syllabus, familiarize yourself with your University's processes and policies regarding cheating. Additionally, you should also consider what you will do as an Instructor if you catch someone cheating; most university processes on cheating work in tandem with academic freedom which will give you the leeway to either trigger the University policies or to follow some other resolutions.

Before we talk about some potential ways to handle cheating, it is instructive to consider that putting methods in place to prevent cheating can help tremendously in developing a positive learning environment in your class. With exams, maintaining the security of your exams is paramount to working to reduce cheating in your class. The fewer people that handle your exams, from their construction, through their copying, to their completion, and through their grading, will cut down on the chance or temptation for students to cheat. For example, how do you copy your exams? Do you give the exam to an office worker and ask for copies or do you make copies yourself? While every staff member I've worked with I would trust implicitly, I'm also very aware the copy of the exam I give to the staff member can be lifted off a desk or otherwise compromised. You must get in the habit of thinking about how to maintain the security of your test from the time you put it down on paper to when you enter the exam grade into your grade software. Along this line comes our earlier discussion about reusing old exams. Chances are, if you reuse old exams, someone 'out there' will build a compilation of your old exams and thus, some students could have an advantage on your exams.

Another area to pay attention to with your exams is during the administration of the exams. I've seen far too many faculty give out exams and then settle behind a desk with other reading material, effectively zoning out to what is going on in the classroom. Don't disengage after you give out the exam; walk around the classroom and watch your students. You'll be amazed at the behavior you'll see, and the attention you give your classroom *during* an exam will help you keep cheating to a minimum and will be noticed and respected by the students. Part of managing your exams is to prevent actions that may lead to cheating during the exam; for example, if a student has a question would you let them come to you and ask, or would you go to them? I'm betting most of you already have guessed going to the student keeps them sitting down and reduces the chance they'll see other students' exams or efforts. Yes, it is tempting to zone out when your students are taking exams, but if you zone out or do something else while they are taking the test, you are increasing the chances they'll cheat.

So far, the discussion has been about cheating during exams; however, there are often opportunities for cheating to occur during other types of assignments, such as writing assignments. Putting procedures in place to prevent cheating during outside class assignments will also help prevent problems. For example, one of the University Instructors I worked with, who was a great Instructor and had been a State-wide Teacher of the Year in the public schools, gave a class an assignment to do an observation on an external event.[86] Upon receiving the written reports from her students, this Instructor quickly realized there was a problem with many of the reports. It appeared almost 75% of the students in the class had copied from each other, or from external sources. Given this class had over 40 students in it, you can quickly see the magnitude of the problem in this class. While the students were solely responsible for their actions, there were some actions the Instructor could have taken that would have helped tremendously in the outcome.

First, the Instructor needed to be clear that plagiarism was not tolerated and would be considered cheating and be punished fully according to all the University rules and regulations in place. You may be shocked that as an Instructor you would have to tell your students this, but understand, once lawyers get involved, which they did, if you do not have these types of common-sense things described somewhere (such as in the syllabus), you can't prove the students knew this behavior was not tolerated.

Secondly, if the Instructor had also told the students what constituted plagiarism, this would have helped the case because many of the students claimed they didn't know what plagiarism was. Yes, really. While you may consider both of these precautions as being more appropriate for middle-schoolers, understand if you accuse a student of cheating, especially a large number of students cheating at the same time, then the lawyers will probably get involved and they will quickly devolve to questions such as "did you tell the students plagiarism wasn't acceptable" or "did you tell the students what

---

[86] If you are frustrated I'm not giving more detail, please be aware not only does FERPA impact the events of this story, so does the confidentiality of personnel processes. The details wouldn't add much to the take-home message or to the severity of what happened!

plagiarism was?" So, while it may seem trivial, officially telling students what you define as plagiarism, that you do not allow it, and it is considered cheating will go a long way toward providing a foundation upon which you can hold students accountable if you catch them cheating.

In fact, to prevent that type of cheating in the future, the department made an online plagiarism tutorial available for each faculty member to use in their classes. Most of our faculty required their students to take the plagiarism tutorial at the beginning of the semester with a tracking of who took the tutorial, so if any instance of plagiarism arose, we would have proof the student had done the tutorial, knew plagiarism wasn't appropriate, and knew what constituted plagiarism. That type of action, requiring each student to take a plagiarism tutorial, may seem to be unnecessary, but in fact, not only was that tutorial instructional, it helped us deal with other plagiarism issues we had later, so it was preventative as well.

Another preventative method to use if you are giving out of class assignments, especially written work, is to inform the students you will submit their work to one of the many plagiarism checkers that exist. Most Universities have subscriptions to these services, often through the library, and I would encourage you to use this service on the written assignments from your students. It is interesting that as you read students' written work, you will quickly get a sense of what is an appropriate writing level for your students and as a result, work that is too smooth and too professional-appearing will stick out. Those well-done writing samples are the ones I usually submit to plagiarism checking services. If those samples come back clean, I'm happy because not only does it mean the student didn't plagiarize, but it also means they can write well and as such, I'm going to think about asking them to join my lab group. But the beginning point – informing your students in your syllabus you'll submit samples to a plagiarism checker – will be enough to warn them not to plagiarize.

So, there are some easy approaches you can take to help prevent cheating amongst your students. But what do you do if you find a student has cheated? As unpleasant as it is, if you do anything other than following your established procedure, then you have just let this student know, as well as the student's friends, they can get away with cheating in your class. And while you may have just had one student cheat this time, it will spread and you will have multiple students cheating in the future. So, if you discover cheating, you must take care of the issue immediately.

As noted above, as a faculty member, you have academic freedom to handle your class the way you think is appropriate, and this includes dealing with cheating. While I continue to recommend you note in your syllabus you'll pursue the University process if you catch cheating, I've found in the universities I've worked in the University process to deal with cheating is a blunt instrument that is often onerous and often doesn't provide much support for the Instructor.

Remember the story from above about the class with 30 instances of cheating on a written report? As we worked through the University process with that group of students, the process was so onerous and so unsupportive of the Instructor, our Instructor actually resigned at the end of the semester. Not all student misconduct processes are like that, but nonetheless, most university processes dealing with cheating are legalistic, as they should be, and as a result, onerous. Because of that, I believe there should be a middle-ground between letting stuff go and invoking the University process. In my experiences, almost without exception, students, whatever their reason for cheating, are horrified when they are caught. As a result, I have worked to use these situations as teaching opportunities when they arose. For example, when caught, I have often assigned the student an expanded written assignment regarding whatever item they were working on with an extra assignment of writing about why plagiarism hurts scientific knowledge.

My one caveat on any type of extended assignment is the student cannot do as well (grade-wise) on the expanded assignment than they could have done on the original assignment. For example, if the student could have received 100 points on the original assignment if the paper had been perfect, on the expanded assignment, they can only receive a maximum of 90 points so there is a punishment for the cheating. However, this is not a 'one-size-fits-all' solution; cheating situations vary vastly and you'll need to respond in a wide-variety of ways, always keeping in mind your need to protect the integrity of your assignments and grading system. For example, I once had a student write exam material on his arms and hands that was exposed when he reached to get the exam from me. (Yes, really.) Invoking the University cheating procedure would have done no good (in fact, he hadn't taken the exam yet, so there had been no cheating yet). I simply had him go to the bathroom, wash his arms and hands, and then begin the exam.

The take home message is that the cheating situations you will encounter will vary vastly and you will have to use wisdom and discernment when deciding what to do. I would always encourage you to talk to your Department Chair about what is going on as well as document the entire situation. While I will not hesitate to put students through the University process for cheating, I also try to figure out how to make the situation a learning experience for the student so they will not do it again. If you put the extra effort into thinking about how to take a bad situation like cheating and make it a learning experience, you may find the involved students learn more and gain more in the long run.

One last story before we leave the section on student problems. For my last exam as a doctoral student, I decided to blow-off the exam and not to study. I had never done that before; however, I knew I was going to pass the class anyway. So, I blew off the exam and proceeded to start work at Kennedy Space Center where I was completing my doctoral dissertation work. Dr. Ed Howley, who was my doctoral advisor and the Instructor of the course, wasn't going to let me off the hook that easy. Dr. Howley called me up, realize this was before the advent of cell phones and email, to let me know he wasn't accepting my final exam and I had an incomplete in the class until I provided a two-page paper, with citations, on each of the questions I had missed on the final, which were many.

My decision to not study for that final exam meant that I had to locate a medical library close to Titusville, Florida so I could work on my answers, which had me driving to Gainesville, Florida multiple times. Thanks to Dr. Howley, I learned a lesson and I have used similar types of exercises on students over my 30 years as a faculty member. Today, as an Instructor, I appreciate Dr. Howley didn't take the easy way out and just give me a grade. He cared enough to go the extra mile and he wanted to make sure I got my money's worth from his class. Because he cared enough to go the extra mile, I wound up caring enough to go the extra mile as well. Believe me, over and over my experience has been when, as a Faculty member you care enough to go the extra mile for your students' learning, your students will respect your effort and will also go the extra distance with you.

Improving your teaching

I'm closing this rather lengthy chapter on maybe one of the most important topics in promotion and tenure which is how do you get better at teaching? None of us start out as master teachers so one of the points your P/T portfolio will be judged on is how you have improved your teaching over the course of your time as a faculty member. As such, you need to indicate both in words and your deeds, how you've worked to improve your teaching. While there are numerous ways to improve your teaching, I'm going to suggest two primary avenues: 1) Take advantage of any type of teaching/learning opportunity you

> **Critical Teaching Point - 6.4**
> **Importance of Improvement**
> The most important thing you need to do for the teaching-side of your P/T effort is to show efforts to improve your teaching. No one will expect you to be a master teacher at first, but they will expect you to work on your teaching and steadily improve!

have; and 2) Experiment with your own teaching.

There are a huge number of resources available to improve your teaching including many specific articles about teaching improvement in *The Chronicle of Higher Education*.[87] Additionally, every university is concerned about the teaching capabilities of their faculty. You don't have to look at the literature too hard to find many examples of Universities providing workshops, seminars, and groups that focus on teaching improvement. Most Universities now have Teaching Centers on campus that provide many resources to help you with your teaching.

Find the Teaching Center on your campus and take advantage of the workshops and programs they have for you. Make sure you document your participation in these activities since this is a great way to show you have been working on your teaching. If your University has them, take advantage of the Teaching Groups that may be formed on campus. One of the most supportive groups I ever belonged to was a Teaching Circle at the University of North Carolina Charlotte that met monthly. The Teaching Circle was made up of 12 faculty from around the University. There was no one from my College in the Teaching Circle, which was great because I got to make connections around the campus and I could ask 'stupid' questions without being concerned someone from my College would remember my stupid question come P/T review time. You may not have Teaching Circles/Groups at your campus, but take the opportunity to find the Teaching Center and find out what resources they have available to help you with your teaching.

Another suggestion I always give junior faculty is to not be afraid to experiment with your classes. I talked earlier about different things I've tried with class evaluations, but you can also do a large number of other types of experiments in your classes. Try different ways of presenting material such as *not* using digital media or using different approaches like groups instead of the whole class to teach a concept. Don't be afraid to try something different; the best Instructors are those that are always trying different approaches to guiding and interpreting the material for the students. For example, as an Instructor, teaching how hormones respond to and effect exercise responses was always boring to me as an Instructor, which was a sure sign it was boring to my students. So, one semester I reformatted that portion of my course to make it a 'Hormone Survivor' class, where I broke the students up into tribes and formatted the learning activities much like the television show 'Survivor'

---

[87] Again, I would recommend you start with Dr. Boice's book *Advice for New Faculty Members* to get you started, but there is some good material on *The Chronicle's* website (Chronicle.com)!

(you know, the one where people are voted off the island). That's just one example of a different approach you can take to engage your students and keep you sharp. The only thing limiting your teaching, and the opportunity you give your students to learn, is your imagination and creativity. Don't hesitate to use them!

The Take Home Message

Whew! This was a long chapter, but for a good reason. Teaching is a complicated and complex practice and good teachers think about their teaching and they work and experiment to make their classes better for their students. While you can never be responsible for how much your students learn because your students are ultimately responsible for their level of learning, you are responsible for providing the best learning environment you can for your students. You are truly responsible for giving your students their money's worth in your classroom. That is a huge responsibility, and because of that, teaching is one of the critical pieces of your academic furniture you are putting together. There's often much more work involved in great teaching than most people realize, but I know you will excel at it if you care enough and work at it.

7

SERVICE:
NECESSARY, YET LEARN TO SAY 'NO'

The third traditional 'piece' of your academic furniture that you are putting together is service[88]. Being a good departmental citizen who participates in the life of the department, university, and the profession is critical, both for the faculty member's future and for the health of your Institution and profession. Further, it can be argued it is critical faculty engage with the community and so, community professional service can also be vital. As such, there are a myriad of ways faculty members can participate in service. However, as a junior faculty member if you are not careful, you can become overwhelmed by service obligations, so much so your teaching and research production spiral downward. In this chapter, I'm going to covers tips for identifying service that will help you move positively toward P/T[89] as well as methods to tactfully and gently turn down service participation requests.

What is service?

'Service' can be a catch-all phrase that includes everything you do professionally other than research and teaching. 'Service' designates activities you do to support the functioning and advancement of your profession and your Institution. These types of activities are considered 'professional service' and contribute directly to your profession in a broad-sense, or in specific ways to your Institution.

Professional service can be very broad and multifaceted. Within every university there are literally hundreds of ways to get involved and do professional service,

This Chapter:

What is service? 175

Why is service important? 176

Importance of service in getting P/T 178

Protecting your time from service 178

Service opportunities you should consider 180

The Take Home Message 181

---

[88] If you are keeping count, Service is actually the fourth 'piece' of your academic furniture we are describing. However, traditionally, only research, teaching, and service have been counted with funding being relatively new.

[89] As in past chapters, P/T stands for Promotion and Tenure and includes those up for contract renewals as well!

ranging from being in Faculty Senate to being an Advisor for Student Clubs. Also, professional service includes activities you do for your profession, including the professional organizations you belong to, serving on committees, being a manuscript reviewer for a journal, and/or moderating symposiums and talks at scientific meetings.

Community service are activities that are related to your professional knowledge and expertise, but are directed to individuals *outside* your profession or your University. This type of service can take several forms such as you being asked to give community talks on your area of expertise, or being asked to participate in community activities directly related to your profession such as health fairs, or being asked to testify or give informed opinion in trials or in political deliberation. Community service can be broad and not related to your profession, like singing in your church choir, and unless your professional discipline is vocal performance, these types of non-professional community service activities would not be counted as community service for P/T.

You will find an overwhelming number of ways you can get involved in service with the difficulty becoming how to manage the number of service opportunities you agree to do so your service obligations do not supersede your research and teaching priorities.

Why is service important?

You may be questioning why you should even do service if it might overtake your research and teaching priorities. Simply put, if faculty members stopped doing professional service, most universities, professional organizations, and scientific journals would probably cease to function. All these entities depend a great deal on the volunteer labor faculty provide.

As an individual, doing professional service is critical to your career advancement. Through service, you will develop collaborative networks, ties with other professionals, and get access to resources that will allow your career to continue to grow and flourish. One of the critical reasons for you to do professional service is to develop and establish those collaborative and collegial relationships that will help you not only further your career, but will help you have an impact on your profession. This same rationale goes for doing service within your University; who you meet and who you know will help you navigate your University system more easily.

Since I have served on compliance committees at every University I've worked at, I've often known whom to call for help with research problems, compliance issues, or for resources. If I had just sat in my office working on my research or teaching as opposed to being on the compliance committees,

I would not have been as productive just because being involved with service gave me contacts I could use if I needed help.

As much as service can help your career, as I noted earlier, service is also vital to the continued health of your Institution as well as your profession. Just within your Institution, professional service is needed for such things as search committees, promotion and tenure committees, and curriculum committees, just to name a few. Without faculty participating in these efforts, faculty would be left without a voice in these processes. This is one reason most universities have what is called 'faculty governance', which is defined as the faculty having an opportunity to work with the administrators to run the university. Faculty governance is critical to the proper functioning of every educational unit, from departments, through colleges, and up through the university and system organizations. Faculty governance wouldn't exist without faculty doing service.

In a similar manner, most professional organizations wouldn't exist without faculty participating in the various activities that are endemic in a professional organization. My primary professional organization, the American College of Sports Medicine, currently has 64 different committees that work to make the organization function. Most professional organizations are like mine; they have a small number of paid administrative professionals running the organization on a day-to-day basis, but depend on many volunteers from the membership to make the organization function well. Those volunteers are all doing professional service and as such, are contributing to helping the organization function.

Lastly, I believe it is critical faculty take their knowledge and expertise into the community. As an academic, you have been given a position of trust in our society; that is part of the exchange our society has with our institutes of higher education. We train people in various disciplines and then those people we train are supposed to help make our communities and society better for everyone. However, if you just sit in your office writing scientific papers all day, society in general does not get the benefit of your training or for paying for institutes of higher education. As a result, society may start to question why they pay so much for higher education in the form of tax support or tuition-cost.

If you've paid attention to the national news over the last several years, you can see politicians questioning higher education; state legislatures are not as willing to fund higher education, and more often, the high cost of tuition is being targeted as a problem. While this is not the place to debate either of these issues, when these types of issues arise it should be a warning that

Universities are not doing a good job of serving the community or of helping society understand what we are doing. So, it is critical that you as an academic look for ways to serve your community with your professional expertise. Anything that will help the public understand what you do as an academic and why it is important does a service not only to your community, but also to the greater cause of education in general.

Importance of service in getting P/T
There is an adage in academia that says "No one ever got promotion and tenure based on service. However, not doing service will insure you don't get promotion and tenure." That adage seems to be a contradiction doesn't it? Don't do service and you won't get P/T, but do service and it may not count much toward P/T? How is this seeming paradox rectified?

First, the core concept to remember is while research and teaching primarily are about you, service is about what you do for your Institution, profession, and community. In other words, research and teaching are mostly selfish activities, research more so than teaching, while service is primarily about serving others. Your colleagues, as they consider your P/T packet, want to see you have been engaged and you have been a 'good departmental citizen'.

I said earlier service is necessary for the University to run. If you don't do service, you're basically letting everyone else carry the load of running the University for you while you benefit. Your colleagues want to see you are also engaged in helping the University run. As a result, you must show you have been engaged and have been willing to help your educational community grow and move forward. I have been in many P/T committee meetings where in discussing a candidate, especially for promotion to Full Professor, the topic arises about whether the candidate has been a good department citizen and carried their share of the load. Again, while service will not be the primary factor that gets you P/T, whether you've helped and participated in necessary service is always a discussion point in the deliberations.

Protecting your time from service
While I made the point above that Service was an important part of your P/T portfolio, I am now going to argue that as a junior faculty, you need to zealously guard your time from doing service. Further, I'm going to encourage you to surround yourself with colleagues that will help you guard your time against service. Your focus during your first five years as a faculty member should be first and foremost to establish your research program and teaching skills and lastly, to engage in service. Ultimately, your P/T fate will largely depend on your research and teaching and so, you would be foolish to allow service to become a large part of your day-to-day faculty activities.

I had a colleague who because he was bright, well-informed, and a hard worker, wound up on 13 different committees the year he came up for P/T. If it hadn't been for his incredibly strong research record, including an NIH grant, and his stellar teaching, that much service would have torpedoed his P/T bid. With that much service, the P/T committee could have questioned his priorities as a faculty member. The take-home message is while service is important, during your first five years as a faculty member it can also be deadly to your promotion and tenure bid.

So, how do you protect your time from service commitments? First, learn how to say "no". You may think if you say "no" you'll displease, offend, or upset people. This couldn't be further from the truth. As an academic, you'll find you'll get turned down many times and because of that, most academics are used to hearing "no". Don't think if you say "no" you are going to hurt your future chances at other opportunities. However, as you say "no", it is important to learn how to say "no" appropriately.

Table 7.1 – Ten Ways to Say 'No'
1. That sounds like a really great opportunity, but I just cannot take on any additional commitments at this time.
2. I am not comfortable with that _____ (situation, task, group of people involved).
3. I feel overwhelmed by service right now, so I am going to have to decline your generous invitation.
4. I am in the middle of _____, _____, and _____ and, if I hope to get tenure, I am unable to take on any additional service.
5. I am not the best person for this. Why don't you ask _____?
6. If you can find a way to eliminate one of my existing service obligations, I will consider your request.
7. I would rather say no to your request than do a halfhearted job on the committee.
8. Right now, I need to focus on my research agenda and publications. When I have tenure, I hope to be able to say yes to requests like this one.
9. I cannot serve on your committee right now. But why don't you ask me again next year?
10. No. (Look the asker in the eye and sit in silence.)
From Rockquemore, K. A. and T Laszloffy. *The Black Academic's Guide to Winning Tenure – without losing your soul.* Lynne Rienner Publishers, Inc. Boulder Colorado, 2008 (used by permission of Dr. K.A. Rockquemore)

You should always make sure you say "no" by referring to the importance of you fulfilling your other priorities (i.e., research, teaching). Do not use a generic 'I'm too busy' excuse to turn-down service opportunities; you'll find everyone is busy in academia and so, using this excuse becomes trite and meaningless. Instead, learn how to say "no" in a positive manner. Table 7.1[90] offers 10 different ways to say "no". Practice these different responses and you'll find saying "no" becomes easier and easier.

The second way to protect yourself from service obligations is to surround yourself with colleagues and mentors that will help you protect your time from service requests. Ask your Chair or your senior mentor if they would be willing to be a buffer between you and service requests as well as a sounding board for you when you get service requests. Then, when you get service requests, talk to your Chair or Mentor and see what they think. Not only will they be a good buffer for you, but you'll also get the benefit of their experience. Asking for input can help you determine the advantages and disadvantages of each service request. Plus, you'll have an opportunity to learn how senior faculty handle such requests.

Service opportunities you should consider

You may be saying to yourself, "Wait, you just said don't do much service as a junior faculty member and now you're saying I should do service?" Yep, that's exactly what I'm saying. You need to do some service to show you are a good departmental citizen. Just don't do too much service. Be selective and choosy about the service you perform. In general, a good rule of thumb to follow is to do any service that will help you establish collaborations, a network, or give you access to other resources that will directly support your research efforts. This includes some forms of professional service (e.g., being a manuscript reviewer when asked) as well as some forms of university service (e.g., Compliance service).

As you consider service opportunities, remember that there are many service opportunities that occur at the department, college, and the university level. At your Department level, there are service opportunities in curriculum approval and review, faculty hiring, graduate student evaluations, and a wide variety of other ways to get involved. At your College level, there are often the same type of service opportunities, but related to the whole college versus just the department. At the University level, besides being similar opportunities as at the department and college level, you begin to see

---

[90] Table 7.1 comes courtesy of Dr. Kerry Ann Rockquemore, from Rockquemore, K. A. and T Laszloffy. *The Black Academic's Guide to Winning Tenure – without Losing Your Soul.* Lynne Rienner Publishers, Inc. Boulder Colorado, 2008

university-wide opportunities that can give you insight across the whole institution.

For example, I would encourage you to consider serving on one of the federally-mandated compliance committees at your University. These compliance committees are commonly known by their acronyms: IRB = Internal Review Board (or Human Subjects Committee); IACUC = Institutional Animal Care and Use Committee; and Institutional Biosafety = Biosafety. Every university must have these committees and they provide a great avenue for you to meet researchers across the campus, as well as being privy to the research that is being done on campus. In particular, the IRB and the IACUC sit at the nexus of most research activity on campus and as a member, you will see most, if not all of the research being done with humans and animals on your campus. Serving on the IRB or the IACUC helps you get to know and work with the compliance office staffs that are so important in helping get research approved so it can be conducted. More than once I've called my contacts within the compliance office to ask questions, deal with protocol approval issues, or just to solve problems. I would not have had these contacts if I had not served for many years on both IRB and IACUC committees. One last advantage of serving on the IRB or IACUC is that you become a resource for your fellow faculty. In today's era of compliance, it helps to have someone you know on these committees so you can find out the latest changes and details needed to get approval of your work. With your participation, you can become a valuable resource for your colleagues. In short, serving on one of the compliance committees will not only support your research program, but will also increase your value to the department, college, and university.

You may find there are other service opportunities that will support your career and if so, go for them. But carefully weigh out the advantages and disadvantages for each opportunity[91], check with your Department Chair and/or mentor, and then go for the service that will not only show you are a good department citizen, but will help further and support your research program.

The Take Home Message
Service is critical to the smooth functioning of any higher education institution and faculty are the ones that do most of the service. You can't dodge

---

[91] Dr. Manya Whitaker wrote a great piece in the *Chronicle of Higher Education* (How to Advocate for Yourself as an Early-Career Scholar, July 20, 2018) proposing a classification scheme for service requests you get as a junior faculty member. It's well worth reading.

service because you must do your part, but you need to work to limit your service obligations, especially in the first five years of your position. You should always work to establish your research and teaching first and then develop your service. Learn to say "no" and surround yourself with colleagues that will help you limit your service. But, if you get an opportunity to serve in an area that will support your research program, go for it. You may find resources you didn't know you had access to.

8
BUILDING TOWARD PROMOTION AND TENURE: THE TIME TO START IS NOW!

The excitement of a new faculty job can provide motivation and enthusiasm when you start assembling your career furniture. Fairly soon though, the normal day-to-day items a faculty member is responsible for will take all your attention and time. Before you know it, your Department Chair will be asking for your review portfolio in either your third year or fifth year, and you'll realize how quickly the time has gone by. Suddenly you'll be faced with the reality that while you've been playing with the different parts of your academic career, the time has come when you have to show what your 'piece of furniture' looks like!

Reducing the anxiety of the process

For junior faculty, the anxiety of the P/T process can be overwhelming and all encompassing. It's hard not to be anxious when you know your job, your career, and your future could be riding on the outcome of the mysterious review process. After watching and working with junior faculty as they navigated the P/T process for over 25 years in conjunction with my own experiences with P/T, there are some keys I have seen that will help you transit the P/T process with a minimum of anxiety.

To a large extent, the anxiety you will feel as you go through the process is largely self-generated. Yes, you are often the source of your own anxiety. Granted, the process can be mysterious and confusing with a lot riding on it which can lead to tension and anxiety, but in the end, how you approach the process, how thorough and diligent you are with your scholarship, and what you allow yourself to feel will ultimately determine how much anxiety you have during the process.

One of the reasons for this whole book, as I stated way back in the Preface, was to work to demystify and clarify what the P/T process really was, how you go through it, what you'll need, and what you'll have to present. The more you

> **This Chapter:**
>
> Reducing the anxiety of the process 183
>
> Getting Started on Your Documents 185
>
> The Process 186
>
> Your Portfolio 189
>
> External Reviewers 209
>
> Work / Life Balance 213
>
> The Take Home Message 214

know about the process and how the P/T decisions are made, the less anxiety you should feel because you'll know exactly how things will be handled. Because each university has their own 'unique' version of the P/T process, besides reading this book, you will have to learn and understand how the process works at your Institution. You'll find much of what we've talked about in this book will apply to your own P/T efforts, but you'll also likely find additional things you'll have to do or items from this book you'll have to tweak. My point here is that learning everything you can about the process at your Institution is something you'll have to do; not knowing the process and what will happen during the review will just make it more of a mystery to you which will ultimately add to your anxiety.

Besides knowing the process, the next best way to avoid anxiety is to make sure you have good mentoring, both locally within your Department and University, but also external to your University. Take advantage of the knowledge your mentors have about the process, their experiences with P/T, and the advice they give you. It really is a wasted opportunity if you do not tap into the expertise and experience your mentors have in regards to P/T. In addition to listening to your mentors, you need to put what they say into action. I've had many junior faculty ask for my opinion and advice on their P/T efforts; most of the successful ones have listened and put into play my suggestions. The ones that have struggled with P/T are the ones that either didn't ask or didn't listen to the advice their mentors gave them.

Anxiety is often the result of not understanding the process, not feeling like you have control, or having regret because you don't feel you have accomplished what you should have accomplished. When you understand the process you'll have to go through, you'll find you do have some control because you have control of how good your portfolio is, plus, you get to suggest potential reviewers. With these understandings, the amount of anxiety you feel about the P/T process is ultimately completely up to you.

If you have done all you can do on a daily basis to have a strong academic record, you need to release the unknowns. It is a well-tested and practiced method in athletics to get the athletes to focus on the process and not the outcome.[92] If you focus on what you must do to fulfill your side of the P/T process and not on possible outcomes, you'll have greater peace of mind. This is just another way of bringing it all back to having confidence about what you've done daily. However, if despite everything written above, you are still overwhelmed and highly anxious about P/T, I would encourage you

---

[92] If you want to know more about this approach, check out Dr. Jacques Dallaire's book *Performance Thinking: Mental Skills for the Competitive World...and for Life!* 2012.

to seek counseling[93]. But don't forget, if you understand the process and focus on your work and not on possible outcomes, this will go a long way toward reducing the anxiety P/T or contract renewal can invoke.

Another way to prevent anxiety during the promotion and tenure process is to realize you've done all you can do. I am assuming when you get to the P/T stage, you will have been diligently building your research and funding record, will have been developing into a master teacher, will have provided service, and will have been a good department citizen. If you have worked hard, then you should take comfort you have done all you can do.

Faculty are often their own worst critics. We all know where our portfolios are weak and the areas we wish were stronger. Every day of your academic career you must make choices as to what to focus on that day. Many questions can arise in your head that cause anxiety: Would my teaching record be stronger if I'd focused more on teaching than on research; Would my research record be better if I didn't teach as much? These types of questions we may ask ourselves, but in the end, these questions are meaningless and do not help either your portfolio or your mental state. You must accept the portfolio you will put forward will reflect your hard work and as such, will have to be satisfactory.

Info to Know – 8.1
Reducing P/T Anxiety
1. Know the P/T process thoroughly – focus on the process, not potential outcomes
2. Have good mentoring
3. Focus on doing what is most important in your Institute (e.g., research or teaching)
4. Accept that you've done all you can do
5. Get counseling if the anxiety is overwhelming

Getting Started on Your Documents

Because the time can pass so quickly and the need for the development of your P/T documents can creep up on you, I would advocate that you start thinking about your P/T portfolio almost as soon as you hit campus. What you need to do immediately, especially if you are early in your career, is to make sure you are cognizant of what will be required when you do come up for P/T review. In particular, you must keep in mind the items you'll need to include in your portfolio so when you're putting your portfolio together you'll have these items handy to give you plenty of time to work on your portfolio without scrambling for material.

---

[93] Most university counseling centers will see faculty and most have methods to keep your visits confidential. P/T anxiety is probably one of the more common issues most university-based counseling centers deal with. So, don't suffer alone, get help!

To that end, I would suggest you set aside two areas where you'll put potential P/T items and documents. One area should be a physical file folder where you can easily drop all items that come in hard copy form (e.g., class evaluations, peer evaluations, thank you notes from students, etc.). However, since there are fewer and fewer documents existing in hard-copy form, you also need to set aside a folder on your computer for all the digital documents you'll receive you'll need easy access to (e.g., annual evaluations, published papers, written grants, etc.). If you'll set up this simple filing system as soon as you hit campus, it will be a relatively easy task for you to pull out all the appropriate material when it is time for you to put together your portfolio(s). An intriguing suggestion was made recently by Dr. Pam Whitfield[94] to also put together a 'Be Kind Portfolio' which contains all the positive notes, letters, and articles you accumulate over the years. Certainly, the items in this Be Kind Portfolio can be used in promotion and tenure, but primarily can be used as positive validation for you when you need positive validation (e.g., after you've received not-so-positive student evaluations).

In the end, your discipline in putting items you'll use in your evaluations in places where you can find them easily will be a tremendous time-saver and a useful reference for you as you go through the review process.

The Process

Figure 8.1 is a review of the general timeline of the P/T process that we covered in Chapter 1. If you'll note, you will usually come up for comprehensive reviews in your third year and in your fifth year of employment. In most cases, this review schedule means you'll have to have your portfolio ready to go at the end of your *second year* and at the end of your *fourth year*. So, it won't be long between when you start your job and when you'll have to submit your portfolio.

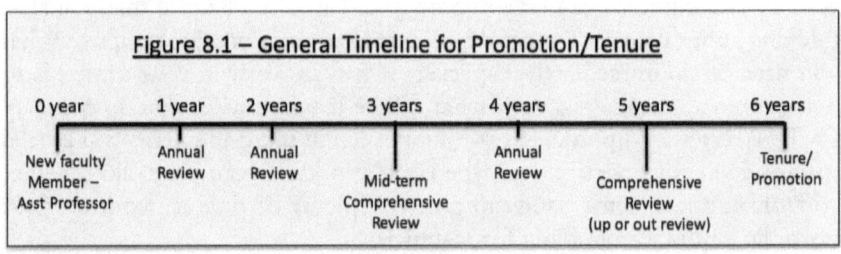

[94] You can find Dr. Whitfield's suggestion about a Be Kind Portfolio in an article titled, "A Self-Care Strategy for Beleaguered Academics", in the archives at the *Chronicle of Higher Education,* from May 29, 2018.

In general, the evaluation process is usually straight forward. When you are up for review, whether it be your third-year review, your P/T review, or a contract renewal review, you will normally be asked to assemble and submit your initial portfolio in late summer, usually July or August of the year of your review (see Fig. 8.2). Some universities ask for an initial portfolio during the Spring semester around March-April, so the P/T committee and the administrators can review it and provide you feedback so your portfolio is the best it can be before the official start of the review process in late summer.

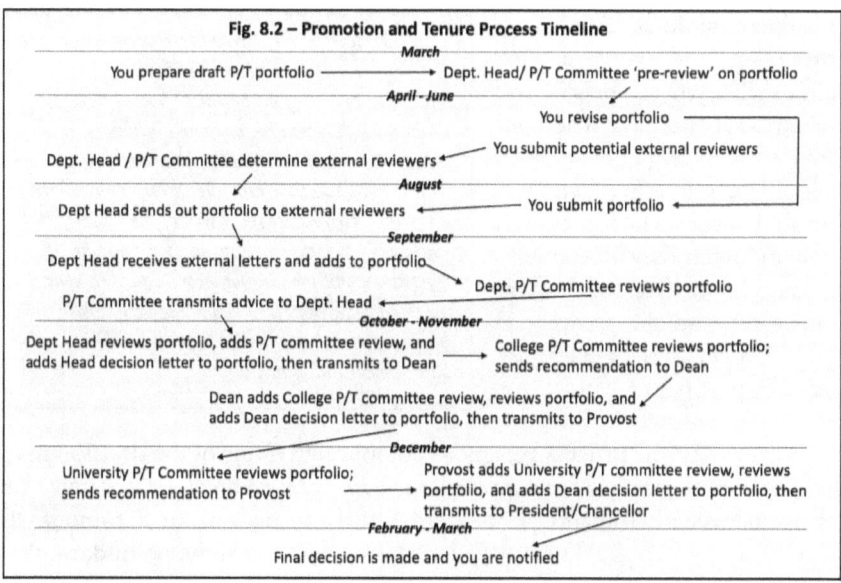

Your portfolio will likely be submitted to your Department Chair, who will then send out invitations for external reviews of your portfolio. When the external review letters come back, those letters will be added to your portfolio which will then be transmitted to the Department P/T Committee. The Department P/T Committee will normally have about one month to complete their advisory review and transmit their recommendation to the Department Chair via a letter that is included in your portfolio. The Department Chair will then have about a month to complete their review and add their recommendation letter to the portfolio. This process (P/T Committee advises, Administrator recommends), will then repeat sequentially at the College (usually November/December) and then the University level (January/February), where the Provost is usually the last to add a recommendation to the portfolio. If the recommendations are all positive, then your portfolio and recommendation will usually be forwarded to the President/Chancellor of the University and the Board of Regents/Trustees for confirmation (March-May) with contract renewal or promotion and tenure being effective at the beginning of the next academic year (≈ August).

Note the process, if it has a positive outcome, will take at least 9-12 months, so understand this is a slow process. You will probably be given updates along the way; most university P/T processes require you be officially notified of the various decision makers' recommendations as the process unfolds, so you will have some idea of how your evaluation is going during that 12-month period. However, you should also understand due to legal considerations, often the feedback you'll get on how your portfolio is fairing will be relatively minimal. Most P/T processes are very explicit about what you can be told and when, so if you have read your P/T processes guidelines, you should have an idea of who will be able to share outcomes with you and what they'll be able to share. If you are still unclear and can't find the answers in your University's policies, ask your Department Chair.

> **Critical P/T Process Point – 8.1**
> **It Takes Time**
>
> *The P/T process (and contract renewal process) takes time. Depending on your University, it may take 9-12 months from when you first turn in your portfolio until all the Deciders have rendered decisions. Because of the length of the process, you'll need to start working on your portfolio at least six months before you have to turn in your portfolio. Developing your portfolio does not happen overnight; a rushed portfolio will not be the best representation of you!*

Unfortunately, the process gets more complicated if one of the decision makers in the process does not support your P/T application. One negative vote is not necessarily the end of your bid, but it can be a major detriment. In most cases, again, you'll be notified of this outcome at some point during the process.

If you are denied P/T, all Universities have a grievance procedure you can enter into to have your case reviewed. This review is usually conducted by a University Grievance Committee that is made up of faculty members. Grievance proceedings take various forms at different Universities so if you find yourself in this situation, you need to be thoroughly aware of the grievance procedure at your University which should be detailed in your University policies. Additionally, for something as important as this process, I would encourage you to seek legal representation outside of the University. Most Universities allow for the individual grieving to have legal counsel available, but often counsel can only be advisory; in other words, they can't argue your case for you in front of the Grievance Committee. If you must go this route, look specifically for legal representation that has experience with your University's grievance process; in most college towns, there is at least one attorney that has experience dealing with your University in personnel matters. Toward this end, if your University has a faculty-union, there may be stipulations allowing for the union to have a representative for you present. Again, make sure you understand all facets of the process!

If you are on a fixed-term contract and you were not recommended for *contract renewal*, you will most likely not have a job at the end of the semester when the process is occurring. If you were turned down for P/T, in most cases you will have another year *after* the year of your review to look for another job.

Not being renewed or being denied P/T can be due to a wide-variety of reasons, some of which you may have control of (e.g., non-production of research) and some of which you may not have control of (e.g., funding to support your academic program has dried up). As such, and even if you are going through a grievance procedure, if you are staying in academia you should immediately start looking for another job as soon as you find out your P/T is going to be denied. Even if your grievance turns out positive, you still may want to leave the University. Also, because grievance procedures can take several months, if you wait until the outcome of the grievance procedures to start looking for another job, you may miss one or more academic hiring cycles. Maybe most importantly, not getting P/T or a contract renewal can lead to a wide range of emotional responses for you. Sometimes it is better to move on and work to have a fresh start somewhere else. Chapter 9 has a section just on this.

Despite the last two paragraphs, Universities today work very hard to make sure, as much as possible, to put checks and evaluations in place that will help you be successful when you go up for P/T. Believe me, universities do not *want* to deny faculty P/T, because these outcomes can significantly impact not only the faculty involved, but also the department, the other faculty, and students in that department. So, the best you can do is work hard, listen to your mentors, stay in touch with your Department Chair, and put together the best portfolio you can.

Your Portfolio

In most cases, your P/T portfolio, which is sometimes called a 'dossier', is a collection of documents the P/T committee and the various decision-makers will use in determining whether to renew your contract or give you promotion and tenure. In general, your portfolio should give evidence of your performance, productivity, impact, and the quality of your accomplishments during your time as a faculty member. As such, the reviewers of your portfolio are going to be looking for evidence in four general areas:

    1. Evidence of an exemplary level of accomplishment in either research or teaching, depending on the mission of the Institution;

2. Evidence of professional conduct conducive to a collegial work environment;
3. Evidence of specialization that is germane to your Department and Institution;
4. Evidence that indicates a commitment to maintaining and/or elevating your level of research, teaching, and service in the future[95].

As such, each university has specific items required for your portfolio that will be used to probe the four areas above, so you'll need to ask for guidance very early in your time as a faculty member as to what documents and items will be required for your portfolio. Within your portfolio, there will be documents you put in and there will be documents the University puts in. Certainly, the only thing you can control is what you put in your portfolio, and that's what this section will focus on. The good news is that while each university has different requirements for documents to include in your portfolio, there are usually some basic documents most Universities will require.

> **Info to Know – 8.2**
> **Basic Documents You Will Likely Put in Your P/T Portfolio**
> 1. An updated CV
> 2. Narrative impact statement regarding your research, teaching, funding, and service (usually no more than 3-5 pages long).
> 3. Copies of published papers
> 4. Copies of submitted/funded grants
> 5. Summary tables of teaching, research, funding, and service activities

Given the P/T evaluation will focus on your accomplishments in teaching, research, and service, your portfolio will contain some type of summary of your accomplishments. Certainly, you will have to provide a current copy of your CV[96] and copies of any publications you've had during your time as a faculty member. In many Universities, to keep the portfolios from being huge, you are asked to provide summary tables of the courses you've taught, with these tables also providing basic information about each course like the number of students and your overall average class evaluation. Additionally, you'll be asked to provide summaries of your research, fund development, and service activities. In many instances, some of the summary information may duplicate at least partially what you have in your CV and that's okay. If the University asks for it, give it to them. However, the most important

---

[95] These came out of notes from the many P/T Committee workshops I attended at Texas A&M. The four categories aren't original to me, but the original source was likely one of the four Deans of Faculty I worked with at Texas A&M.
[96] I've provided an example CV as a model (see Example 8.1). If you've read Book 1 in this series, you're familiar with our example academic Katherine D. Whitt. Katherine continues to provide examples for this book – but of course, since she's now had the job for five years (in Book 1), her CV is a bit more extensive!

document you'll be asked to provide is a narrative summary of your work at the University with an emphasis on your impact as a scholar. Overall, all these documents must be as perfect as possible and factually correct. When you have it completed, theoretically the portfolio will represent your career so far as an academic, and as such, the review committees and decision makers will look at it as your representation of what has occurred. That's why it is so important to make sure the portfolio is as accurate as possible. You do not want reviewers to find any misstatements or omissions.

Tips on your CV (example 8.1): All academics have a CV[97] and more than likely, you've also had to keep that CV updated during your time as a faculty member because many universities require faculty to turn in an updated CV every year with their annual evaluation reports. But in preparing for your review, you need to pull out your CV and look at it carefully. You must make sure every item listed on your CV, titles, dates, and co-author names, are exactly correct with no misrepresentations regarding what you have done or accomplished. In essence, you want to make sure anyone could pick up your CV and if they wanted to, confirm every item on your CV by other means. It is your responsibility to be sure that every item on your CV is clear and correct.

I've seen issues arise on P/T committees over the past several years regarding the role a faculty member played within research grants that are listed on the CV. So many research grants now are collaborative and many of us may not only be the Principal Investigator (PI) on grants, but also are probably co-investigators or collaborators on other grants. When you list funding on your CV, you must be very clear about what *your role* was on the grant as well as the percent effort you exerted on the grant. If you leave your role off, you leave it up to the search committee to determine your role. If they can't easily figure out what you did, you stand the chance of losing credit for grant activity.

> ### *Critical P/T Process Point – 8.2*
> ### *Accuracy and Full Descriptions Matter*
>
> *It is critical that your CV is an up-to-date and <u>accurate</u> reporting of what you've done as a faculty member. Check all the entries to make sure they are as accurate as possible.*
>
> *Also, be clear as to your role on all multi-investigator activities like grants and papers. You will need to indicate what you did on each and how much money you actually brought in (especially with grants).*
>
> *Having an accurate and fully described CV will help the P/T committees and Deciders know exactly how impactful your faculty accomplishments have been.*

---

[97] If you want more information on developing your CV, check out Chapter 5 in Book 1 of this series.

For example, in reviewing CVs as part of evaluation packets, candidates will often list large grants they are on (multiple millions of dollars) and will leave off their role, especially if it is a minor role, in the hopes of getting more credit for the grant. Heck, it does look good to list a multiple million dollar grant on your CV. However, in most cases, the actual responsible investigators for these large grants can be easily found through a quick online search, so reviewers can quickly find out what role you played on that grant. If you played a minor role on a grant, or even worse, are not listed in the investigator list, and you did not indicate that on your CV, this omission will raise multiple red flags with the reviewers. So, save yourself trouble and list exactly what your role was on each funded grant, even if your role was fairly minor. And if you aren't the PI on the grant, list the name of the person who was PI. Believe me, getting some credit for a grant by being honest about your involvement is a lot better than getting no credit and raising suspicion about your honesty because you left off your actual role on your CV.

One last item about your CV. I've yet to meet an academic that thinks their CV is as extensive as they would like. However you feel about the length of your CV, resist the temptation to add fluff to your CV to make it look bigger. Yes, you can list every guest lecture you've done at your University and/or every individual class session you've taught, but these types of items are not going to add substantially to your CV. All the 'stuff' you list isn't going to matter if you don't publish, develop funding, and teach well. So, resist the temptation to throw everything into your CV to make it look bigger than it is.

I know some academics take great pride in the length of their CV which is sad because in the end, it's not about the length of the CV, it's about the substance of what you've done and the impact you've had. Remember your CV is a record of your academic life and in the end, review committees are looking for substantial contributions in research, funding, and teaching, with proof you are a good department/professional citizen in service. Don't make it harder for your review committee to review your portfolio by making them dig through extraneous information.

When it comes to your CV, make sure everything is as clear and accurate. Additionally, make sure you list all your accomplishments on your CV that show your impact on your profession. Managing your CV on a regular basis will pay dividends when your portfolio is reviewed.

Example 8.1 (this is a CV from a fictitious person!)

Katherine D. Whitt, PhD
Curriculum Vitae

Make sure your CV is as accurate and up-to-date as possible!

I. Contact Information:
Department of Kinesiology
Metropolitan Academic University
Chicago, IL 60637
(847) 555-1212 (office)
(515) 555-1212 (cell)
email: WhittKD@mau.edu
web: https://en.wikipedia.org/wiki/Katherine_Whitt

II. Education and Training:

School	Degree	Yr of Degree
Midway High School	Diploma	May 2004
Southeast University	B.S. Exercise Science Minor: Mathematics	May 2009
Northeast University	M.S. Exercise Science	August 2011
Midwest University	PhD Kinesiology	May 2015
Northwest University	Post-doctoral Fellowship	August 2017

III. Professional Experience and Qualifications

A. Positions
  2008-2009 Southeast University Athletic Trainer Women's Basketball
  2009-2010 Northeast University Athletic Trainer Track / Cross-Country
  2010-2011 Northeast University Graduate Teaching Assistant Physical Education/Activity Program
  2011-2013 Midwest University, Graduate Teaching Assistant
  2013-2015 Midwest University, Research Teaching Assistant (Dr. Warren, Supervisor)
  2015-2017 Northwest University, Division of Physiology, NIH funded post-doctoral fellowship (Dr. John Forsith-Smythe, supervisor)
  2017-current Metropolitan Academic University, Assistant Professor

B. Honors and Awards
  2009 – Southeast University, Outstanding Undergraduate Major, Exercise Science
  2011 – Northeast University, Outstanding Graduate Teaching Assistant, Health and Kinesiology
  2014 – American Physiological Society, EB Conference Travel award
  2014 – Elected Student-Representative to the Board, Midwest American College of Sports Medicine

Example 8.1, p2 (continued)

    2016 – American Physiological Society, EB Conference Travel award
    2020 – American College of Sports Medicine, Fellow
    2021 – Metropolitan Academic University, Outstanding Young Faculty member.

C. Professional Society Memberships
    2008-current American College of Sports Medicine
    2008-2009 – Southeast Regional American College of Sports Medicine chapter
    2009-2011 – Northeast Regional American College of Sports Medicine chapter
    2011 – current – American Physiological Society
    2011-2015 – Midwest Regional American College of Sports Medicine chapter
    2015-current – Northwest Regional American College of Sports Medicine chapter

D. Professional / Clinical Certifications and Registrations
    2007 – current American Red Cross – Basic First Aid and CPR
    2011 – Certified Strength and Conditioning Specialist, National Strength and Conditioning Association
    2015 – Certified Clinical Exercise Specialist, American College of Sports Medicine

E. Other Relevant Training
    Spring 2015 – University Course Construction and Delivery workshop – conducted by Midwest University Graduate Programs office
    Fall 2016 – NIH and NSF Grant Writing workshop – conducted by Grants Central Development
    Spring 2018 – University Best Teaching Practices workshop, Metropolitan Academic University, Teaching Development Center
    Fall 2020 – Teaching Large Sections, Metropolitan Academic University, Teaching Development Center

IV. Research:
  A. Grantsmanship and Fund Development
    1. Funded grants and contracts
      2009 – Southeast University, Dept. of Exercise Science Student travel award - $350. (for attendance at SEACSM meeting)
      2011 – Northeast University Student travel award - $200. (for presentation at TACSM meeting)
      2014 – Midwest University College Student Research grant - $500 – *"The role of hip angle in determining ACL reinjury rates"*
      2015 – Midwest University College Student Research grant - $1000 – *"Turf rebound effect on soccer ACL injuries in the Big 12"*
      2016 – American Physiological Society – Travel award - $1200 (for attendance at EB conference)
      2017 – Metropolitan Academic University – Young Faculty Pilot award - $50,000.

Example 8.1, p3 (continued)

Your role on grants needs to be clear!

2018 – 2023 – Co-investigator, NIH NIHMS R01-8790 – *Functional analysis of protein variants in mental health status in group homes.* ($1.25 million direct costs; $1.92 million total costs). Director of protein variant core facility. (IM Smart, PI)
2019 - 2022 – NIH NIAMS – R15-34785 – *Causal biological mechanisms of elderly falls* ($450,000 direct costs, $675,000 total costs) Principal Investigator
2021 – 2024 – NIH NIDDK – R21-8734 – *The role of calsequestrin 1 in elderly falls* ($100,000 direct costs, $150,000 total costs) Principal Investigator

2. Unfunded grants and contracts

Showing unfunded grants shows your efforts!

2008 – University student travel award (Southeast University, College of Human Sciences)
2010 – Northeast University Student Research grant – *"Lower back injury rates in volleyball players"*
2015 – National Institutes of Health, NIDDK F32 – *"Genetic variation associated with type II diabetes incidence"*
2016 – American Physiological Society – Porter Minority Fellowship grant
2017 – NIH NIAMS K00 award – *Biological mechanisms of Falls* (unfunded)
2018 – NIH NIDDK R21 – *Protein recognition of skeletal muscle* (unfunded)
2019 – NIH NIHMS R01 – *Protein variants associated with aging* (unfunded)

B. Pending grants (as of Aug. 5, 2021)
- National Institutes of Health, NIDDK R01 – *"Efficacy of physical training based on genotype in reducing fall rates in the elderly"* Total = $1.95 million (submitted June 6, 2022)

C. Publications
   1. Books and invited chapters
   Forsith-Smythe, JB and KD Whitt. *Chapter 13 - Fall prevention in elderly populations through social media interaction.* In: Modern Techniques of Orthopedic Treatments. CM Dunwright (ed). Presyncopal Publishing, 2016.

   Whitt, KD. *Chapter 39 – Systems genomics of fall prevention in elderly.* In: Routledge Handbook of Sport and Exercise Systems Genetics. JT Lightfoot, M Hubal, S Roth (eds). Routledge, 2019.

   2. Peer – reviewed articles (*indicates student author)
   Cano, AI, GR Fuller*, SZ Scotty*, KD Whitt. *Integrating psychological and physiological data to predict elderly fall rates.* Science News. 78(12): 1596-1600, 2021.

   Granados, JZ*, H Vellers, AC Letsinger*, B Briedenbach, KD Whitt. *Clinical guidelines in applying arginine metabolism findings from elite athletes to elderly patients.* Medicine and Science in Sports and Exercise. 53(8): 829-838, 2021.

   Fuller, GR*, B Bridenbach*, AC Letsinger*, JZ Granados*, H Vellers, KD Whitt. *Misfolding of protein resulting from genomic variation in the heat shock protein 90.* Cell. 156(3): 598-611, 2021.

Example 8.1, p4 (continued)

Letsinger, AC*, B Bridenbach* JZ Granados*, GR Fuller*, KD Whitt. *Metabolome metabolites associated with increased fall risk in the elderly.* Journal of Applied Physiology. 128(1): 154-163, 2021.

Scotty, SZ*, AC Letsinger*, JZ Granados*, AI Cano, KD Whitt. *Mental acuity of elderly is improved with fall training and regular physical activity.* Biological Psychology. 110(11): 1256-1263, 2020.

Granados, JZ*, AC Letsinger*, AI Cano, GR Fuller*, KD Whitt. *Metabolism of arginine leads to an increased muscle strength in elite female rowers.* British Journal of Sports Medicine. 55(9): 897-905, 2020.

Fuller, GR*, SZ Scotty*, JZ Granados*, AI Cano, KD Whitt. *Chaperone protein involvement in destabilizing lumbar muscle architecture with aging.* PLoS One. 15(2): e0211460. 2020.

Whitt, KD, GF Fuller*, SZ Scotty*, JZ Granados*, AI Cano. *A transbiological model of fall prevention in elderly patients.* Journal of Theoretical Biology. 450(7): 94-102, 2019.

Scotty, SZ*, GF Fuller*, AI Cano, KD Whitt. *Fall prevention training improves physical activity affect state in elderly.* Journal Applied Psychology 126(9): 1029-1038, 2019.

Fuller, GF*, Scotty, SZ*, AI Cano, KD Whitt. *Calsequestrin 1's role in stabilizing lower lumbar indices.* Physiological Genomics. 14(8): 452-463, 2019.

Scotty, SZ*, AI Cano, KD Whitt. *Anxiety reduction with fall prevention training in older populations.* Journal Applied Psychology. 104(3): 345-352, 2019.

Whitt, KD, CR Dombsky, JP Forsith-Smythe. *Proteome associated with fall incidence in the elderly.* Journal of Applied Physiology. 125(5): 815-822, 2018.

Whitt, KD, TL Turner, WR Gossage, JP Forsith-Smythe. *Fall prevention training reduces mortality in older populations.* Medicine and Science in Sports and Exercise. 50(4): 563-570, 2018.

Whitt, KD, TL Turner, WR Gossage, JP Forsith-Smythe. *Genomic variants associated with fall prevalence in the elderly.* Journal of Athletic Training. 54(2): 758-763, 2017

Turner, TL, KD Whitt, CR Dombsky, JP Forsith-Smythe. *SLC4A3 is associated with fall loss and balance in the elderly.* Annals of Improbable Research. 23(4): 545-553, 2017.

Whitt, KD, FA Wojteski, GE Warren. *Turf hardness effect on incidence of ACL injuries.* Journal of Sport Science. 15(2): 235-243, 2015.

3. Articles in review / preparation (as of Aug. 5, 2021)

Granados, JZ*, AC Letsinger*, B Bridenbach*, KD Whitt. *Arginine metabolism is slowed in circadian clock degredation.* Frontiers in Neuroscience. *(in second review).*

Show ms in review and prep in a separate section

Example 8.1, p5 (continued)

Bridenbach, B*, AC Letsinger*, JZ Granados*, KD Whitt. *Development of an elderly rodent molecular model to simulate human falls.* Journal of Biomedical Engineering. *(in second review).*

Letsinger, AC*, JZ Granados*, B Briedenbach*, KD Whitt. *Evolution of the T>C variant in the heat shock protein 90.* PLoS One *(in initial review)*

Whitt, KD, JZ Granados*, AC Letsinger*, B Briedenbach*, GF Fuller, SZ Scotty, AI Cano. *The multiple facets of balance control and translation to clinical practice.* Frontiers in Public Health. *(in initial review)*

Briedenbach, B*, JZ Granados*, AC Letsinger*, KD Whitt. *The microbiome communicates with the balance system through intermediate metabolites.* *(in preparation)*

Letsinger, AC*, B Briedenbach*, JZ Granados*, KD Whitt. *Bacteria in a giant mech-suit: control and determination.* *(in preparation)*

4. Non-peer reviewed publications

Whitt, KD. *Decreasing falls: it's all in the balance.* Northeast Dispatch (newspaper). June 5, 2017

5. Abstracts and Presentations

Granados, JZ*, AC Letsinger*, B Bridenbach*, KD Whitt. *Arginine metabolism is slowed by circadian clock degradation.* Experimental Biology, Indianapolis, IN, 2021.

Bridenbach, B*, AC Letsinger*, JZ Granados*, KD Whitt. *Development of an elderly rodent molecular model to simulate human falls.* Experimental Biology, Indianapolis, IN, 2021.

Cano, AI, GR Fuller*, SZ Scotty*, KD Whitt. *Integrating psychological and physiological data to predict elderly fall rates.* American College of Sports Medicine, San Francisco, 2020.

Granados, JZ*, H Vellers, AC Letsinger*, B Briedenbach, KD Whitt. *Clinical guidelines in applying arginine metabolism findings from elite athletes to elderly patients.* American College of Sports Medicine, San Francisco, CA, 2020.

Fuller, GR*, B Bridenbach*, AC Letsinger*, JZ Granados*, H Vellers, KD Whitt. *Misfolding of protein resulting from genomic variation in the heat shock protein 90.* Experimental Biology, San Diego, CA, 2020.

Letsinger, AC*, B Bridenbach* JZ Granados*, GR Fuller*, KD Whitt. *Metabolome metabolites associated with increased fall risk in the elderly.* Experimental Biology, Orlando, FL, 2019.

Scotty, SZ*, AC Letsinger*, JZ Granados*, AI Cano, KD Whitt. *Mental acuity of elderly is improved with fall training and regular physical activity.* American College of Sports Medicine, Orlando, FL, 2019.

> **Example 8.1, p6 (continued)**

Granados, JZ*, AC Letsinger*, AI Cano, GR Fuller*, KD Whitt. *Metabolism of arginine leads to an increased muscle strength in elite female rowers.* American College of Sports Medicine, Orlando, FL, 2019.

Fuller, GR*, SZ Scotty*, JZ Granados*, AI Cano, KD Whitt. *Chaperone protein involvement in destabilizing lumbar muscle architecture with aging.* National Athletic Training Association. Las Vegas, NV, 2019.

Whitt, KD, GF Fuller*, SZ Scotty*, JZ Granados*, AI Cano. *A transbiological model of fall prevention in elderly patients.* Experimental Biology, 2018.

Scotty, SZ*, GF Fuller*, AI Cano, KD Whitt. *Fall prevention training improves physical activity affect state in elderly.* Experimental Biology, 2018.

Fuller, GF*, Scotty, SZ*, AI Cano, KD Whitt. *Calsequestrin 1's role in stabilizing lower lumbar indices.* American College of Sports Medicine, Minneapolis, MI 2018.

Scotty, SZ*, AI Cano, KD Whitt. *Anxiety reduction with fall prevention training in older populations.* American College of Sports Medicine, Minneapolis, MI 2018.

Whitt, KD, TL Turner, WR Gossage, JP Forsith-Smythe. *Fall prevention training reduces mortality in older populations.* American College of Sports Medicine, Denver, CO., 2017.

Whitt, KD, CR Dombsky, JP Forsith-Smythe. *Proteome associated with fall incidence in the elderly.* Experimental Biology, Chicago, IL, 2017.

Whitt, KD, TL Turner, WR Gossage, JP Forsith-Smythe. *Genomic variants associated with fall prevalence in the elderly.* National Athletic Training Association, Houston, TX, 2017.

Turner, TL, KD Whitt, CR Dombsky, JP Forsith-Smythe. *SLC4A3 is associated with hair loss and balance in the elderly.* Experimental Biology, 2017.

Whitt, KD, TL Turner, WR Gossage, JP Forsith-Smythe. *Genomic variants associated with soft tissue injury.* Experimental Biology. San Diego, CA, 2016.

Whitt, KD, GE Warren. *Stretching program including plyometrics reduces ACL injury in female athletes.* American College of Sports Medicine. San Diego, CA, 2015.

Whitt, KD, GE Warren. *Stretching program including plyometrics reduces ACL injury in female athletes.* American College of Sports Medicine. San Diego, CA, 2015.

Warren, GE, MJ Smoteski, KD Whitt. *Anatomical predictors of female ACL injury rates.* Midwest ACSM, Boyne Mountain, MI, January 2014.

Example 8.1, p7 (continued)

Whitt, KD, MJ Smoteski, GE Warren. *Plyometric stretching exposure effect on ACL injury rates.* American College of Sports Medicine. Orlando, FL. 2014.

Warren, GE, MJ Smoteski, KD Whitt. *Anatomical predictors of female ACL injury rates.* Midwest ACSM, Boyne Mountain, MI, January 2014.

Whitt, KD, MJ Smoteski, GE Warren. *Plyometric stretching exposure effect on ACL injury rates.* American College of Sports Medicine. Orlando, FL. 2014.

Wojteski, FA, MJ Smoteski, KD Whitt, GE Warren. *Stretching and heat effect on ACL injury incidence.* Midwest ACSM. Boyne Mountain, MI, Feb. 2013.

Whitt, KD, MJ Smoteski, FA Wojteski, GE Warren. *Measuring turf hardness on soccer fields.* Midwest ACSM. Boyne Mountain, MI, Feb. 2013.

Whitt, KD, MJ Smoteski, FA Wojteski, GE Warren. *Grass vs. artificial turf rebound and friction coefficient.* American College of Sports Medicine, Indianapolis, IN, May, 2013

Warren, GE, KD Whitt, FA Wojteski. *ACL injury incidence in female soccer players.* Midwest ACSM meeting. Boyne Mountain, MI, Feb. 2012.

Whitt, KD, GZ Forner. *Walkability of grocery store parking lot structures.* Mid-Atlantic ACSM meeting, Hersey, PA, Nov. 2011.

6. Invited Talks and Keynotes

Iowa State, Department of Kinesiology. *I can dance, but then I fall down: the environment and genetics.* August 2021.

University of Kentucky, Department of Exercise Science and Physiology Seminar. *Can your genes make you fall down?* March, 2020.

University of Swansea, Wales. Departmental Seminar. *Snow on the head and falls: preventing injury in seniors.* January, 2019.

Southeast University Exercise Science Departmental Seminar. *Artificial turf, ACLs, and Post-docs: Science in the field.* Young Alumni Award, May 2016.

Example 8.1, p8 (continued)

V. Teaching:
A. Undergraduate Courses (overall class evaluation score: 4=Outstanding; 1=Poor, with departmental mean in brackets)

Northeast University
- Fall 2010 – Beginning Racquetball (2 sections; 3.57, 3.75)
- Fall 2010 – Walk, Jog Run (2 sections: 3.6, 3.34)
- Strength Training (1 section: 3.97)
- Spring 2011 – Beginning Racquetball (2 sections: 3.43, 3.75)
- Exercise Physiology Lab (2 sections: 2.9, 3.45)

Midwest University
- Fall 2011 – Exercise Physiology Lab (4 sections: 3.5, 3.65, 3.43, 3.78)
- Spring 2012 – Beginning Bowling (2 sections: 3.24, 3.56)
- Exercise Physiology Lab (2 sections: 3.65, 3.72)
- Fall 2012 – Exercise Physiology Lab (4 sections: 3.48, 3.74, 3.78, 4.0)
- Spring 2013 – Beginning Bowling (2 sections: 3.42, 3.65)
- Exercise Physiology Lab (2 sections: 3.92, 3.83)
- Fall 2013 – Exercise Physiology lecture (team-taught with Dr. Warren; 1 section: 3.22)

Metropolitan Academic University
- Fall 2017 – Exercise Physiology (2 sections: 3.4, 3.78, [3.6])
- Spring 2017 – Exercise Prescription (1 section: 3.3, [3.55])
- Fall 2018 – Exercise Physiology (2 sections: 3.6, 3.4, [3.48])
- Spring 2018 – Exercise Prescription (1 section: 3.4, [3.5])
- Fall 2019 – Exercise Physiology (2 sections: 3.22, 3.65, [3.53])
- Spring 2019 – Exercise Prescription (1 section: 3.5, [3.48])
- Fall 2020 – Exercise Physiology (2 sections: 3.5, 3.9, [3.62])
- Spring 2020 – Exercise Prescription (1 section: 3.6, [3.4])
- Fall 2021 – Exercise Physiology (2 sections: 3.55, 3.83, [3.64])
- Spring 2021 – Exercise Prescription (1 section: 3.8, [3.68])

B. Graduate Courses
- Spring 2017 – Advanced Exercise Physiology (1 section: 3.78, [3.55])
- Spring 2018 – Advanced Exercise Physiology (1 section: 3.6, [3.5])
- Spring 2019 – Advanced Exercise Physiology (1 section: 3.4, [3.48])
- Spring 2020 – Advanced Exercise Physiology (1 section: 3.85, [3.4])
- Spring 2021 - Advanced Exercise Physiology (1 section: 3.9, [3.68])

C. Doctoral Students (completed)
- Sarah Z Scotty – *Psychological protection of physical training to prevent falls in the elderly.* 2021
- Greg F Fuller – *Genomic variants functionally associated with increased falls in the elderly.* 2021

Example 8.1, p9 (continued)

VII. Professional Service:

A. International, National, and Regional
2021-2023 – President-Elect, New England ACSM
2018-2021 – Member, Grant Review Committee, American College of Sports Medicine
2018-2020 – Executive Board, New England ACSM
2018-current – Manuscript reviewer for:
  Medicine and Science in Sports and Exercise (n=10 articles)
  Journal of Applied Physiology (n=3 articles)
  Exercise and Sport Science Reviews (n=4 articles)
  Journal of Athletic Training (n=9 articles)
2016-2017 – Member, Student Awards Committee, American Physiological Society
2015-2016 – Member, Student Advisory Board, Midwest ACSM

B. State
2020 – Member, New York State Kinesiology Curriculum Standards Committee
2009 – Student representative, Alabama Athletic Trainer Association

C. University
2018-2021 – Metropolitan Academic University – Human Subjects Committee
2010-2011 – Treasurer, Northeast University Graduate Student Organization
2013-2014 – Secretary, Midwest University Graduate Student Organization
2014-2015 – President, Midwest University Graduate Student Organization
2016-2017 – Vice-President, Northwest University Post-doctoral Fellow Organization

D. College
2020-current – Faculty Senator, College of Allied Health Science
2019 - 2020 – Member, College of Allied Health Science Graduate Curriculum committee
2015 – Student Member, Search Committee, Dean of Health and Human Services

E. Department
2019-2020 – Chair, Department Graduate Curriculum committee
2018-2021 – Member, Department Environment and Diversity Committee
2018 – Member, Athletic Training search committee
2008-2008 – President, Southeast University Exercise Science Student Organization
2017 – Student Member, Search Committee, Assistant Professor in Exercise Science, Northwest University

F. Community
2021 – Twitter series aimed at fall prevention
2020 – Newspaper/web series on Fall prevention – Greater New York Eagle
2019 – Speaker, Greater New York Library system "Meet the Experts" Seminar
2015-2016 – Speaker, Northwest Community Center (Four talks on "Ways to Maintain Joint Health")

> **Example 8.1, p10 (continued)**
>
> **VII. Statement of accuracy and authenticity**
> This statement of accuracy and authenticity certifies that all the information in this CV is accurate and represents the education, experiences, and accomplishments of Katherine D. Whitt.
>
> Date: 8/5/2021   *Katherine D. Whitt*

The Summary and Impact Statement: Probably the most important document you'll be asked to provide in your review portfolio is a written narrative summarizing your time as a faculty member. One of the newer trends in many universities is to ask you to write this narrative in the context of the 'impact' you've had in each area (example 8.2). This 'impact' statement is usually brief by academic standards, in many cases being limited to 2-5 pages in length. This impact statement, because you are writing about your work and achievements, is often hard to write because it feels like you are bragging as you write it. In my experience, most academics leave this statement to the very end or write very weak impact statements because they do not like talking about themselves. While I appreciate and empathize with how hard it is to write this type of document, as someone coming up for P/T, you need to get over it. In many cases, your impact statement may be one of the most important documents you've written to this point in your career, and as such, you need to approach the writing of this document because your job depends on it. Just because the subject of the impact statement is 'you' and the impact of your work, it should not discourage you from writing the strongest possible document.

> **Critical P/T Process Point – 8.3**
> *Your Impact Statement is the Most Important Document in Your Portfolio*
>
> *While tough to write, understand that your Impact Statement is a critical document to help reviewers <u>understand</u> how your activities as a faculty member fit together to represent your total activities as a faculty member. You can think of your Impact Statement as providing an overall picture of your 'academic furniture' you've been assembling. Because of its importance, remember that the Impact Statement is an overview and not an item-by-item list. Work to make the Impact Statement read well and show the importance of your work as a faculty member.*

As you develop this impact statement, some of the guidelines you used to write your original job application letter should also be used. You must remember since the reviewers will have your CV, you do not need to list specific items from your CV. One of the reasons for this impact statement in your portfolio is to help your reviewers 'tie-together' the accomplishments listed on your CV, i.e., help the reviewers understand how the things on your CV 'fit together' to fulfill your research, teaching and service obligations. Besides providing context for your work for the reviewers, the impact statement also allows you to describe your production over time, the quality of your scholarship/teaching, and the impact your work has had. Additionally, just like in your job application letter, you need to explain any difficulties you've faced or gaps that may show in your CV during your time as a faculty member. The tone of your writing for the impact statement should be factual and not come off as complaining or whining, but rather straight-forward 'this is what happened, this is how I responded, and this was the result' type of approach.

Your impact statement will be broken into four sections that cover research, teaching, service, and a summary. If you have room, you can also put a short introductory section that will set the overall context including the workload requirements of your position. Within each of these sections, you want to cover your major accomplishments (your impact), how you've learned and grown (your trajectory), and how this all fits into a larger package (your future promise). As such, in each section, you want to focus on your production over time, the quality of your work, and the impact of your work. If you composed a teaching philosophy and/or research statement/philosophy for your job application package, these are perfect documents from which to start the appropriate sections in your impact statement.

The research section of your impact statement will include both your fund development activities (if they were related to research) and your research production. Remembering what we covered in Chapter 5 regarding the qualitative evaluation of your research, remember that you will need to orient the reviewer as to the context of your science. As such, your research section should start with a brief statement regarding your research focus (see example 8.2). You can then cover your various funding efforts and experiments and how they relate to the fulfillment of your research focus. In this way, the reviewers can tie the scholarly products listed in your CV with how you believe they each have fulfilled your research focus. Further, if you have any data regarding your impact on science, this is the place to mention it. How many citations have you had, what is your H-index, and what are the impact factors of the journals you have published in or reviewed for?

Example 8.2 – Sample P/T Impact Statement

Tenure and Promotion Statement of Dr. Katherine D. Whitt, August 5, 2021

Overview: I arrived at Metropolitan Academic University (MAU) in the Fall of 2017 with an appointment in the Department of Kinesiology. While my research focus has been on the factors – both biological and environmental – that lead to lower extremity injury, my assigned teaching focus has been on Exercise Physiology and Prescription, both at the undergraduate and graduate level. Further, my service activities within the University have concentrated on curriculum, instruction, and compliance efforts, while my professional service activities have been increasing to include leadership roles. Given the expectations of **Associate Professor**, as outlined in the MAU Faculty Guidelines, I believe that the quality of my work, my productivity over my 4.5 years at MAU and the impact of my work on MAU and my profession – all delineated below – demonstrate that I am meeting the expectations of the Associate Professor rank.

Research: As noted above, my research focus has been on biological and environmental factors that lead to lower extremity injury. While this research focus is often thought of in narrow terms (e.g. pick a factor and study it), our findings have led to considering this area in more holistic terms. Specifically, when I arrived at MAU, my research was transiting from 'built-environment' factors that are involved in falls and lower extremity injuries (e.g. types of surfaces), to biological factors that may be associated with a higher fall rate. As such, we have identified several genetic factors, that when present in an individual, predispose them to a higher incidence of falls. Having this rudimentary information has allowed us to develop specific training programs, using both physical and mental training, that reduce the incidence of falls in all individuals across various population (e.g. young, elderly). In essence, using genomic information, we can customize training to fit the individual. Further, we have continued to do in-depth studies of the mechanisms of how these genetic factors influence fall rates, with the hope that this knowledge will allow us to provide even better training in the future. Interestingly, as an instance of serendipity arising from some of my collaborations on campus with human performance psychologists, one of my graduate students became very interested in the potential psychological benefits – especially in an elderly population – that might arise after they experienced our customized fall prevention training. As a result, we have found that our genomically informed customized training approach also provides significant positive psychological benefits, including an increase in confidence which subsequently increases the individual's physical activity level. As a result, our efforts to understand the factors that lead to lower extremity injury and falls, has allowed us to not only better understand the potential genetic and environmental mechanisms at play, but has also been the springboard to our development of customized fall prevention training which provides large psychological benefits AND increases physical activity in our subjects.

Details of my lab's scholarly production during my time at MAU are detailed in my CV. Briefly, while at MAU, I and my lab have published 14 peer-reviewed articles and one book chapter, with either myself or one of my students

Example 8.2, p2 (continued)

being first author on each of these studies. This is an average of 3.11 articles per year which is greater than the expectation for Associate Professors at MAU (2 articles/year) detailed in our College's Faculty expectations guidelines. Basic metrics of quality indicate that in general, our articles have been published in journals that have high impact factors (average impact factor = 5.45). Given that the median impact factor in the Sport Science journals (where most of my publications are found) equals 1.863 (source, InCite Journal Citation Reports), the average impact factor of journals my publications are in was 2.9 times higher than the median, suggesting that our publications are of high quality. While citation rates often lag behind publications by 2-3 years, the total non-self-citations of our articles during my time at MAU has been 224 which averages out to 49.8 citations per year, with my h-index currently standing at 8, which is a high percentage of my current total publications (n=16). I expect that our citation rates as well as my h-index will grow with time. While there are no guidelines which to compare our citation rates/h-index against, it is worth noting that the current average h-index of the Associate Professors in our College at MAU is 7.8 which suggests that my publications are having a similar impact in my discipline as compared to other faculty at the Associate Professor rank in my College.

Another indication of our lab's progress is our development funding to support our research program. Initially, I used my start-up funds to purchase equipment and pay doctoral student stipends. My initial project results, as well as data I collected previously, were the foundation for my MAU Young Faculty Pilot award. This award allowed me to conduct several studies that formed the basis for my unsuccessful grant applications in 2017-2019, as well as the basis for both of my successful NIH R15 and R21 grants (both regarding biological and genomic mechanisms triggering falls in the elderly). These successful grants totaled $825,000 and provided funding for my doctoral students, support for my lab, as well as providing $275,000 in indirect costs to the University. Both of these grants were ranked by the study sections below the 10-percentile level indicating broad national support for the ideas in the grants. I have used the results of these grants to submit an NIH R01 and believe that our previous research provides a solid foundation for this R01, as well as future grants.

My research activity, while providing publications and funding that are above the expectations for Associate Professor level (Kinesiology's Expectations document), has also provided important opportunity for cross-disciplinary collaboration within MAU. For example, I continue as a co-investigator on an NIH R01 project (PI: Smart) which is housed in MAU's College of Medicine. Because of these collaborative connections, I am also currently involved as a co-investigator on an effort to develop an NIH-funded Center related to the biological aspects of aging (anticipated submission date: May 2022). Thus, my research is not only having an impact on my scientific discipline, it is allowing me to contribute to cross-disciplinary efforts which are considered a science-marker of excellence by the most recent MAU Strategic Plan (section X.II).

> **Example 8.2, p3 (continued)**
>
> Lastly, my research efforts are impacting my teaching through my direct work with undergraduate, master's, and doctoral students in the lab. During my time at MAU, I have had ten undergraduate students work in my lab group, six of which were in the lab group for at least three years. Of the 10 undergraduates, 8 of those went on to graduate school in various degree programs. Of the six master's students that have been in the lab, four have graduated (two are still in the lab), with two of the graduated students moving on to PhD programs (one in Physical Therapy and one in Biomedical Engineering). Lastly, I have graduated two PhD students (Scotty, Fuller) with both landing post-doctoral research fellowships, and one (Scotty) recently accepting a tenure-track position at an R2-University. Additionally, I currently have three doctoral students at various stages of their programs (Letsinger, Granados, and Bridenbach) and generally add one doctoral student per year to the lab. While my work with the students in my lab bridges my teaching (below) and my research efforts, the progression of my lab students onto further graduate degrees and eventual faculty positions is another indication of not only the impact of my scholarship, but also of my teaching.
>
> In summary, my research program has shown indices of production over time, quality, and impact through the number of publications, the quality of the journals they were published in, as well as through the number of citations they've garnered. Further, the impact of my science can be directly seen in the amount of external funding that I've been awarded as well as in the number and progression of the students that have been in my laboratory. While research impacts the body of knowledge transiently, the impact of my students on science will be long-lasting, as will be the impact of their students on science.
>
> Teaching: As can be seen in my CV, as well as in the Teaching Summary Table elsewhere in this portfolio, I have been assigned a common 2/2 teaching workload during my first 4.5 years at MAU. The classes I have been assigned to teach have focused on Exercise Physiology and Exercise Prescription at the undergraduate and graduate level. As can be seen, my student classroom evaluations have generally been at or above the departmental mean each semester, with my lowest evaluations occurring early in my time at MAU, with gradual improvement seen across the semesters I've taught. In particular, I believe that the undergraduate Exercise Physiology course, which is a common prerequisite for all of our departmental programs that must be passed before students can progress in their degree plan, shows my skill as a teacher. Because Exercise Physiology is a common prerequisite course, there is a lot of pressure on students to pass the course, which often makes it difficult for a professor to be rigorous in their grading because of potential effects on class evaluations. However, despite ≈10% of my Exercise Physiology students making non-passing grades the first time they take the class, my class evaluations in Exercise Physiology have been consistently at or above the departmental average. I attribute both the improvement in my teaching scores during my time at MAU and my good evaluation scores in the common prerequisite class I teach to several factors. First, my approach to teaching as a 'guide and translator' of the material as well as my basic education philosophies of perennialism and pragmatism, allow me

Example 8.2, p4 (continued)

to be more interactive with the students which translates into a more engaging classroom. Secondly, I believe my continuing improvement has been due primarily to the feedback I've received from peer- and supervisor-evaluations that I've requested every semester. I have appreciated the honest feedback I've received from my colleagues and my Department Chair which has allowed me to try different approaches in class. Lastly, my involvement in the MAU Teaching Groups, as organized by the University Teaching Center, have been invaluable in expanding my teaching network, which has provided valuable feedback and ideas from other faculty. I look forward to continuing the improvement of my teaching using similar mechanisms in the future.

As noted at the end of the Research section, I also believe that 'out-of-the-classroom' teaching is incredibly valuable for many students, and as such, I work to involve undergraduate and graduate students in my lab's research efforts. As noted above, I've had several undergraduate and graduate students in the lab during my 4.5 years at MAU, with most going on to either higher graduate programs or becoming academics themselves. I truly believe that the time I spend with my students out of the classroom has the greatest impact on students and that ultimately, my impact as a researcher and a teacher will be greatest through the teaching and research that my students ultimately do. In that sense, I believe that my teaching efforts, both in and out of the classroom, support the research programs of the department and university by helping train the next generation of researchers and teachers.

Service: I believe strongly that as a faculty member, I should be providing service to both MAU and my profession. However, shortly after arriving at MAU, I was advised that my service activities should be limited over my first 2-4 years at MAU, so that I could establish my teaching and research programs. In general, I have followed that advice and only recently began to take on more service opportunities (which are all listed on my CV). As such, I have begun to establish a professional service record at both the regional and national levels, as well as providing service to my Department and University. In particular, I have recently been elected as President of the New England chapter of the American College of Sports Medicine (NE-ACSM), which I believe portends future service not only in guiding the regional NE-ACSM chapter, but also at the national level. In recognition of my early efforts at professional service (both in leadership and scientific review), I was recently awarded Fellowship in the national American College of Sports Medicine. These are exciting developments and I look forward to helping guide my professional organization in the future.

I also strongly believe that service does not stop when I come on campus. As can be seen from my CV, I am involved in several service opportunities ranging from participation on search committees, to representing the College at the University Faculty Senate, to work on curriculum issues in the department and college, and to work in the research compliance area by being a member of MAU's Human Subjects Committee. These service opportunities give me the opportunity to provide service to my colleagues and provide and develop leadership skills that I can use in the future.

> **Example 8.2, p5 (continued)**
>
> In total, I believe that my service activities provide both service to MAU and my profession, while also allowing me to grow and improve my professional abilities. I believe that these activities will continue to help me be an asset to both MAU and my profession.
>
> Summary: In considering the University, College, and Departmental guidelines for promotion and tenure in research, teaching, and service, I believe that my record shows that I am functioning at the Associate Professor level. The data shows that my research program is productive, is having an impact on my field, and is recognized through the external funding that I have received. My teaching has been judged by students, peers, and supervisors to be excellent, and my production of graduate students and future professionals is a further indication of my teaching skills. Lastly, my service record shows that I am developing as a leader, both within my profession and within MAU, suggesting that I will continue to be a good departmental and professional citizen. In light of my progress in all three of these areas, I believe that the foundation I've established will allow me to continue to function at the level of Associate Professor as I work to develop into a Full Professor.

Many of the same items listed in Chapters 4 and 5 as being indices of research production should be used in this portion of the impact statement because they can quantitatively indicate both *quality* and *impact* of your work. Additionally, if you are starting to do professional research service, such as reviewing manuscripts, serving as an officer of a professional society, or regularly organizing and presenting seminars and symposiums at scientific meetings, these are all factors you should mention as showing you are having an impact on science. Lastly, while it overlaps with teaching, and thus, makes a great segue into your teaching impact statement, any of your students' scholarly products such as abstracts and presentations should be generally described here. If your students are participating in science, those activities show your science impact is not just limited to your contributions, but you are also having impact on your field through your students.

In a similar manner, you can start your teaching impact section with your general area of content and your overall teaching philosophy you developed for your teaching philosophy documents (example 8.2). Your teaching philosophy grounds your impact statement in your teaching context, and allows the reviewers not only to see why you teach the way you do, but sets a great foundation by which to consider the other teaching evidence you are going to present. That 'other' evidence can include classroom evaluations, peer evaluations of your teaching, supervisor evaluations of your teaching, and even informal evaluations you may have done.

Good teaching is notoriously hard to evaluate, so you just need to put in as much data as possible that reflects your teaching ability. Make sure you give a general overview of the efforts you've made to improve your teaching, including any workshops, courses, or other activities you've done to improve. Lastly, if you have any emails, cards, or other laudatory notes from your students, reference those in your impact statement, and make sure you put copies of these notes in your portfolio so the committee can verify the students made those comments.

Even though it shouldn't be a big part of your activities to this point, you'll include a section on service (example 8.2). This section should be your shortest section because as a junior faculty member, your primary focus should be on research and teaching. However, you do need to show you are a good departmental citizen and you've participated in the functioning of the department and your profession, so make sure you address and remark on the impact your service has had. For example, if you've served on the compliance committees, you can talk about the impact of that service on helping expedite and move forward other researchers' projects on campus.

If you're involved in curriculum and instruction committees, you can speak about the impact of the courses you worked to approve. Ideally, every service you do should have some impact and you should not hesitate to explain what you consider that impact to be. Additionally, if you have any data that reflects your service, share that data. For example, if you are reviewing articles for journals, note how many reviews you've done in a specific period. If you are on a compliance committee, put in how many protocols you've reviewed or been lead reviewer on. You are trying to paint a picture for the reviewers as to the importance of your service. While you may not have done much service to this point, you need to make sure you do highlight what you've done and the impact you believe that service has had.

Lastly, you'll need to provide a very short summary section (example 8.2). This section is where you can take a couple of sentences to wrap up and conclude how you see the impact of your time as a faculty member. Maybe more importantly, you should put in a sentence or two about what you perceive your future impact will be if you stay on the same trajectory. Again, don't be shy and don't exaggerate. Just summarize succinctly and you'll be fine.

External Reviewers

As noted earlier, your review documents will probably include evaluations by professionals outside of your University. These so-called 'External Reviewers' will review your portfolio, evaluate your progress as an academic primarily focused on your scholarship, and write a letter of evaluation that is placed in your portfolio. External reviewers are part of the system to try and prevent any positive- or negative-biases regarding your evaluation that may arise from inside your University. Because these reviewers are external to the University and are supposedly free of most biases against you, these external evaluations are given much weight in the review process. For example, when I was Chair of the Departmental P/T Committee several years ago, one flippant sentence in one of five external reviews for one candidate was almost enough to derail this candidate's application for tenure. In fact, that one sentence cost many of us many extra days of effort to get our higher administrators to disregard what was obviously a flippant remark. So, the external reviewer letters play a critical role in your evaluation and as such, are an important part of the P/T process.

> **Critical P/T Process Point – 8.4**
> **External Reviewers**
>
> *External reviewers are a part of most P/T reviews. You will be asked to provide a list of possible external reviewers that do not have a conflict of interest with you (e.g., they haven't worked with you, published with you, studied with you, etc.). This list will be combined with a list from the P/T Committee and your Department Chair. The final list will be a combination of your list and the list from the P/T committee with the Department Chair having final say over the external reviewers selected.*

While you do not have any control over *what* external reviewers say about your portfolio, you do have control over having an excellent scholarly record and portfolio. In most Universities, you will be allowed to suggest names of individuals that could be external reviewers. In most cases, the P/T committee will select half the reviewers from your list and the other half of the reviewers from a list the P/T committee develops. On your list, you will be asked to provide names of individuals in your professional discipline you do not have close ties with, i.e., people you haven't worked with, studied with, and/or published with. Further, these individuals will usually have to be at the same rank or higher than the one you are applying for and at a university that is of a similar type as yours. Thus, if you are going up for Associate Professor and your University is an R1 institute, you'll need to suggest names of individuals in your discipline that are already at the Associate Professor level at an R1 institute.

One of the reasons you must select individuals from universities like yours is these individuals are more likely to have the same workload and research expectations as you do and can speak directly to whether you've met expectations or not. If you are at a Masters Institution, it would be an unfair evaluation for someone at an R1 university to evaluate your portfolio and vice-versa. The rationale is the same for picking individuals that are of the same rank. So, with these stipulations, how do you pick external reviewers?

First, you need to make sure that you believe any reviewers you name can do a fair and unbiased review. In many cases, whether a potential reviewer can do a fair and unbiased review is a subjective determination informed by your acquaintances and experiences with others in your field. During your first five years, pay attention to the other professionals in your field that you interact with at conferences, on committees, and in other professional venues. Your interaction with these people will be a great indication for whether they would be fair and unbiased. In a similar fashion, pick people that have some knowledge of your work already. Again, you must be careful not to pick potential reviewers that have an obvious conflict of interest, but there is usually no stipulation against picking someone you are acquainted with due to professional interactions. In fact, I would encourage you to start to build those networks as soon as you can as a new faculty member, so by the time you come up for review, you'll have a ready list of potential reviewers.

Additionally, while you will not participate in the P/T Committee's external evaluator list determination, you should not hesitate to discuss potential external reviewers with your Department Chair and your mentor(s) *before* you put in your portfolio and the P/T process begins. Not only can these types of discussions help you refine your list of potential evaluators, but they can also help the Chair or your mentor get clarity on individuals that may or may not be on their list and thus, would be on the P/T committee external reviewer list.

Another consideration in picking external evaluators is to know who you do not want as a reviewer. If you know professionals in your field you do not believe would give you an unbiased review or with whom you have other professional or personal disagreements with, you should give this list to the Department Chair or P/T Committee Chair. It is important if you compose a 'do not ask' list of potential evaluators you have solid rationale for the potential elimination of these individuals. For example, as mentioned earlier in this book, as a junior faculty member, I had severe professional and personal disagreements with another professional in the field. When I came up for P/T, I would clearly and non-emotionally share my concerns with

---

Info to Know – 8.4
How to Pick External Reviewers
1. Pick colleagues in your field that you trust will do a fair and unbiased review.
2. Reviewers need to be at a similar type of Institution as yours, as well as at the rank you are being considered for.
3. Use your professional network that you've been developing for potential names of reviewers.

having this individual as a potential external reviewer. While this individual was never asked to review my portfolio, I can only imagine I would have received a very negative and probably nasty evaluation if they had been asked.

Lastly, as you pick external reviewers, accept that one of the ways unbiased reviewers can be recruited is through the promise of confidentiality. So, you will never be able to see the reviews the external reviewers write or discuss with them the reviews they wrote about you. It would be considered unprofessional to ask people who may or may not have reviewed your portfolio about what their review was. There are many evaluations done in academia that are confidential, so just accept that your portfolio external reviews will fall into that same category.

In conclusion, other than putting forward the best portfolio you can, you will have no control over what your external evaluators say about your portfolio. Where you will have some input is who are picked to be external evaluators of your portfolio. So, start making a potential reviewer list, meet and interact with as many professionals as you can to add or subtract from that list, and by the time your portfolio is up for review, you'll have a solid list of potential external reviewers.

Other items in your portfolio: While your CV and your impact statement are the two most common documents found in your P/T portfolio, they are by no means the only documents you may be asked to provide. As noted earlier, you may be asked to develop and submit summary tables of the various areas of your academic life such as teaching evaluations and grant funding applications. While different universities ask for different items in your portfolio, the best thing you can do is to make sure you have documentation for everything you do as an academic.

Shortly after you arrive at your new position, as I mentioned earlier, I would encourage you to immediately set up filing systems, both paper-based and digital, that will allow you to both list and deposit items that directly relate to your duties as a faculty member. Over the course of your duties as a faculty member, you will be given many documents reflecting on your productivity and impact as a faculty member. These items are wide-ranging but include things like classroom evaluations, peer-teaching evaluations, thank you notes from students (yes, you'll get these), and thank you letters for professional service. Whether these items are paper-based or digital, having one place to deposit them is helpful when you develop your portfolio or your annual reviews so you don't have to dig through your files to find these items and so you don't forget items.

In a digital file, for example in a word processing document, list anything you do as a faculty member as soon as you do it. What you put in this document is up to you, but at minimum, put a basic short listing of each item as it occurs so you can remember all you do as a faculty member. This is an approach I personally use and it is amazing how many items I would have otherwise forgotten if I hadn't put them in this summary file. These simple organizational steps will save an incredible amount of time and anxiety as you develop your annual reports and your P/T portfolio[98].

Work / Life Balance

Lastly, I would encourage you, especially as a junior faculty member, to pay particular attention to your work/life balance. The 'life' side of the equation is too often ignored because junior faculty believe they will have a better chance for P/T if they just *focus* on work. I can directly attest to that belief after I put in regular 13-16-hour days as a post-doc and as a junior faculty member. It is too easy to do nothing but work. However, if you do not pay attention to your work/life balance, you will probably sacrifice many relationships or other life enriching opportunities. As a human, your life is not just about work, it's about the totality of the experiences and relationships you have. This balance includes your family, your hobbies, and your faith. You shouldn't ignore any of these just because you are new to academia.

As a junior faculty member, you have worked very hard to obtain a terminal degree. You've possibly completed post-doctoral research, have an esteemed position at an institute of higher education, and you are getting paid a good salary on a regular basis. However, the University is not paying you to sacrifice your life or your well-being. Yes, there are times you'll have to work hard and put in long hours; in this business, that is a given. But now is the time to start living and enjoying your life. If all you do is work long hours without doing anything else, you'll quickly become one-dimensional, boring, and will miss all that life has to offer!

> *Critical P/T Process Point – 8.5*
> *Work / Life Balance*
> *You will not have succeeded if you get P/T and have no work/life balance. Remember that while your career is important, you shouldn't sacrifice relationships, your faith, or other opportunities for professional growth for your job. Sometimes you will have to work long hours; just don't make a habit of it. The University does not own every minute of your day. Besides, 'all work and no play, makes Jack/Jill very dull'!*

---

[98] Since I mentioned and described setting up these systems twice in this chapter, I'm not just being redundant but think these systems are incredibly important. And now I've mentioned them three times….

Taking a break from work will often give you a new perspective on your job, will help you learn and experience new things, which in turn, may help you add to your professional growth. For example, my wife and I once owned a type of stock-car racing team because we both love racing. I spent a lot of time working on the car, going to tracks, racing, and working on the car again. Could I have been working *more* on my research or teaching during that time? Sure, but I wouldn't have had as much fun with my wife and family as I did by racing. Taking a break and doing something fun gave me time to develop and utilize skills necessary for racing, but more importantly, I created deeper relationships with family and friends.

In addition to having fun and being with folks I love and care about by racing, a funny and interesting thing happened. Because of my motorsports experience, I wound up being on a joint NASCAR/ACSM task force on driver safety, my lab developed connections with several NASCAR teams, we started doing driver and pit crew testing, and before I knew it, I had a whole other aspect to my research program.

This new research aspect led to having students in the lab who were interested in the physiology of motorsports, which recently led one of those former students to publishing the first book on the physiology of motorsports![99] Because I made the decision to have work/life balance and do something that I enjoyed, it resulted in an augmentation of my research program and had a significant impact on future students! You never know how and where the pursuit of work/life balance will take you, but you should know you'll miss out on a lot if you don't make time for friends, family, and other interests in your life.

The Take Home Message

Going through the P/T process can be tiring, anxiety-producing, and excruciatingly long. Understanding how the process works and how to best put forward your accomplishments for review can help with the anxiety of the P/T process. Additionally, paying attention to your work/life balance is critical. While work and academia are important, you can't forget there are other phases of life that are just as important. Family, your faith, and your hobbies should never take a back-seat to your career or academia. Remember to learn as much as you can about the process, work hard so you have a great P/T portfolio, but also play and enjoy life to get the most out of your time as a faculty member.

---

[99] *The Science of Motorsport*, from Routledge, October 2018. The author is Dr. David P. Ferguson, now an Assistant Professor at Michigan State University!

9

AFTER PROMOTION/TENURE: WHAT TO DO WHEN THE SMOKE CLEARS AND THE FOG LIFTS

All too quickly, your first five years as a faculty member will come to an end. You will have worked diligently on your research, your teaching, and your service. You will have gone through at least one, if not two comprehensive reviews during those five years. Your academic furniture will be what you built it to be. But what do you do next? What happens next will depend not only on the outcome of your P/T[100] review, but on other factors external to P/T that may affect you personally or professionally.

This chapter is organized around three main themes. The first two themes are fairly obvious: what do you do if you don't get P/T and what do you do if you do get P/T. A third theme is what you do if you decide you want to look for a position in a different University, or even in a different industry. Certainly, while the third theme is tied particularly into the first theme, you may find there are other situations arise that lead you to decide you need to find another position.

Given I'm a positive guy, I'm going to lead with the potential negative outcome and finish up with the other two positive themes. In fact, I would recommend you skip the 'not getting P/T' section and only read that section if you need it.

> **This Chapter:**
>
> What if you don't get promotion and tenure (or contract renewal) 215
>
> What if you have a Positive P/T Outcome? 222
>
> Should you go or stay? 224
>
> Factors to consider when looking for a new job 226
>
> The Take Home Message 233

What if you don't get promotion and tenure (or contract renewal)
I was fortunate my first academic position was in a University that allowed faculty members to go up early and repeatedly for P/T until the end of their fifth year. After encouragement by my colleagues and administration, I did

---

[100] As in past chapters, P/T stands for Promotion and Tenure and includes those up for contract renewals as well!

just that; I went up for P/T early at the end of my third year. I was told I had a strong and positive case, the data in my portfolio seemed to support that conclusion, and indeed, the Department Chair and Dean supported my P/T bid. However, the University P/T Committee did not support me for P/T. When I did not get P/T, I was crushed. Here was an Institution I'd worked so hard for saying I wasn't good enough. It is said that "anger is really love disappointed"[101] and in my case, there was a lot of anger.

It didn't help that the Provost, who I really liked, relayed that while it wouldn't show up in the written documentation, the University P/T Committee just thought I hadn't been at the University long enough to deserve P/T. I was stunned; here I had done everything I was asked, my scholarship record was quantifiably better than most others in my College (even the Full Professors) and yet, an unwritten standard had been imposed on me. As I said earlier, I was lucky I was in an Institution that allowed early P/T review *and* repeated attempts; in other words, I was lucky I wasn't constrained by a 'one and done' approach to P/T many universities have.

While I went back up for P/T the next year and got it, the sting of that first rejection which was the result of unwritten rules I knew nothing about, lasted throughout my time at that University and probably contributed to me moving on from that University three years later. Interestingly, I ran into a similar situation the first time I went up for promotion to Full Professor: Denied. I just wound up recycling the feelings of anger, hurt, and betrayal I had experienced six years earlier which gave me the experience once again of what it is like to work hard, but yet, be told you aren't good enough. Getting denied P/T, no matter when it happens during your career, is still a slap in your face.

As an Administrator, I've also had to deny faculty P/T. While I know it was devastating for those faculty, I also know it was no picnic for me either, or for the other Administrators and P/T Committees that were involved. Certainly, a negative outcome on a P/T review leads to emotional angst not only for the faculty involved, but also to the University involved. The trauma a negative P/T decision can induce is reflected in the huge number of articles written about 'what to do if you get denied P/T' versus the fewer articles written about what do you do if you are successful. For example, just in the *Chronicle of Higher Education* alone, if you do a quick search on 'denial of tenure', you'll find there have been 2,129 articles published in the *Chronicle* since 1989 having something to do with the topic (that's an average of almost 30

---

[101] The quote is from the song "Hole in the World Tonight" by The Eagles which is about the 9/11 attacks. There are several similar quotes in the literature, but I believe this quote is original to this song.

per year). Clearly, not getting P/T can be a difficult blow, and the purpose of this section is to help you figure out what your next steps should be.

Often individuals that have been denied P/T will say or do things that will hurt their job options, their reputations, and their relationships with their colleagues and families. Being denied P/T can invoke the same stages of grief[102] that are seen in any other traumatic life experience: Denial, Anger, Bargaining, Depression, and Acceptance. Understanding you will move through these stages as you emotionally and personally deal with being denied P/T will help you monitor your actions. In my experience, the denial stage moves rapidly because often, you are denied P/T in writing and there is little point in denying it is really happening. The anger stage is the most dangerous for faculty that have been denied P/T because it is natural for any of us that are deeply hurt to lash out or strike back when we are angry. And academics, especially because of their verbal and writing abilities, can lash out in ways that have serious ramifications for their futures.

I once had a colleague that had not received a promotion and I counseled him that it didn't matter what he had done in the past, but it is what he would say and do over the next two years that would determine what people remembered about him. Unfortunately, that faculty member lashed out in anger at many people, and suddenly, someone who had had a great reputation and was thought of a valuable colleague before the review process became someone who was not considered a good colleague and subsequently, hurt their chances for positive references for other positions. As such, the anger stage after a negative P/T review can do the most subsequent damage to your career and needs to be guarded against.

> **Info to Know – 9.1**
> *What to do if you don't get P/T or contract renewal*
> 1. Gather all the information you can; see if you can get copies of the letters from the various P/T committees and Deciders;
> 2. Consider initiating the grievance procedure (optional);
> 3. Get legal representation (optional);
> 4. Begin looking for another job as soon as possible;
> 5. Remain professionally graceful; how you act will determine how your colleagues respond to you;
> 6. Get counseling if you need it.

It is extremely difficult to continue to be 'professionally graceful' after a negative review. However, you must remember while you may not have a future at your current Institution, a new job and collegial relationships – many of

---

[102] These five stages of grief are often known as the Kübler-Ross model which were popularized in Dr. Elisabeth Kübler-Ross' 1969 book *On Death and Dying*.

which that will remain intact regardless of whether you stay at the University or not – can often depend on how you react to a negative review. I'm not advocating suppressing your feelings, anger, and/or disappointment, but I am advising you to work hard to maintain your professional attitude while you are at work.

As advocated in other places in this book, if you have negative emotions you can't deal with by yourself, make use of the counseling services at your University. Your colleagues will often feel sympathy and sometimes empathy for you. However, if you act out, you'll quickly find sympathy turning into either apathy or hostility reflected back at you. Further, while it might be tempting for you to marshal colleagues or even students to your cause, this type of move puts both your colleagues and students in an awkward position because now you're making them choose sides, either your side or the University's side. While colleagues may be empathetic, you must remember they have to work at the University and it is *not* appropriate for you to expect them to burn their bridges for you. Further, while there is a long list of injustices at universities students have helped to overturn, your personal P/T in most cases will not be a systemic injustice students need to get involved in. Once again, being an example of professional grace, even when you have received a negative P/T evaluation, will have greater positive impact on your students and colleagues than if you act out.

Despite how you handle a negative review, the process in most universities is that after a bridge-year, you will have to leave the University. In most cases, if you are on a tenure-track line and get denied P/T, you will be given a year to continue to work, look for other positions, and to allow any appeal/grievance processes to play out. As such, as soon as you receive a negative P/T decision, I would advocate that you start looking for another job immediately.

If you begin the job search immediately, you have a better chance of landing a new position that will start at the beginning of the coming academic year, thus allowing you to skip the awkward bridge year. Given most negative P/T decisions are finalized within the December – March timeframe, getting immediately back onto the job market will allow you to hit the second wave of job postings that usually occur in the January – March timeframe. If you wait to start looking during your bridge year or you wait until any grievance processes are completed, which can often take many months, you run the risk of missing most of the job postings for the current academic year and will be forced to wait until the Fall hiring cycle starts. Waiting this long means you may not land and start a new job for over 12 months.

As I mentioned in Chapter 8, all universities have thorough grievance/review processes for individuals that are denied P/T. These grievance processes are usually handled through a faculty-led grievance committee, and if your University has a faculty-union, it is likely that a union representative will be assigned to you as an advisor. The grievance process is always a stressful and emotionally draining process; however, if you believe that you were treated unfairly during the P/T process or think that the process as conducted was flawed, going through the grievance process will give you another avenue of review for your materials. While the procedures are usually difficult, stressful, and emotionally-draining for everyone involved, grievance proceedings play a valuable role in making sure the University has made the right (or wrong) decision. The grievance process varies markedly between universities, so make sure you have read and understand all the grievance process procedures.

As I mentioned in Chapter 8, you need to find out whether you are allowed representation at the grievance hearings and the extent of the participation your representatives are allowed. While you may balk at paying extra money to have an attorney advise you, again, for your own peace of mind, it does not hurt to have someone on your side who clearly understands the process, is experienced with the grievance process, and someone who can give you calm, clear advice on the process and the findings of that process. It has been my observation most faculty never or rarely deal with a grievance process, so, it is likely if you choose to go through the grievance process, it will be the first time you've experienced such a process. Help yourself out and find an advocate that has experience with the process and understands the process. As mentioned earlier, everywhere I've worked, there's always been at least one attorney in the area that specializes in employment law for university faculty. If you have to go through the grievance process, find that person and consult with them.

If you get a negative P/T decision, you may decide you don't want to go through the grievance process. There is no doubt that even if you take advantage of the bridge year, your relationships with your colleagues, your administrators, and your University will be strained. Thus, many faculty that get negative P/T decisions often look for a job and move on as soon as they can without going through the grievance process. Just know if you have any doubts about the validity of the P/T decision in your case, you should not hesitate to invoke the grievance process.

It is incredibly difficult not to take a negative P/T decision personal because if you are passionate about your teaching and research and you get denied P/T, it's a refutation of all your effort and time. That being said, a negative P/T decision should not define who you are. Get counseling if necessary, maintain your professional grace, start the grievance process, and look for another job. While those four actions may not completely alleviate the emotional sting of what you are going through, you'll be acting to heal yourself while working to keep your professional reputation and career intact.

The flip side of a negative decision

Faculty that have been denied P/T often see administrators as callous and cruel, with little regard for the negative emotions they cause in faculty that are denied P/T. In my experience, no administrator that I have known that had to render a negative P/T decision ever did it lightly or without considerable concern about the individual involved. While those administrators often must take a seemingly hard, non-emotional approach, it is difficult to make a negative P/T decision when you know the turmoil you will cause in an individual's life.

In my years as a Department Chair, there were two instances where I had to make negative P/T decisions. Also, as the Chair of both Department and College P/T Committees, I've had to write negative advisories regarding faculty coming up for P/T. From an administrative standpoint, these are very hard decisions to make. However, administrators are tasked with enforcing the standards the University, College, and Department set for P/T, and so to do their job, they must at times make negative decisions. Additionally, administrators often have access to information others in the decision chain don't have, so their decisions are shaped by all information, not just what the candidate puts into the portfolio. While it may not help your distress, you should understand that at least in every negative P/T case I know of, the administrators involved were often distressed by the turmoil they knew would result from the P/T decision because administrators are human also.

You should also be aware that the administrators often wrestle with negative P/T decisions for several weeks knowing they will need to be prepared for negative behavior from the individual not getting P/T. While administrators would most certainly like to not have to deal with the anger behaviors faculty exhibit when they are denied P/T, administrators usually have clear guidelines as to how they must act, what they can or cannot say, and how they can direct your inquiries.

When you are denied P/T, the University becomes very mindful that any actions on the part of their employees, including your Department Chair and Dean, could cause further justification for a grievance or a lawsuit. That's why you'll often find the administrators you deal with during a P/T denial seem very officious and 'by the book'; they're working to protect themselves and the University. These are all reasons that if you can maintain a professionally graceful attitude during the process, you may find the administrators involved will be more amenable to considering your points, even during a grievance. However, if you have a 'slash and burn' mentality after your negative P/T decision, you should expect the administrators involved will do everything they can to prevent any damage you could do to the morale, environment, and individuals in your Department and College.

Are there positives in not getting tenure? It depends on who you talk to or what you read. Some writers have suggested that there may be positives in not getting P/T. Not being awarded P/T may speed your movement to an institution better suited to your strengths and skills. For example, assume you were employed in an R1 institution that required you to develop a large amount of external funding. However, you found during your first five years you didn't like or have the knack for getting large amounts of funding. A P/T denial could speed your finding a job at a different research institution where funding is a lesser piece of total faculty responsibility.

There are many stories of academics who found they had a better life outside of academia in some other career path.[103] As I noted in book 1 of this series, there are several career paths available to people with PhDs that don't necessarily involve research or teaching. You may find as you ponder what happened during your P/T bid, you would be happier and more fulfilled in a non-faculty job. Finding an institution better suited to your strengths or finding an alternate career path could be the positive that comes out of your P/T denial. As an anonymous professor wrote in *The Chronicle*[104], "After I was denied tenure, I didn't believe my friends and colleagues when they tried to reassure me that things would turn out fine. I could not imagine a scenario in which my professional and personal life would be improved. I am blessed to say that I was mistaken."

Understand that a P/T denial does not define who you are as a professional or as an individual. In fact, it may open career paths you had not considered when you focus on moving through the process of recovering from your P/T denial and seeking further career options.

---

[103] Here's an excellent article to start with to show there are successful careers outside of academia after a tenure denial. From the *Chronicle of Higher Education*, James M. Jasper, "Moving On After You Are Denied Tenure". June 1, 2001.
[104] "Life After Tenure Denial" Peter Ellenbogen. *The Chronicle of Higher Education*, Feb. 03, 2010. You also might want to read the series of articles Peter Ellenbogen wrote while he was going through his tenure denial. There is emotional distress in those articles which is understandable because they were written several years prior to the article quoted above. But once you are through the P/T denial, you can go through the grieving process and move on – often to better situations!

What if you have a Positive P/T Outcome?

Promotion and tenure characterize the accomplishment you have been working on for at least five years, if not longer. After all the time you devoted to preparing documents and then the months of waiting, you finally hear from the Provost. You got it – promotion and tenure! Celebrate, enjoy the moment and share the good news with friends and family!

So, what do you do now? The post-P/T time can give you the opportunity to make sure you've got a healthy work/life balance. If something or someone has been neglected in your personal life, now is the time to address the situation. You'll certainly want to regain a healthy work/life balance so you can continue to nurture your relationships, family, friends, and spiritual faith.

Once you have tenure, your career options begin to open up. Suddenly you will find academic leadership opportunities will become available. However, you have to balance your desire to take on leadership roles against your desire to pursue Full Professorship rank. In most universities, you can stay as an Associate Professor for the rest of your career if you are continuing to contribute to the mission of your Department, College, and University. There are a multitude of reasons why some faculty stay at Associate Professor rank for most of their career. And while you will have additional career growth opportunities as an Associate Professor, the largest career opportunities open once you become a Full Professor. So, while not advocating for one path or the other, you should recognize if you are going to work toward Full Professorship, immediately after P/T is the time to start planning your next promotion.

> **Info to Know – 9.2**
> *If you get P/T or contract renewed*
> 1. Celebrate!
> 2. Start planning for the next rank (Full Professor)!
> 3. Make sure your work/life balance is appropriate.
> 4. Enjoy your new rank!

Whatever path you decide to embark upon after a positive P/T decision, the one thing you don't want to do is disengage and shut down. Unfortunately, some faculty members' research production becomes minimal in the years after P/T. You will certainly have peaks and valleys in your research production over the years, but resist the temptation to rest on your laurels after P/T.

Whether you continue to aggressively build your career or not, you should be aware many universities have now implemented what are called 'post-tenure review processes' that are meant to help faculty continue to be productive over the course of their careers. Post-tenure review processes arose in the mid-90's as a reaction to the perception that many professors, after gaining P/T, became unproductive and just coasted (some used the term 'dead-wood' to describe this stereotype).

While most of the faculty I've known continued to produce after they received P/T, there have been some that decided it was better to coast, or turned their attention elsewhere and just showed up to teach and do little else. In essence, this stereotype of the dead-wood professor became ingrained in legislators' minds and as a result, the post-tenure review process was born.

In most institutions, post-tenure review applies to both Associate and Full Professors and occurs either at a particular time - once every four years is a time course I've seen most frequently - or if a professor falls below a particular production standard. If a post-tenure review is triggered, this review can range from being a fairly simple review of the Professor's work in the past year to a full comprehensive review including the assembling of a portfolio and the use of external reviewers.

If a Professor, after going through this Review is judged to only be minimally productive, they are often put on a multi-year 'work-plan' with regular evaluations of their progress at defined intervals. In the majority of cases, if the Professor doesn't meet his/her work-plan objectives, the University will often pursue termination of some form which can include outright termination or encouraged retirement. While the post-tenure review process is often a long process, it gives the faculty member every chance to rectify their performance issues. Additionally, the post-tenure review process also gives the University an opportunity to remove faculty that have become non-productive.

As was the case with other processes in the University, you may or may not agree with post-tenure review. However, whether you agree or disagree, post-tenure review has become a part of the rules of the faculty work environment. One of the best ways to prevent falling into the post-tenure review process is to understand what triggers post-tenure review in your University and make sure you don't activate any of those triggers.

Once promoted and tenured, you should start to work toward the Full Professor designation. To do so, in most cases you need to begin to make sure you establish yourself within your profession as having national and international impact; having just regional/state impact often won't cut it. You must be seen as an expert in your area. You should also work toward the final polishing of your teaching skills as well as increasing your contribution in the service areas. Now is the time you should consider being Chair of department, college, and/or university committees. You must establish yourself as an academic leader, not only in your profession, but in your Institution. If it is boiled down to one phrase, you must stay engaged and involved to move to Full Professor. Besides being on the correct track toward Full Professor, you'll also stay marketable if you remain engaged and involved. And marketability may lead to other job opportunities.

Should you go or stay?

It is inevitable at some point, you'll start to think about pursuing another faculty position. For me, it was about two months into my first position; I kept thinking "It can't be this bad at other places!". Assuming the grass was greener elsewhere, I started looking seriously very soon after I started my first job. Interestingly, almost every junior faculty member I've worked with has admitted to thinking the same thing in the first year of their first faculty position. Some people are successful in changing jobs relatively quickly, some aren't (I wasn't). So, if early on in your faculty experience, you have the desire to look for other jobs, just know you're not alone. The first year as a faculty member is often filled with so many surprises and so much pressure most junior faculty assume there will not be as many surprises or pressures elsewhere (spoiler alert: there are always surprises and pressures in academia).

While it may not be wise to immediately change jobs as a junior faculty member, there are fewer and fewer faculty that work only at one university during their career. As a faculty member, I have worked at three universities across 30 years in the business. My moves, as is the case for many faculty that change Universities, were caused by a variety of reasons. Not surprisingly, scholars have studied why faculty change jobs and have found in general, faculty change jobs for five basic reasons:

1) "They didn't get or weren't going to get tenure;
2) A new job was in a more favorable geographic location;
3) Family obligations;
4) For professional opportunities; or
5) Because of work environment and fit."[105]

Before we jump into the reasons why you may want to change universities, let's cover a couple of drawbacks to changing universities as a junior faculty member.

When you change universities, you will immediately lose the navigational

---

[105] From the great article "To Heaven or Hell: Sensemaking about Why Faculty Leave" by KerryAnn O'Meara, Andrew Lounder, and Corbin M. Campbell. The Journal of Higher Education, 85(5): 2014, pp. 603-632.

knowledge you've gained regarding how to get things done in your University. Most universities have different ways of doing things, from getting paper and pencils, to spending grant money, and so, if you change your University, just accept you'll be a newbie all over again when it comes to getting things done. This is not usually problematic, but critical facets of your job, especially in regards to research and teaching, may suffer as you figure out a new system. Re-establishing yourself, especially with the research compliance committees on campus can take time and as a result, can hold up your research efforts.

Another drawback you may find when changing your University is there is the real possibility you will lose the University's contribution to your pension plan. You may wonder why I am talking about pensions because you are many years away from retiring; however, you leaving your position may affect your pension. Let me explain: most pension plans are set up with a 'vesting period', which means you don't get the employer's contribution to your pension unless you work there a specific amount of time, usually, two to five years. Certainly, the longer you stay at a university, the more you would lose if you move and you are not fully vested.

As an example, using general numbers, let's suppose you are paid $70,000 per year, your University kicks in 6.5% toward your pension, and your vesting period is five years. If you left that University at 4.5 years after you started, you would *lose* $22,750 in your pension; if you left during your first year, you would *lose* $4,550. These amounts may not seem like much money to lose, but also understand the total amount you would lose is not just those amounts, but all *future* earnings on those amounts. As a rough estimate, over a 35-year career, if we use the general financial rule of thumb that amounts in a pension plan double approximately every 7 years, what you'll lose will range from $22,750 (if you leave after one year) to $114,000 (if you leave at 4.5 years)! So, while the financial factor should not be what primarily drives your decision, you should consider what you may lose in your pension if you leave before you are vested.

Lastly, you must consider what your leaving early will say about you as a professional. If you leave early, or do this often in your career, when you apply for other positions, other professionals will start to wonder if you will commit to be with their Institute for very long. To search and hire a faculty member takes a lot of money and a lot of faculty time. If you leave early, the department has to go through the search and hire process all over again. I can assure you that search committees think about this if you have a record of starting positions and then leaving early.

So, as you think about applying or taking a new position, consider both the positive and negative consequences of your decision.

Factors to consider when looking for a new job

If you are faced with a P/T denial or other departmental challenges, you may consider looking for a new university to call home. Many reasons faculty leave a university revolve around the idea of not being a good 'fit' at your institution[106]. 'Fit' issues at a university can include such things as the Institution having too much bureaucracy, bosses that micro-manage, a lack of resources, the requirement to do too much service, or job requirements that change or aren't supported by the resources you have. If you are under stress due to institutional fit issues, you may find your health diminishes, you are working too much, and you begin to suffer emotional detachment, such as feeling isolated and undervalued. All these fit issues can lead you to start investigating new positions.

As you investigate new positions, you need to consider whether a new position at a different university will actually 'solve' the institutional and personal fit issues you are experiencing. As such, the *Chronicle*[107] suggests if you are entertaining a new job offer, you should answer four questions:

1) How stable is your current job;
2) What are the personal aspects of the new job that may solve your current issues (or exacerbate them);
3) How much support can you reasonably expect at the new position; and
4) How good is the fit?

Regarding this last question, if you are struggling with both institutional and personal fit issues at your current University, consider carefully whether moving will solve those issues. All universities have their issues and quirks. You want to make sure when you change universities, you are not just trading one set of 'fit' problems for a different (or the same) set of problems.

I would always encourage you *before* you start looking for other jobs to have an open and honest discussion with your Department Chair regarding the reasons you are considering looking for another job. If your current University can provide the support you need to be successful, having a discussion with your Chair about these issues may be the first step toward solving the

---

[106] From Maya Whitaker's great article "*Warning Signs that You and Your Campus Are a Bad Fit*". (*The Chronicle of Higher Education*, 9/19/2018).
[107] From the *Chronicle's* Quick Tip column (no author noted) "How to Decide Whether to Take a New Job". Feb. 22, 2019.

issues. You don't have to be so blunt as to say "fix this or I will look for another job" but you should give your current administration a chance to fix the issues before you go to the trouble of looking for other positions.

In the end, deciding whether to search for and/or accept a new job can be a difficult process and decision. I have done this twice (so far), and in both cases, I constantly felt like it was a 'devil you know versus one you don't know' decision. In the end, all you can do is gather as much information as you can, consult with your trusted mentors and your spouse or significant other, and if you have a religious faith, pray on it.

How to look for a new job: You may be tempted to think looking for a new academic position is just a repeat of what you did to get your first academic job. To a large extent, you are correct in that the method of finding a position, the necessary application materials, and the process will be the same as they were the first time you did it. However, past the basics, looking for a job when you already have a job has some added complications. These complications include how you should structure your application materials and whether you should make it known in your current position you are searching for another job.

If you were denied tenure, you should understand that the members of the Search Committee where you are applying for the new job, will either know or will find out you were denied tenure. If the Search Committee that is considering your application doesn't know or ask, one of the administrators above them will find out that you were denied P/T. Since you cannot keep it a secret that you were denied P/T, in your application materials you should acknowledge the fact and let the Search Committee and hiring Administrators know you have moved on. In an excellent column, Dr. David Perlmutter[108] suggests candidates write in such a way that they give the impression of a positive, forward-moving colleague. Even if you aren't looking for a new job because of a P/T denial, it is still good practice to emphasize your positivity and future plans, because remember Search Committees and Departments are looking for someone that has potential and will bring a positive energy to the position and their Department.

Your materials, especially your CV and your cover letter, need to focus on your positive career path; it is helpful to highlight any upcoming papers, projects, or grants you are working on. In your cover letter, you may note you were denied tenure, but don't dwell on in it, and as Dr. Perlmutter suggests

---

[108] David D. Perlmutter, "You Didn't Get Tenure: Part 2" *The Chronicle of Higher Education,* Sept. 24, 2007.

"explain in a sentence or two that you fell short of your goals in your previous job".

Additionally, prepare the people that will serve as your references so they can address the situation if they get asked for either letters or receive phone calls. Preparing your references for these questions could be as simple as asking them directly how they would handle a question about your tenure denial and (gently) suggesting to them different responses that would help the new University understand you are moving forward and are functioning well as an academic.

If you've continued being professionally graceful, even after the tenure denial, this positive attitude will be reflected in your references' views of you and their recommendations. Even if you feel awkward asking for their reference, if you approach the individual the correct way, you may be surprised how willing they are to help. Even telling your references honestly, as Dr. Perlmutter observes, "I accept that things didn't work out; I could use your help to find another job" can work wonders in having people decide to help you with a very positive reference. In short, in your materials, be upfront, but have a positive and moving-forward approach, as well as choosing your references carefully.

If you have decided to leave your University even without a P/T denial, you are essentially striving to end one relationship to begin another. As such, you should understand the University where you are working has invested time and money into your career, the people in your department have invested time in you, and leaving may be seen as an act of betrayal, unfaithfulness, or impatience. Thus, it is imperative if you decide to change positions, you be discreet about your searches, interviews, and negotiations. If you aren't discrete, you run the risk of being considered a 'short-timer'; someone who will not be on the team for the long term. As a short-timer, you'll find people stop asking your opinion, your advice, or including you in departmental considerations.

Critical Point – 9.1
Discretion When Looking for a New Job

If you decide to look for a new position, regardless of P/T/ contract status, understand that you are looking to end your place in the community. This is akin to breaking a relationship. As such, if you let people know you are looking, you may be faced with negative emotions from other faculty as well as being shut-out of departmental conversations and discussions. It is always best to keep your job-searching quiet until you have to reveal it – most often when you have to give a hiring University references. Be discrete; it will pay dividends, especially if you don't get a new job!

By letting it be known that you are looking for a new position, you are telling your colleagues you are dissatisfied and have decided to move on. While it is 'only' a job you are looking to change, you will be also changing your relationship with your Department and your colleagues. As such, in many ways, looking for another job while you still have a job is a type of breakup. Since searching for a new job can be perceived as a betrayal by some, you need to be careful not only in what you say in your current job, but how you structure your application materials.

Crafting your cover letter: As noted earlier, with a P/T denial, you want to acknowledge the point in your cover letter, but then focus on your future positives. If you are beginning a job search and still have P/T at your current location, while you should still be positive and forward looking in your materials, you also should focus on the positives of why you are applying for the new position versus why you are looking to leave your current position.

For example, in the first paragraph of your cover letter you should indicate why you are interested in the position. Here are two different approaches to that paragraph (from our hypothetical candidate Kathryn D. Whitt). If you were on the search committee, which paragraph would make you more interested in interviewing Dr. Whitt?

> 1) "Please accept the enclosed materials for consideration for the Associate Professor position in Exercise Physiology at Middle-Sized State University advertised in the *Chronicle of Higher Education.* I am excited for this opportunity because my career growth goals have been repeatedly stymied in my current position and I have come to realize Metropolitan Academic University has not and cannot support my academic aspirations. However, I do not believe this would be the case at Middle-Sized State University. Thus, I believe my job experiences, past teaching and research accomplishments, and my record of service would fulfill the job description of your position at MSSU."

Or

> 2) "Please accept the enclosed materials for consideration for the Associate Professor position in Exercise Physiology at Middle-Sized State University advertised in the *Chronicle of Higher Education.* I am excited for this opportunity because it appears from colleagues and published articles Middle-Sized State University

(MSSU) is supportive of faculty development and has a tremendous record of helping faculty succeed. Thus, I believe my job experiences, past teaching and research accomplishments, and my record of service would fulfill the job description of your position at MSSU."

If you selected 'paragraph 2', you are correct; it is more positive and focuses on a generally positive point of view regarding the hiring University, versus a negative viewpoint of Dr. Whitt's current University. This positive approach will help prevent the Search Committee from seeing you as a malcontent just looking to change positions.

While I have emphasized staying positive and not commenting on your current employer, you should be prepared to address the issue of why you want to leave your current University if it is brought up in an interview situation. It is common for Search Committees or administrators involved with the search to ask you why you are interested in leaving your current institution. Again, I would emphasize your verbal answers to this question, whenever it is asked, focus on the positive aspect of the hiring University versus your negative perception of your current University.

When I was Chair of a Search Committee in a mid-level University (an R2 Institution), we once had a job applicant that was currently employed at a very prestigious R1 university and by all signs, was on track for P/T at that institution. During the phone interview I asked the candidate, "Why do you want to leave 'research nirvana' at your current institution to come work where your workload is 50% teaching and 50% research?". The candidate responded "You're right, my current institution is research nirvana and is extremely supportive of my efforts. I have many great colleagues here. But what I've realized about myself is teaching is incredibly important to me; teaching allows me to feel like I am giving back to society. Thus, I think your University would allow me to facilitate my research aspirations and to also fulfill the need I've discovered to be in the classroom. Also, we are expecting our first child soon, and all our parents live within 100 miles of your University. So, while some might perceive I am losing professionally, I actually see this move as increasing the opportunities I have to be professionally fulfilled as well as allowing us to be near our parents." This candidate's response was a perfect mix of respect for his current institution and emphasis of the positive about the hiring institution. Additionally, this applicant threw in a deeply personal reason for wanting to move which further eliminated any doubts the Search Committee had about why he was considering our University.[109]

---

[109] And yes, we hired this candidate!

You don't necessarily have to have a personal justification for your job search, but if you do, there is no reason not to emphasize there are personal positives for why you are looking. In fact, the most difficult thing for most of my students to do as we practice job-talks in class, is to share the personal reasons why they are interested in a position. Sharing personal reasons can give the Search Committee more assurance you will become part of the community and you are not just running from your current position.

If you begin looking for another position, but want to keep it quiet you are looking, it's always difficult to figure out how to handle references. Surely, if you list your current Department Chair, or other colleagues at your current institution as references, you'll have to tell them you're looking, which will defeat the goal of being discrete. However, if you don't list your current administrators or colleagues, the Search Committee may believe you are hiding something. It is a difficult situation.

One approach to rectify this difficult situation is to put together a list of references that do not include your current administrators or colleagues, but does include a statement like the following in both the end of your cover letter and on your reference page.

> "Due to the confidential nature of my application for this position, I have not listed any of my current colleagues from my current University and would request none be contacted unless I am an on-campus interview finalist for the position. At that time, I would be happy to share the contact information for my current Department Chair and/or other colleagues at my current University."

With this type of statement, along with the standard confidentiality statement I recommended in Book 1 for these documents[110], the Committee will understand they should not talk to your current institution until you are a finalist. In most cases, since you made a clear and straight-forward request, the employing University must follow your wishes. If they do not follow your wishes, this will also tell you something about those individuals involved and then you should question whether you want to work somewhere where individuals would ignore a straight-forward request that could impact you in your current position.

---

[110] That standard confidentiality request the end of your cover letter <u>and</u> at the top of your reference list is: "All of the listed references have been contacted and are aware I am applying for this position; however, other than contact with the listed references, I would ask my application be kept confidential until such a time the Committee needs information from other sources."

In the end, there is no guarantee your current University will not find out you are looking for another position in the early stage of the search and they certainly will find out if you are a finalist for the position! As a result, you should be prepared for how you will handle that difficult conversation with your Department Chair when the time comes.

Assuming you apply for a new position and you get an on-campus interview, if you are looking because of P/T denial, then your colleagues at your current University will already know you were looking and may have been actively helping you find a new position. However, if you choose to leave the University and you were looking for another position, when you get an on-campus interview request, you'll need to consider whether to share this information with your current Department Chair.

The search committee and Department Chair at the hiring University will eventually want to talk with your current supervisors as a reference. This conversation sometimes occurs before you are brought on campus, but most likely, will occur after you have been on-campus, and usually only if you are the number one finalist.

I have seen a few situations, especially with faculty that already have tenure, where the hiring department will not contact your current Department Chair; the hiring department figures that since you already have promotion and tenure, you are an acceptable hire. Thus, they may just go ahead and offer you the position. However the hiring University handles this situation, if you are the finalist for a position, at some point, you will find yourself having to tell your current Department Chair you have been looking for a new position and you are either interviewing or have a job offer.

Whatever your feelings about your current position, I would always recommend having a discussion with your Department Chair *before* you sign any offer, even if you must move due to any of the institutional/personal fit issues covered earlier. With that Department Chair conversation, a couple different scenarios may play out:

> 1) The Department Chair wishes you good luck and asks about when the change will be effective. With this outcome, it will be clear to you the Department is not going to counter-offer and is willing to let you go. If this outcome occurs, you should then have a clear conscience to sign your offer from the new University and move forward. But after you have this conversation, sign your offer immediately and get it back to your new Chair as soon as possible

to prevent interference from your current Institution in your new position.

2) Another scenario – especially if you've been productive - is the Department Chair will ask to see your offer and may want time to generate a counter-offer. This is one of the rare times you will have leverage with your University, so if you are considering staying at your current University, I would suggest you not accept the new offer and wait to see what type of counter-offer your current Department Chair can generate.

Universities that have top-flight, productive faculty understand that other universities will try to poach their best faculty; in fact, that has been a strategy at some universities in the past 10 years where instead of building up their faculty ranks from recruiting good junior faculty, they will go out and recruit mid- and later-career faculty that have been very successful. To combat this trend, some university systems have set up special funds they can use to retain faculty. Thus, getting a counter-offer from your current University is not unusual if you have been a productive faculty member and have the potential to be even more productive in the future, especially in the external grant funding area. However, I would not condone using job searches as a way of increasing your salary or support unless you are serious about taking a new job. This type of action – applying for jobs just to get written offers so you can negotiate with your current University – is inherently dishonest and it will be perceived that you are trying to deceive the hiring University just to further your own agenda.

You should also be aware your University will not generate any counter-offers unless you have a written offer from another University. It should be obvious the written offer has to be genuine; recently there is at least one example of a faculty member forging written offer letters to increase his pay and support at his University.[111] Not only did this professor lose his job when it was discovered his 'written offers' had all been faked, he faced both extensive professional and legal difficulties afterward. So, make sure your offer letter is genuine, and then feel free to share with your current Department Chair if you want to stay at your current University.

The Take Home Message
The title of this chapter could have applied to the whole book because your first five years will be a combination of new experiences, hard work, and

---

[111] The case of Bryan McNaughton as described by Jack Stripling and Megan Zahneis (The Big Lie) in the Sept. 4, 2018 *Chronicle of Higher Education*.

becoming a part of a new community. Your first five years will be a constant drumbeat of working on research, teaching classes, interreacting with colleagues and students, and trying to figure out the best ways to be a great faculty member. That first five years will go quickly and you shouldn't be surprised if you find yourself thrilled, terrified, or overwhelmed at different times.

If there is one take-home message I hope you take away from this whole book, is that while you should learn everything you can about the process and work diligently toward your goals and you shouldn't sacrifice your life for your work. Look for mentors and colleagues that are knowledgeable and supportive and remember the priorities of your Institution. In some ways, academia is a simple business; we teach, we discover new knowledge, and we provide service to our profession and to society. However, humans are involved in academia which can make it more complicated, more dramatic, and more traumatic.

Even though it is complicated and full of drama and trauma, if you strive to stay positive, be professionally graceful and keep moving forward, you'll be just fine.

Academia has been good to me and I know it'll be good to you if you stay professionally graceful, work to understand the process, and keep a sense of humor! Just know that you now have an open invitation from me; never hesitate to say "hello" if we're at the same conference, email me, and/or join us online for discussions about academic careers and the questions you may have[112]. I have no doubt, that once assembled, your academic 'furniture' will look great! Enjoy it!

---

[112] Reach out and join our community at AcademicCareerDevelopment.com. You'll find classes, blogs, and videos that will augment the material in this book, as well as allowing you to connect with others at your same level and in your same situation. See you online!

INDEX

A

AcademicCareerDevelopment.com, 234
Annual evaluations, 5
authorship, scientific
   guidelines, 108

B

bridge year, 6
building your resarch team
   don't have money, 106
   hiring, 103
building your research team, 103
buying out of teaching
   with grant, 69

C

Carnegie Classification
   defined, 11
   Masters Universities, 12
   more information, 11
collaborator, 18
collaborators, 30
   developing, 30
colleagues, 18, 29
Communication
   colleagues, 45
   external world, 54
   general guidelines, 36
   staff, 39
   students, 42
   supervisors, 50
counseling center, 27

D

Deciders
   who they are, 8
Delegating
   research tasks, 101
Delivering material, 138
   appearance / dress, 138
   attitude in classroom, 139
   dropping powerpoint, 141
   real-time presentation, 143
Denial P/T, 215
   administrative view, 220
   bridge year, 218
   positives, 221
   seeking counseling, 218
   stages of grief, 217
Dr. Carol Greider
   Nobel prize winner and NIH reviews, 84

E

esearch is a team sport, 102
Evaluation of your research, 110
   Altmetric, 119
   changing research focus, 111
   citations, 113
   external reviews, 116
   focus, 111
   H-index, 114
   impact factor, 113
   impact statement, 118
   K-index, 119
   number of publications, 113
   qualitative factors, 118
   quantitative factors, 110
Evaluation of your teaching, 157

peer- supervisor-evaluations, 162
student class evaluations, 158
expectations
tenure/promotion, 6
external fund development
advantages, 70
amount needed, 60
contracts, 77
department view, 82
disadvantages, 72
do you have to have it?, 67
endowments, 77
extra salary, 68
grant applications, 76
internal funding, 75
leverage, 71
relation to Carnegie Classification, 67
External fund development, 59
external reviewers
choosing, 210
External Reviewers, 209, *See* Evaluation of your research

F

Finding another job, 224
crafting application letter, 229
discretion, 228
drawback financial, 225
drawbacks, 224
factors to consider, 226
negotiating with your current University, 232
processes, 227
references and confidentiality, 231

G

Grading, 146
24-hour moratorium, 154
bonus points, 156
getting help, 150
giving back exams, 152
item analysis, 151
quizzes, 155
types of exams, 147
grant writing tips, 81

H

hard money programs, 68
higher education funding decreases, 60
humanities
different from sciences, ii
Humanities
different from sciences, 85
hypercompetitive, 73

I

IDC
full or partial, 64
how spent, 64
IDC rate
calculation, 62
example, 63
example, business, 63
expression, 62
imposter syndrome, i
Improving your teaching, 172
experiment with your class, 173
Indirect Costs (IDC), 61

J

J. Timothy Lightfoot, 239
journal impact factor (JIF)
defined, 92
disadvantages, 93
example of use, 93

K

kaizen, 23

Katherine Hayhoe
   climate science, 55

L

learning environment
   don't let students hide, 127
   learning student's names, 127
   not a democracy, 124
   not student friend, 124
   setting expectations, 126

M

mentors
   asking, 26
   location, 27
Mentors, 18
   defined, 10
   finding, 25

N

network
   definition, 23
   developing, 24
Nine month contract
   related to funding, 68
non-tenure-line
   timeline, 5
non-tenure-track
   definition, 4
non-tenure-track line
   types, 12

P

P/T accomplished, 222
   career options, 222
   post-tenure review, 222
   working toward Full Professor, 223
P/T denial, 188
P/T documents, 185
   filing system to organize, 186

P/T portfolio
   CV tips, 191
   defined, 189
   Impact statement, importance, 202
   Impact statement, sections, 203
   impact statement, what it does, 203
   required documents, 190
   research impact. *See* Evaluation of your research, impact statement
P/T process
   reducing anxiety, 183
   seeking counseling, 185
   timeline, 186
page charges, 67
peer-review, 87
   function of, 87
Perception is reality, 35
Post-tenure review. *See* P/T accomplished, post-tenure review
predatory journals
   defined, 95
preparing for teaching
   'just enough' tips, 136
   class prep, 135
   grading. *See* grading
   overpreparing, 136
   syllabus development, 128
pre-print archives. *See* 'pre-review archives'
pre-review archives, 96
   P/T consideration, 97
professionally graceful, 21, 22, 50, 217, 228
professionally graceful'
   defined, 20
promotion/tenure
   pausing clock, 6
promotion/tenure clock, 3

R

Reasons to look for another job, 224
research
    abstracts, 88
    books / chapters, 90
    defined, 85
    dissemination, 87
    open-access journals, 94
    original data papers, 89
    review papers, 89
    scholarly products, 86
    where to publish, 91
Research Cycle, 100

S

Schedule time to write, 99
Scientific stage name, 89
Senior Faculty, 10
Service
    defined, 175
    importance of, 176
    opportunities to consider, 180
    protecting your time, 178
    role in P/T, 178
soft money institution, 68
start-up money
    relation to IDC, 64
Student Issues, 166
    cheating, 167
    plagiarism, 169
Supervising your research team, 107

T

teaching
    professor not responsible for student learning, 123
Teaching
    preparing, 128
    what it is today, 122
Tenure
    definition, 4
tenure/promotion
    comprehensive review, 6
    definition, 4
tenure-track
    definition, 4
    timeline, 4
third-year review, 6

W

Work / Life Balance, 213

Y

your research story, 32

ABOUT THE AUTHOR

J. Timothy Lightfoot completed his PhD at University of Tennessee after a stint at NASA. He completed an NIH sponsored post-doctoral fellowship at Johns Hopkins University in the Division of Physiology. He took his first faculty position in 1989 at Florida Atlantic University, where he received tenure and was promoted to Associate Professor in 1994 and became Department Chair shortly thereafter. He took the Department Chair position at the University of North Carolina Charlotte in 1996, was promoted to Full Professor in 2001, and remained as Department Chair until 2005. In 2010, he became the Omar Smith Endowed Chair in Kinesiology and Director of the Huffines Institute for Sports Medicine and Human Performance at Texas A&M University. Additionally, he has held a variety of leadership roles at all three Universities where he has worked, as well as in the American College of Sports Medicine. He has been named Teacher of the Year at all three Universities he has worked at, was named the Distinguished Graduate Mentor for Texas A&M in 2018, and was the recipient of the American College of Sports Medicine's Citation Award in 2018. His research work has been in the areas of the genetic mechanisms regulating daily physical activity level, as well as the physiological stresses of performance in extreme environments.

www.ingramcontent.com/pod-product-compliance
Lightning Source LLC
Chambersburg PA
CBHW031642170426
43195CB00035B/365